GENETICS AND INTELLIGENCE

Other Books in the Current Controversies Series:

GENETICS AND INTELLIGENCE

David L. Bender, *Publisher*
Bruno Leone, *Executive Editor*

Scott Barbour, *Managing Editor*
Brenda Stalcup, *Senior Editor*

Tamara L. Roleff, *Book Editor*

CURRENT CONTROVERSIES

No part of this book may be reproduced or used in any form or by any means, electrical, mechanical, or otherwise, including, but not limited to, photocopy, recording, or any information storage and retrieval system, without prior written permission from the publisher.

Cover Photo: Will and Deni McIntyre/Photo Researchers

Library of Congress Cataloging-in-Publication Data

Genetics and intelligence / Tamara L. Roleff, book editor.
     p. cm. — (Current controversies)
    Includes bibliographical references and index.
    ISBN 1-56510-409-9 (lib : alk. paper). — ISBN 1-56510-408-0
(pbk : alk. paper)
    1. Intellect—Genetic aspects. 2. Nature and nurture. 3. Intelligence
levels—Social aspects. 4. Intelligence tests. I. Roleff, Tamara L.,
1959-   . II. Series.
BF431.G39   1996
155.7—dc20   96-11546
                                        CIP

Every effort has been made to trace the owners of copyrighted material.

Contents

Children with a higher social status score higher on IQ tests than children with a low social status. The younger a child is, the more impact environment has on his or her intelligence.

Arthur R. Jensen's evidence that genetics is responsible for IQ differences between blacks and whites is based on faulty reasoning. The heritability of intelligence within one race cannot be applied across races, nor can the importance of the environment's effect on intelligence be ruled out.

Researchers have not proven that IQ tests measure heritable intelligence rather than learned knowledge. People's answers to questions on IQ tests reveal their experience or education rather than their innate intelligence.

Chapter 2: Do IQ Tests Measure Intelligence?

Part of the controversy over genetics and intelligence concerns the issues of whether general intelligence, or *g*, can be measured and whether IQ tests provide a valid assessment of intelligence. Most psychometricians, those who specialize in the measurement of intelligence, believe IQ tests are accurate. Other psychologists, however, believe that there are many types of intelligence besides *g* and that existing IQ tests only measure a small amount of total intelligence.

Yes: IQ Tests Measure Intelligence

Intelligence is heritable and can be measured by IQ tests. IQ test results also correlate strongly with personal achievement and socioeconomic status.

IQ tests serve a useful purpose: They identify which students are gifted and which need extra help, as well as which employees are best suited for certain jobs. IQ test data also help researchers to understand why some people succeed while others do not. However, because IQ research demonstrates that various groups test lower than others, it is opposed by those who mistakenly believe that these findings will be used to obstruct equal rights.

IQ scores can be used to explain much of a person's behavior. People who have low IQs are not as likely as those with high IQs to learn from their experiences and to foresee the consequences of their actions. There are strong correlations between low IQs and undesirable social behaviors, such as criminality.

adopted black and interracial children should have considerably lower IQ scores than their white siblings. However, a follow-up study of black, white, and interracial children adopted by white parents showed no significant difference in IQ scores between the parents' biological white children and the adopted children.

Yes: IQ Differences Between Races Are Genetic

Chapter 4: How Should IQ Research Affect Social Policies?

Foreword

By definition, controversies are "discussions of questions in which opposing opinions clash" (Webster's Twentieth Century Dictionary Unabridged). Few would deny that controversies are a pervasive part of the human condition and exist on virtually every level of human enterprise. Controversies transpire between individuals and among groups, within nations and between nations. Controversies supply the grist necessary for progress by providing challenges and challengers to the status quo. They also create atmospheres where strife and warfare can flourish. A world without controversies would be a peaceful world; but it also would be, by and large, static and prosaic.

The Series' Purpose

The purpose of the Current Controversies series is to explore many of the social, political, and economic controversies dominating the national and international scenes today. Titles selected for inclusion in the series are highly focused and specific. For example, from the larger category of criminal justice, Current Controversies deals with specific topics such as police brutality, gun control, white collar crime, and others. The debates in Current Controversies also are presented in a useful, timeless fashion. Articles and book excerpts included in each title are selected if they contribute valuable, long-range ideas to the overall debate. And wherever possible, current information is enhanced with historical documents and other relevant materials. Thus, while individual titles are current in focus, every effort is made to ensure that they will not become quickly outdated. Books in the Current Controversies series will remain important resources for librarians, teachers, and students for many years.

In addition to keeping the titles focused and specific, great care is taken in the editorial format of each book in the series. Book introductions and chapter prefaces are offered to provide background material for readers. Chapters are organized around several key questions that are answered with diverse opinions representing all points on the political spectrum. Materials in each chapter include opinions in which authors clearly disagree as well as alternative opinions in which authors may agree on a broader issue but disagree on the possible solutions. In this way, the content of each volume in Current Controversies mirrors the mosaic of opinions encountered in society. Readers will quickly realize that there are many viable answers to these complex issues. By questioning each author's conclusions, students and casual readers can begin to develop the critical thinking skills so important to evaluating opinionated material.

Current Controversies is also ideal for controlled research. Each anthology in the series is composed of primary sources taken from a wide gamut of informational categories including periodicals, newspapers, books, United States and foreign government documents, and the publications of private and public organizations. Readers will find factual support for reports, debates, and research papers covering all areas of important issues. In addition, an annotated table of contents, an index, a book and periodical bibliography, and a list of organizations to contact are included in each book to expedite further research.

Perhaps more than ever before in history, people are confronted with diverse and contradictory information. During the Persian Gulf War, for example, the public was not only treated to minute-to-minute coverage of the war, it was also inundated with critiques of the coverage and countless analyses of the factors motivating U.S. involvement. Being able to sort through the plethora of opinions accompanying today's major issues, and to draw one's own conclusions, can be a complicated and frustrating struggle. It is the editors' hope that Current Controversies will help readers with this struggle.

Introduction

Ask a dozen people to define "intelligence" and you will probably receive a dozen vague generalizations about being smart or receiving good grades in school without having to study hard. Even psychometricians—researchers who study and measure intelligence—do not agree on a definition of intelligence. Some define intelligence as the ability to reason, learn quickly, analyze and solve new problems, and grasp abstract or complex concepts—skills that are measured by standard intelligence tests. Other intelligence experts include in their definition of intelligence such task-specific abilities as musical, spatial, and practical skills, as well as creativity and innovation—talents that are not tested for on standard intelligence tests.

The first intelligence test was invented in 1905 by French psychologist Alfred Binet as a way to identify students who needed extra help in class. He developed a series of problems that a majority of "normal" children for each age could answer correctly. According to Binet, if children being tested could answer all the questions for their age correctly, they were "normal." Those children who could not, Binet maintained, were "backward" and needed additional help from their teachers.

After Binet's death in 1911, Stanford University professor Lewis M. Terman expanded upon Binet's intelligence tests. Terman developed the intelligence quotient, or IQ, as a means of determining a person's mental age. An IQ score of 100 is average, 70 or below is retarded, and 130 or above is gifted. When a population's IQ scores are mapped on a graph with the IQ scores on the x-axis and the number of test-takers on the y-axis, the spread of points will resemble a bell curve. Nearly 70 percent of the IQ scores will fall between 85 and 115, and 95 percent will fall between 70 and 130.

Even while the intelligence tests were being developed and revised, debate over their use, their accuracy, and their purpose erupted among scientists and researchers. Two arguments emerged: whether intelligence was hereditary and therefore fixed, or due to environment and therefore changeable; and whether some ethnic groups or races were more or less intelligent than others. In the decades since the intelligence test was developed, these debates remain unresolved.

Controversy over these two questions broke out again in 1994 when Richard J. Herrnstein and Charles Murray published their book, *The Bell Curve: Intelligence and Class Structure in American Life*. Herrnstein and Murray argue that cognitive ability (their word for intelligence) is substantially inherited and, therefore, it is nearly impossible to permanently raise IQ. Their critics, however, maintain that environment has an important role in determining intelligence and that by changing a child's environment, IQ can be significantly changed.

Herrnstein and Murray concede that placing children with low IQs in an improved environment through adoption or in an enriched learning program such as Head Start may raise their IQ scores as much as 10 points at first, but the authors insist that these gains are temporary. After being out of the Head Start program for a few years, the children experience what Herrnstein and Murray call "fade-out": The test scores of the children who participated in the program gradually fall until they converge with the test scores of low-IQ children who did not participate in Head Start and similar programs. Any gains in group averages of IQ test scores totally disappear by the time the children are in the sixth grade, the authors maintain.

Herrnstein and Murray also contend that IQ is highly correlated with behavior and that because of this correlation, the national IQ average is declining (an effect known as dysgenesis). Herrnstein and Murray claim that social scientists and researchers can predict the performance of a group based on the group's IQ average. They argue that groups with a low IQ average tend to be poor, unemployed, or on welfare; are often involved in criminal activities; and have more children, frequently illegitimate. However, they assert, groups with high IQs are often middle- or upper-class, tend to do well in school and at work, and have fewer children, illegitimate or otherwise. What worries Herrnstein and Murray most about these correlations, they write, is that "when people die, they are not replaced one for one by babies who will develop identical IQs. If the new babies grow up to have systematically higher or lower IQs than the people who die, the national distribution of intelligence changes." Herrnstein and Murray fear that the national IQ average is declining because "dull" people generally have more children than "bright" people. If, as the authors believe, IQ is mostly hereditary, then "dull" people will outnumber "bright" people, thus lowering the nation's average IQ.

But like Terman and other early intelligence researchers, Herrnstein and Murray's most explosive contention is that cognitive ability varies among the races. Herrnstein and Murray cite IQ test scores to support their thesis: East Asians (those of Japanese, Chinese, and Korean descent), whether in the United States or in Asia, score, on average, a few points higher on IQ tests than do whites. Whites score, on average, 15 points higher on IQ tests than do blacks. Because the black/white (B/W) gap does not decrease when test takers are matched for socioeconomic status (in fact, the B/W gap increases when test takers are matched for high socioeconomic status), Herrnstein and Murray attribute these differences in test scores to genetic differences:

> The universality of the contrast in nonverbal and verbal skills between East Asians and European whites suggests, without quite proving, genetic roots. Another line of evidence pointing toward a genetic factor in cognitive ethnic differences is that blacks and whites differ most on the tests that are the best measures of *g*, or general intelligence.

13

Introduction

Some detractors of Herrnstein and Murray's theory of the heritability of intelligence in *The Bell Curve* claim that environment is largely responsible for IQ scores. Blacks, they say, have had to endure a long history of slavery and racism, the effects of which are still felt today on black IQ scores. According to author John B. Judis:

> The past 400 years provide ample reason to believe that imputing innate inferiority to a group will affect its "encounter" with other groups. In the United States, theories of racial inferiority were the justification for slavery and for restrictions on American immigration. In Europe, these theories were a justification for Nazi genocide. If Murray and Herrnstein's views gain currency, they will deepen the chasms separating whites and blacks.

As blacks are slowly accorded an equal place in American society, their average IQ scores will rise, Judis asserts.

Some critics claim that the B/W gap is already closing. Richard Nisbett, a psychometrician and psychology professor at the University of Michigan, contends that black IQs have shown a slight increase since the civil rights era of the 1950s and 1960s: Black IQ scores have gained on the white IQ average at the rate of 2.5 IQ points per decade. He cites a 1991 review of four studies using well-known IQ tests that found the B/W gap to be 7 to 10 points, not 15 points as claimed by Herrnstein and Murray. In response to the statistics showing that the B/W gap is greatest at the highest socioeconomic levels, Nisbett maintains that the highest socioeconomic status for blacks is not equivalent to the highest socioeconomic status for whites. When adjustments are made to match white and black test takers by such criteria as neighborhoods and resources, Nisbett argues, the B/W gap nearly disappears. Based on this observation, Nisbett concludes that environment is more responsible for the differences in black and white IQ scores than is genetics.

Other critics argue that Herrnstein and Murray are wrong in their contention that the national IQ average is declining. They cite the well-documented phenomenon known as the "Flynn effect," which reveals that average IQ scores have risen by approximately 3 points per decade since the tests were developed. Researchers have noticed that test takers earn successively higher scores on IQ tests each year until the tests are restandardized to make it more difficult to earn an average score of 100. After the tests are restandardized, the test scores initially fall, but then slowly rise again until the next restandardization. The upward drift has been substantiated on many different IQ tests and in several countries. Psychologist Robert Sternberg of Yale maintains that the Flynn effect disproves dysgenesis. "You can't say IQ is going up *and* going down," he asserts.

The controversy over nature versus nurture in determining IQ may never be resolved. Scientists who support the genetics theory of intelligence will continue to put forth studies proving their thesis, while those who support the environment's role will do the same. *Genetics and Intelligence: Current Controversies* explores the history of the debate, whether intelligence can be measured, whether genetics is responsible for the B/W gap, and how theories about genetics and intelligence should guide social policies.

Chapter 1

Historical Debate: Does Genetics Influence Intelligence?

Historical Debate over Intelligence and Genetics: An Overview

by Daniel J. Kevles

About the author: *Daniel J. Kevles, the author of* In the Name of Eugenics: Genetics and the Uses of Human Heredity, *is a historian of the eugenics movement and a prominent writer on eugenics.*

Although attempts to quantify intelligence began in several countries, the most influential effort was mounted in France by the psychologist Alfred Binet. In 1904, the French government, expanding its educational system, asked Binet for ways to detect mentally deficient children. Binet drew up a series of tests consisting of numerous short problems designed to probe such qualities as memory, ratiocination, and verbal facility. In collaboration with a colleague, Théodore Simon, he also devised a scheme for classifying each test taker according to his "mental age." A child's mental age was defined as that of the chronologically uniform group of children whose average test score he matched. Thus, if a six-year-old's test score matched the average score of ten-year-olds, the six-year-old's mental age would be ten; similarly, if a ten-year-old scored the same as the average of six-year-olds, his mental age would be six.

Measuring Feeblemindedness

The Binet-Simon tests were brought to the United States in 1908 by the American psychologist Henry H. Goddard. Goddard was impressed by the tests, not least because they at long last seemed to provide a direct, quantitative measurement of intelligence. He employed the Binet-Simon examinations at the Vineland, New Jersey, Training School for Feeble-Minded Boys and Girls, where he had recently been appointed director of a new laboratory for the study of mental deficiency—one of the first established in this country. The tests seemed to classify the Vineland pupils in a way consistent with his staff's direct

Excerpted from Daniel J. Kevles, "Genetics, Race, and IQ," *Contention*, Fall 1995. Reprinted by permission of *Contention* magazine.

experience with them; the inmates ranged in age up to fifty, yet none scored on the tests at a mental age greater than twelve.

Goddard noted with particular interest that the test results revealed wide variations in degree of "feeblemindedness," a term then used to denote a wide range of mental deficiencies and also of tendencies toward socially deviant behavior; the results provided a way to distinguish among the differences. Turning numbers into categories, Goddard eventually classified as "idiots" those among the feebleminded

> *"The postwar testing vogue generated much data concerning the 'intelligence' of the American public."*

whose mental age was one or two, and as "imbeciles" those whose mental age ranged from three to seven. Those who scored between eight and twelve he dubbed "morons," a word he took from the Greek for "dull," or "stupid."

Further surveys of intelligence, including administration of the Binet-Simon tests, revealed a high incidence of mental deficiency among the inmates of prisons, reformatories, and homes for wayward girls. The feebleminded, Goddard argued, lacked "one or the other of the factors essential to a moral life—an understanding of right and wrong, and the power of control." Children thus afflicted became truants because they lacked the power to "do the right and flee the wrong"; paupers, because they found the burdens of making a living too heavy; and prostitutes, because they were weak-minded and unintelligent. Goddard was unsure whether mental deficiency resulted from the presence in the brain of something that inhibited normal development or from the absence of something that stimulated it. But whatever the cause, of one thing he had become virtually certain: it behaved like a genetic character. Feeblemindedness was "a condition of mind or brain which is transmitted as regularly and surely as color of hair or eyes."

Goddard's tests stimulated other psychologists to experiment with different schemes for the quantitative assessment of mental capacity. Various new testing systems were devised, for normal as well as mentally deficient children. Among the most prominent was the revision of the Binet-Simon tests, published in 1916 at Stanford University by the psychologist Lewis Terman, who had come to mental testing and to a hereditary view of intelligence through research with precocious children, including his own. It was Terman who introduced the term "I.Q." to the language. IQ, of course, stands for "intelligence quotient," which expresses the ratio of a child's mental age to his chronological age.

The U.S. Army Tests

During the First World War, extensive testing was used to sort out the hundreds of thousands of draftees who flooded into the United States Army, "not primarily for the exclusion of intellectual defectives," as a wartime psychologist explained, "but rather for the classification of men in order that they may be properly placed in the military service." There were two types of tests: alpha for literates; beta, for illiterates in English. The alpha tests consisted of the sort of questions—number sequences, word analogies, arithmetic problems, synonym-antonym puzzles, and commonsense queries—that would become familiar to generations of students; the beta tests consisted largely of pictorial problems involving the comparison of forms and the completion of partial drawings.

The tests were biased in favor of scholastic skills, and the outcome was dependent upon the educational and cultural background of the person tested. Robert Yerkes, the head of the testing program, and others claimed that the tests were almost entirely independent of the environmental history of the examinees, and that they measured "native intelligence." But certainly one of the questions on the alpha test—"The Knight engine is used in the: Packard/Stearns/Lozier/Pierce Arrow"—demanded a knowledgeability that could hardly be supplied by native intelligence. Examinees were also bound to fare better with the word analogies and the arithmetic problems of the alpha test if they had had extensive schooling. Illiterates and non-English-speaking recruits had to cope in the beta test with the vagueness and uncertainty of orally communicated directions. Many of the beta examinees had never taken a written test before. "It was touching," one examiner recalled, "to see the intense effort . . . put into answering the questions, often by men who never before had held a pencil in their hands." By the Armistice, some one million seven hundred thousand recruits had been tested.

After the war, a standard national Intelligence Test was drawn up which sold more than half a million copies in less than a year. Intelligence testers examined ever-growing numbers of paupers, drunkards, delinquents, and prostitutes. Business firms incorporated mental tests in their personnel procedures. Intelligence tests were administered annually to a few million primary and secondary school students, and a number of colleges and universities began to use intelligence test results in the admissions process.

> *"[Army IQ tests given during World War I implied that] the average white American . . . had the mental age of a thirteen-year-old."*

The postwar testing vogue generated much data concerning the "intelligence" of the American public, yet the volume of information was insignificant compared with that from the wartime test program. The National Academy of Sciences summarized that experiment in 1921, in a hefty volume entitled *Psychological Examining in the United States Army*. The report, drawn up by Yerkes, Terman, and their colleagues, presented the test procedures and broke down a large sample of the test results by geographical region and ethnic or racial background. Two inches thick, five pounds in weight, and containing more than half a million words, the volume was hardly a best-seller, but it formed the basis of numerous popular books and articles about intelligence tests and their social import.

According to a number of popular analyses of this data, almost four hundred thousand draftees—close to one-quarter of the draft army—were unable to read a newspaper or to write letters home. In a particularly striking finding, the average white draftee—and, by implication, the average white American—had the mental age of a thirteen-year-old.

Immigrants and Mental Abilities

The psychologist Carl Brigham, one of the wartime Army testers, extended the analysis of the Army data in 1923, in his book *A Study of American Intelligence*. The Army data, Brigham said, constituted "the first really significant contribution to the study of race differences in mental traits." In 1917, Henry Goddard had reported—on the basis of the results of the Binet-Simon test given four years earlier to a small group of "average" immigrants at Ellis Island—that two out of five of those who arrived in steerage were "feebleminded." Now Brigham found that according to their performance on the Army tests the Alpine and Mediterranean "races" were "intellectually inferior to the representatives of the Nordic race." He declared, in what became a commonplace of the popular literature on the subject, that the average intelligence of immigrants was declining.

The average intelligence of black Americans appeared to be just as low as most white Americans had long liked to think it. The Army test data, and various test surveys, disclosed that blacks accounted for a disproportionately large fraction of the "feebleminded." The Army tests also appeared to indicate that the average black person in the United States had the mental age of a ten-year-old.

Clearly, a variety of causes, including the cultural bias of the Army tests themselves and the poor education of many of the test takers, might have accounted for the results. Yet the supposedly objective test data further convinced many Americans that both mental deficiency and intelligence were genetically determined. White college students scored very well on the alpha tests, and so did high school students from Anglo-Saxon or white-collar homes. This was taken to mean that gifted students came from homes that, in the words of one educator, "rank high racially, economically, intellectually, and socially." Terman and other psychologists were quick to point out that opening up avenues of opportunity to the children of lower socioeconomic groups probably made no sense; they did not have the IQ points to compete. President George B. Cutten of Colgate University took the Army test results as a starting point to attack the democratization of higher education and wondered aloud in his inaugural address whether democracy itself was possible in a country where the population had an average mental age of thirteen.

All this data fed into the eugenics movement that flourished in the United States (and many other countries) during the first third of the twentieth century. Eugenics centered on the idea that the human race might be improved in the manner of plant and animal breeding—that is, by getting rid of so-called undesirable

19

human beings and multiplying the so-called desirable ones. Eugenicists held desirability and undesirability to be, at base, genetic. A chart displayed at the Kansas Free Fair in 1929, purporting to illustrate the "laws" of Mendelian inheritance in human beings, declared, "Unfit human traits such as feeblemindedness, epilepsy, criminality, insanity, alcoholism, pauperism, and many others run in families and are inherited in exactly the same way as color in guinea pigs."

Prejudice Against Minorities

Class and race prejudice were also pervasive in eugenic science, against lower-income people in general but especially against minority groups, including the Irish Americans, who had been in the United States for several generations, and the then-recent immigrants from southeastern Europe. All were held by many scientists to be biologically inferior to native white Protestant Americans. The data from the Army intelligence tests was taken to provide quantitative affirmation that such people were inferior in native intelligence. It also reinforced the belief that the United States was suffering from dysgenic [biologically defective] tendencies. Eugenicists fastened on British data which indicated that half of each succeeding generation was produced by no more than a quarter of its married predecessor, and that the prolific quarter was disproportionately located among the dregs of society. Before the war in the United States, leading eugenicists had warned that excessive breeding of the lower classes was giving the edge to the less fit. The growth of IQ testing after the war gave a quantitative authority to the eugenic notion of fitness. For the vogue of mental testing did more than encourage fears regarding the "menace of the feebleminded." It also identified the source of heedless fecundity with low-IQ groups, and it equated national deterioration with a decline in national intelligence.

Attempting to encourage the proliferation of good genes in the population, eugenicists sponsored so-called "Fitter Family" competitions at state fairs in the 1920s. These competitions were held at the fairs in the "human stock" section. At the 1924 Kansas Free Fair, winning families in the three categories—small, average, and large—were awarded a Governor's Fitter Family Trophy, which was presented by Governor Jonathan Davis, and "Grade A Individuals" re-

> *"Eugenics centered on the idea that the human race might be improved . . . by getting rid of so-called undesirable human beings."*

ceived a medal that portrayed two diaphanously garbed parents, their arms outstretched toward their (presumably) eugenically meritorious infant. It is hard to know what made these families and individuals stand out as fit, but some evidence is supplied by the fact that all entrants had to take an IQ test—and the Wasserman test for syphilis.

Much more serious measures were advanced to halt the spread of bad genes in the population. By the late 1920s, some two dozen American states had enacted eugenic sterilization laws— which were declared constitutional in the 1927 U.S. Supreme Court decision of *Buck v. Bell*. In 1924, the United States government enacted an immigration restriction law that discriminated against people from Eastern and Southern Europe. IQ test data about the allegedly low intelligence of people from those regions was used to help rationalize the act.

Intelligence Theories Come Under Attack

However, by the 1920s the claims about trends in American intellect were under broadening attack. A growing body of lay and professional opinion held that there had been no progressive intellectual deterioration in the United States. Walter Lippmann, in a series of articles in the *New Republic* in 1922, passionately attacked the conclusions drawn by the Army's IQ testing program, bluntly declaring: "The statement that the average mental age of Americans is only about fourteen is not inaccurate. It is not incorrect. It is nonsense." Lippmann assailed the more fundamental pretension that the Army tests, or any others, measured hereditary intelligence. That claim, he said, had "no more scientific foundation than a hundred other fads, vitamins and glands and amateur psychoanalysis and correspondence courses in will power, and it will pass with them into that limbo where phrenology and palmistry and characterology and the other Babu sciences are to be found."

In Lippmann's view, the basic flaw in any hereditarian interpretation of the IQ test results lay in the insistence of psychologists like Lewis Terman that there was some concrete, invariant entity called intelligence that could be unambiguously measured. "Intelligence," Lippmann insisted, "is not an abstraction like length and weight; it is an exceedingly complicated notion which nobody has as yet succeeded in defining." In the 1920s, American psychologists increasingly came to recognize the notion's complexity, in large part because of the strong links of test performance with social and educational environment. Also troubling was the way that commonsense ideas of intelligence eluded capture by examinations. In 1930, the entire subject was reviewed by Carl Brigham, whose *Study of American Intelligence* had helped so much to promulgate the fear of mental degeneration. The more he studied the data, the more he came to believe that the tests—verbal, mathematical, and behavioral—measured only how well the examinee did on a particular examination. To say that the scores, taken together, indicated something called general intelligence, Brigham concluded, was to indulge in "psychophrenology," to confuse the test name—e.g., "verbal"—with the reality of the trait, and to misidentify the summed traits with intelligence.

By the opening of the 1930s, psychologists were coming to recognize that within given racial or ethnic groups, IQ test results varied widely; a large number in every group scored higher than the middle of the overall highest group. To be sure, whites tended to score higher than blacks, natives outperformed immigrants. But such results began to be seen as indicative of faults in the tests themselves rather than as evidence of innate "racial" differences. In his 1930 re-

21

view of the field, Brigham concluded that "comparative studies of various national and racial groups may not be made with existing tests," and he courageously added that "one of the most pretentious of these comparative racial studies"—his own—was "without foundation."

Environment Affects IQ

Brigham's remarkable mea culpa, based mainly on technical considerations, also suggested a substantive dissatisfaction that was of special importance to assessments of mental differences among racial or ethnic groups. Walter Lippmann had adumbrated the issue in 1923, when in a letter he scolded Robert Yerkes for presuming to think that the test results proved, among other things, that Irish children were inferior to English children. "You are in no position to assess the effects of the history of Ireland upon the Irish intelligence [test] behavior," Lippmann wrote. "You are in no position to disentangle the biological from the traditional causes of the result. You are in no position to disentangle the emotional disturbances of a migration not only across the sea but from a peasant to an industrial environment. You cannot examine the effects of clericalism, or the effects of a disintegration in America of the clerical tradition." Later in the decade, a growing number of American psychologists edged toward Lippmann's position: performance on IQ tests was considerably affected not only by education but by social and cultural environment and history.

In academic circles, criticism of the tests and their discriminatory interpretation was given impetus by a group of social scientists centered on Professor Franz Boas of Columbia University, a German-Jewish immigrant who had become the country's best-known anthropologist. One of Boas's acolytes was Margaret Mead, who studied the children of Italian immigrants and demonstrated that their performance on IQ tests depended on their families' social status and length of residence in the United States, and also on the extent to which English was spoken in the home.

A decidedly more sustained product was the psychologist Otto Klineberg's authoritative body of work on race and IQ. Klineberg noticed that blacks in the urban North had on the average scored higher on the Army IQ tests than certain white groups in the rural South. One of the prevailing explanations of the phenomenon was the theory of "selective migration." People in an urban or sectional region scored better on mental tests because the more intelligent had migrated there from areas where people scored worse. The more intelligent blacks, in short, tended to leave the South for the North. Klineberg was inclined to an alternative explanation: the superior test performance of northern blacks was attributable to their advantageous cultural and educational environment.

> *"Serious measures were advanced to halt the spread of bad genes in the population."*

22

Klineberg devoted his research of the early thirties to deciding between the two theories. He examined school records of black children in three southern cities to determine whether the students who had gone North were any more "intelligent" than those who had remained in the South. He also gave intelligence tests to southern-born blacks who had lived in New York City for different lengths of time, reasoning that if selective migration was at work, length of residence in the North should make no difference in the scores, but that if environment counted, then the scores should rise in proportion to time in the North.

During his travels in the South, Klineberg, a warm human being, partied, picnicked, and became friends with many blacks. The experience was an eye-opener for a white man of that time, even someone who, like Klineberg, already suspected that mental ability had little if anything to do with the biology of race. "I could see some of the ways in which culture and race got confused," he recalled. "I remember being once at a football game between two black college teams, and at every time-out the band would begin to play. Whenever the band played, many black mothers would wave the arms of their babies in time to the music. I said to myself, Well, here you see mothers teaching their children rhythm. You very rarely see that when two Ivy league teams play football. I noticed that same sort of thing with dancing. I also ran into a lot of blacks who had no sense of rhythm and who couldn't sing. The personal experience led me to query all the stereotypical ideas about blacks, and that skepticism came to be rather important in the work."

An Improved Environment Raises Test Scores

In 1935, Klineberg reported the full results of the study in his pathbreaking *Negro Intelligence and Selective Migration*. In his conclusions:

> The superiority of the northern over the southern Negroes to approximate the scores of the Whites, are due to factors in the environment, and not to selective migration. There is, in fact, no evidence whatever in favor of selective migration. The school records of those who migrated did not demonstrate any superiority over those who remained behind. The intelligence tests showed no superiority of recent arrivals in the North over those of the same age and sex who were still in southern cities. There is, on the other hand, very definite evidence that an improved environment, whether it be the southern city as contrasted with the neighboring rural districts, or the northern city as contrasted with the South as a whole, raises the test scores considerably; this rise in "intelligence" is roughly proportionate to length of residence in the more favorable environment.

In numerous subsequent publications, Klineberg continued to press the argument against the biological nature of racial differences in measurements of mental ability, often pointing to the superiority in test scores of northern blacks over various southern whites. "I wasn't the first to notice those data," he remembered with a smile. "But I used them. I did use them. My friendly enemies attributed the discovery to me and called it 'the Klineberg twist.'"

Highly Debatable Claims

The enemies rapidly diminished in force, and so did the advocates of innate mental differences across the broad front of human groups. It must be emphasized that the group differences in intelligence that so absorbed Klineberg's contemporaries were *not* white-black differences; they were differences between what we call ethnic groups but what they understood to be racial groups. Their analyses for the most part pitted not whites against blacks but native white Protestants against Irish, Poles, Hungarians, Italians, Slovenians, and so on. History tells us that the claims made in their day were at the least highly debatable and for the most part wrong. The work of social scientists like Klineberg, whose first major research dealt with differences among European groups, demonstrated that they were wrong. So did advances in genetics, which showed that behavioral traits, to the degree that they are genetic at all, are extremely complex in origin, usually involving powerful environmental inputs and many genes that are not heritable in any simple fashion.

Not all students of the matter believed that there are absolutely no biologically determined mental differences between races, but virtually all held that no such differences had been scientifically demonstrated. By the end of the Second World War, receptivity to that view had been enlarged by the revelations of the Holocaust—the exposure of the barbaric ends to which racism could lead—and had replaced the orthodoxies of Goddard's day. In 1950, UNESCO [United Nations Educational, Scientific, and Cultural Organization] issued a strong "Statement on Race."

> *"Advances in genetics . . . showed that behavioral traits, to the degree that they are genetic at all, are extremely complex."*

It was the product of an internationally distinguished effort—the drafters and commentators included Otto Klineberg, Hermann Muller, and Julian Huxley—and its principal points summarized the new views on the biology of race: The idea of race was merely a convenient tool of classification. Differences between human groups resulted from various combinations of heredity and environment. Racial groupings did not necessarily coincide with ethnic and cultural differences. The results of intelligence tests depended on some combination of innate mental ability and environmental opportunity, and there was no proof that the groups of mankind differ in their innate mental characteristics, whether in respect to intelligence or temperament.

Natural Ability Is Often Inherited

by Francis Galton

About the author: *Francis Galton (1822–1911) was an English scientist and writer who founded the study of eugenics, the theory that the human population could be improved through selective breeding.*

Is reputation a fair test of natural ability? It is the only one I can employ—am I justified in using it? How much of a man's success is due to his opportunities, how much to his natural power of intellect?

This is a very old question, on which a great many commonplaces have been uttered that need not be repeated here. I will confine myself to a few considerations, such as seem to me amply adequate to prove what is wanted for my argument.

Reputation and Ability

Let it clearly be borne in mind, what I mean by reputation and ability. By reputation, I mean the opinion of contemporaries, revised by posterity—the favourable result of a critical analysis of each man's character, by many biographers. I do not mean high social or official position, nor such as is implied by being the mere lion of a London season; but I speak of the reputation of a leader of opinion, of an originator, of a man to whom the world deliberately acknowledges itself largely indebted.

By natural ability, I mean those qualities of intellect and disposition, which urge and qualify a man to perform acts that lead to reputation. I do not mean capacity without zeal, nor zeal without capacity, nor even a combination of both of them, without an adequate power of doing a great deal of very laborious work. But I mean a nature which, when left to itself, will, urged by an inherent stimulus, climb the path that leads to eminence, and has strength to reach the summit—one which, if hindered or thwarted, will fret and strive until the hindrance is overcome, and it is again free to follow its labour-loving instinct. It is almost a contradiction in terms, to doubt that such men will generally become

Excerpted from Francis Galton, *Hereditary Genius: An Inquiry into Its Laws and Consequences* (London: Macmillan, 1869).

eminent [Galton defines "eminent" as having the rank of first among 4,000 men]. On the other hand, there is plenty of evidence to show that few have won high reputations without possessing these peculiar gifts. It follows that the men who achieve eminence, and those who are naturally capable, are, to a large extent, identical.

The particular meaning in which I employ the word ability, does not restrict my argument from a wider application; for, if I succeed in showing—as I undoubtedly shall do—that the concrete triple event, of ability combined with zeal and with capacity for hard labour, is inherited, much more will there be justification for believing that any one of its three elements, whether it be ability, or zeal, or capacity for labour, is similarly a gift of inheritance.

I believe, and shall do my best to show, that, if the "eminent" men of any period, had been changelings when babies, a very fair proportion of those who survived and retained their health up to fifty years of age, would, notwithstanding their altered circumstances, have equally risen to eminence. Thus—to take a strong case—it is incredible that any combination of circumstances, could have repressed [the English statesman] Lord Brougham to the level of undistinguished mediocrity.

The arguments on which I rely are as follow. It will limit their application for the present to men of the pen and to artists. First, it is a fact, that numbers of men rise, before they are middle-aged, from the humbler ranks of life to that worldly position, in which it is of no importance to their future career, how their youth has been passed. They have overcome their hindrances, and thus start fair with others more fortunately reared, in the

> *"If the 'eminent' men of any period, had been changelings when babies, a very fair proportion . . . would . . . have equally risen to eminence."*

subsequent race of life. A boy who is to be carefully educated is sent to a good school, where he confessedly acquires little useful information, but where he is taught the art of learning. The man of whom I have been speaking has contrived to acquire the same art in a school of adversity. Both stand on equal terms, when they have reached mature life. They compete for the same prizes, measure their strength by efforts in the same direction, and their relative successes are thenceforward due to their relative natural gifts. There are many such men in the "eminent" class, as biographies abundantly show. Now, if the hindrances to success were very great, we should expect all who surmounted them to be prodigies of genius. The hindrances would form a system of natural selection, by repressing all whose gifts were below a certain very high level. But what is the case? We find very many who have risen from the ranks, who are by no means prodigies of genius; many who have no claim to "eminence," who have risen easily in spite of all obstacles. The hindrances undoubtedly form a system of natural selection that represses mediocre men, and even men of pretty fair powers—in short, the classes below D; but many of D succeed, a great many of E, and I believe a very large majority of those above. [Galton devised an alphabetical classification system in which "A" is one rank above average and "a" is one rank below average. Each succeeding letter is a higher (or lower) grade until "G" or "g." "X" includes all those ranked above "G."]

If a man is gifted with vast intellectual ability, eagerness to work, and power of working, I cannot comprehend how such a man should be repressed. The world is always tormented with difficulties waiting to be solved—struggling with ideas and feelings, to which it can give no adequate expression. If, then, there exists a man capable of solving those difficulties, or of giving a voice to those pent-up feelings, he is sure to be welcomed with universal acclamation. We may almost say that he had only to put his pen to paper, and the thing is done. I am here speaking of the very first-class men—prodigies—one in a million, or one in ten millions. . . .

Social Advantages Are Not Enough

Social advantages are incompetent to give that status [of eminence] to a man of moderate ability. It would be easy to point out several men of fair capacity, who have been pushed forward by all kinds of help, who are ambitious, and exert themselves to the utmost, but who completely fail in attaining eminence. If great peers, they may be lord-lieutenants of counties; if they belong to great county families, they may become influential members of parliament and local notabilities. When they die, they leave a blank for a while in a large circle, but there is no Westminster Abbey and no public mourning for them—perhaps barely a biographical notice in the columns of the daily papers.

It is difficult to specify two large classes of men, with equal social advantages, in one of which they have high hereditary gifts, while in the other they have not. I must not compare the sons of eminent men with those of non-eminent, because much which I should ascribe to breed, others might ascribe to parental encouragement and example. Therefore, I will compare the sons of eminent men with the adopted sons of Popes and other dignitaries of the Roman Catholic Church. The practice of nepotism among ecclesiastics is universal. It consists in their giving those social helps to a nephew, or other more distant relative, that ordinary people give

> *"Social advantages are incompetent to give that status [of eminence] to a man of moderate ability."*

to their children. Now, I shall show abundantly that the nephew of an eminent man has far less chance of becoming eminent than a son, and that a more remote kinsman has far less chance than a nephew. We may therefore make a very fair comparison, for the purposes of my argument, between the success of the sons of eminent men and that of the nephews or more distant relatives, who stand in the place of sons to the high unmarried ecclesiastics of the Romish Church. If social help is really of the highest importance, the nephews of the Popes will attain eminence as frequently, or nearly so, as the sons of other eminent men; otherwise, they will not.

Distant Kinship and Nepotism

Are, then, the nephews, &c., of the Popes, on the whole, as highly distinguished as are the sons of other equally eminent men? I answer, decidedly not. There have been a few Popes who were offshoots of illustrious races, such as that of the Medici, but in the enormous majority of cases the Pope is the ablest member of his family. I do not profess to have worked up the kinships of the Italians with any especial care, but I have seen amply enough of them, to justify me in saying that the individuals whose advancement has

> *"The nephew of an eminent man has far less chance of becoming eminent than a son."*

been due to nepotism, are curiously undistinguished. The very common combination of an able son and an eminent parent, is not matched, in the case of high Romish ecclesiastics, by an eminent nephew and an eminent uncle. The social helps are the same, but hereditary gifts are wanting in the latter case.

To recapitulate: I have endeavoured to show in respect to literary and artistic eminence—

1. That men who are gifted with high abilities—even men of class E—easily rise through all the obstacles caused by inferiority of social rank. . . .

2. Men who are largely aided by social advantages, are unable to achieve eminence, unless they are endowed with high natural gifts. . . .

Opportunity Keeps Knocking

Even if a man be long unconscious of his powers, an opportunity is sure to occur—they occur over and over again to every man—that will discover them. He will then soon make up for past arrears, and outstrip competitors with very many years' start, in the race of life. There is an obvious analogy between the man of brains and the man of muscle, in the unmistakable way in which they may discover and assert their claims to superiority over less gifted, but far better educated, competitors. An average sailor climbs rigging, and an average Alpine guide scrambles along cliffs, with a facility that seems like magic to a man who has been reared away from ships and mountains. But if he have extraordinary gifts, a very little trial will reveal them, and he will rapidly make up for his arrears of education. A born gymnast would soon, in his turn, astonish the sailors by his feats. Before the voyage was half over, he would outrun them like an escaped monkey. I have witnessed an instance of this myself. Every summer, it happens that some young English tourist who had never previously planted his foot on crag or ice, succeeds in Alpine work to a marvellous degree.

Thus far, I have spoken only of literary men and artists, who, however, form the

28

bulk of the 250 per million, that attain to eminence. The reasoning that is true for them, requires large qualifications when applied to statesmen and commanders. Unquestionably, the most illustrious statesmen and commanders belong, to say the least, to the classes F and G of ability; but it does not at all follow that an English cabinet minister, if he be a great territorial lord, should belong to those classes, or even to the two or three below them. Social advantages have enormous power in bringing a man into so prominent a position as a statesman, that it is impossible to refuse him the title of "eminent," though it may be more than probable that if he had been changed in his cradle, and reared in obscurity he would have lived and died without emerging from humble life. Again, we have seen that a union of three separate qualities—intellect, zeal, and power of work—are necessary to raise men from the ranks. Only two of these qualities, in a remarkable degree, namely intellect and power of work, are required by a man who is pushed into public life; because when he is once there, the interest is so absorbing, and the competition so keen, as to supply the necessary stimulus to an ordinary mind. Therefore, many men who have succeeded as statesmen, would have been nobodies had they been born in a lower rank of life: they

> *"The very common combination of an able son and an eminent parent, is not matched . . . by an eminent nephew and an eminent uncle."*

would have needed zeal to rise. [The French statesman Charles] Talleyrand would have passed his life in the same way as other grand seigneurs, if he had not been ejected from his birthright, by a family council, on account of his deformity, and thrown into the vortex of the French Revolution. The furious excitement of the game overcame his inveterate indolence, and he developed into the foremost man of the period, after Napoleon and Honoré Mirabeau [a French revolutionary leader]. As for sovereigns, they belong to a peculiar category. The qualities most suitable to the ruler of a great nation, are not such as lead to eminence in private life. Devotion to particular studies, obstinate perseverance, geniality and frankness in social relations, are important qualities to make a man rise in the world, but they are unsuitable to a sovereign. He has to view many interests and opinions with an equal eye; to know how to yield his favourite ideas to popular pressure, to be reserved in his friendships and able to stand alone. On the other hand, a sovereign does not greatly need the intellectual powers that are essential to the rise of a common man, because the best brains of the country are at his service. Consequently, I do not busy myself with the families of merely able sovereigns, but only with those few whose military and administrative capacity is acknowledged to have been of the very highest order.

Eminence and Commanders

As regards commanders, the qualities that raise a man to a peerage, may be of a peculiar kind, such as would not have raised him to eminence in ordinary times.

Strategy is as much a speciality as chess-playing, and large practice is required to develop it. It is difficult to see how strategical gifts, combined with a hardy constitution, dashing courage, and a restless disposition, can achieve eminence in times of peace. These qualities are more likely to attract a man to the hunting-field, if he have enough money; or if not, to make him an unsuccessful speculator.

It consequently happens that generals of high, but not the very highest order, such as Napoleon's marshals and Cromwell's generals, are rarely found to have eminent kinsfolk. Very different is the case, with the most illustrious commanders. They are far more than strategists and men of restless

> *"Men who are gifted with high abilities . . . easily rise through all the obstacles caused by inferiority of social rank."*

dispositions; they would have distinguished themselves under any circumstances. Their kinships are most remarkable, . . . [such as those] of Alexander, Scipio, Hannibal, Caesar, [the duke of] Marlborough, [Oliver] Cromwell, the Princes of Nassau [a duchy in western Germany], [the duke of] Wellington, and Napoleon.

Precisely the same remarks are applicable to demagogues. Those who rise to the surface and play a prominent part in the transactions of a troubled period, must have courage and force of character, but they need not have high intellectual powers. Nay, it is more appropriate that the intellects of such men should be narrow and one-sided, and their dispositions moody and embittered. These are not qualities that lead to eminence in ordinary times. Consequently, the families of such men, are mostly unknown to fame. But the kinships of popular leaders of the highest order, as of the two Gracchi [Roman tribunes], of the two Arteveldts [Flemish leaders], and of Mirabeau, are illustrious.

Power of Command Is Not Unusual

I may mention a class of cases that strikes me forcibly as a proof, that a sufficient power of command to lead to eminence in troublous times, is much less unusual than is commonly supposed, and that it lies neglected in the course of ordinary life. In beleaguered towns, as, for example, during the great Indian mutiny, a certain type of character very frequently made its appearance. People rose into notice who had never previously distinguished themselves, and subsided into their former way of life, after the occasion for exertion was over; while during the continuance of danger and misery, they were the heroes of their situation. They were cool in danger, sensible in council, cheerful under prolonged suffering, humane to the wounded and sick, encouragers of the fainthearted. Such people were formed to shine only under exceptional circumstances. They had the advantage of possessing too tough a fibre to be crushed by anxiety and physical misery, and perhaps in consequence of that very toughness, they required a stimulus of the sharpest kind, to goad them to all the exertions of which they were capable.

30

The result of what I have said, is to show that in statesmen and commanders, mere "eminence" is by no means a satisfactory criterion of such natural gifts as would make a man distinguished under whatever circumstances he had been reared. On the other hand, statesmen of a high order, and commanders of the very highest, who overthrow all opponents, must be prodigiously gifted. The reader himself must judge the cases quoted in proof of hereditary gifts, by their several merits. I have endeavoured to speak of none but the most illustrious names. It would have led to false conclusions, had I taken a larger number, and thus descended to a lower level of merit.

Reputation Is a Fair Test

In conclusion, I see no reason to be dissatisfied with the conditions of accepting high reputation as a very fair test of high ability. The nature of the test would not have been altered, if an attempt had been made to readjust each man's reputation according to his merits, because this is what every biographer does. If I had possessed the critical power of Charles Ste. Beuve [French literary critic and poet], I should have merely thrown into literature another of those numerous expressions of opinion, by the aggregate of which all reputations are built.

> *"Men who are largely aided by social advantages, are unable to achieve eminence, unless they are endowed with high natural gifts."*

To conclude: I feel convinced that no man can achieve a very high reputation without being gifted with very high abilities; and I trust that reason has been given for the belief, that few who possess these very high abilities can fail in achieving eminence.

Genetics Influences IQ Differences Between Blacks and Whites

by Arthur R. Jensen

About the author: *Arthur R. Jensen is a professor emeritus of educational psychology at the University of California in Berkeley and the author of many books and articles about genetics, race, and intelligence.*

The important distinction between the *individual* and the *population* must always be kept clearly in mind in any discussion of racial differences in mental abilities or any other behavioral characteristics. Whenever we select a person for some special educational purpose, whether for special instruction in a grade-school class for children with learning problems, or for a "gifted" class with an advanced curriculum, or for college attendance, or for admission to graduate training or a professional school, we are selecting an *individual*, and we are selecting him and dealing with him as an individual for reasons of his individuality. Similarly, when we employ someone, or promote someone in his occupation, or give some special award or honor to someone for his accomplishments, we are doing this to an individual. The variables of social class, race, and national origin are correlated so imperfectly with any of the valid criteria on which the above decisions should depend, or, for that matter, with any behavioral characteristic, that these background factors are irrelevant as a basis for dealing with individuals—as students, as employees, as neighbors. Furthermore, since, as far as we know, the full range of human talents is represented in all the major races of man and in all socioeconomic levels, it is unjust to allow the mere fact of an individual's racial or social background to affect the treatment accorded to him. All persons rightfully must be regarded on the basis of their individual qualities and merits, and all social, educational, and economic institutions must have built into them the mechanisms for insuring and maximizing the treatment of persons according to their individual behavior.

Intelligence and Race

If a society completely believed and practiced the ideal of treating every person as an individual, it would be hard to see why there should be any problems about "race" per se. There might still be problems concerning poverty, unemployment, crime, and other social ills, and, given the will, they could be tackled just as any other problems that require rational methods for solution. But if this philosophy prevailed in practice, there would not need to be a "race problem."

The question of *race* differences in intelligence comes up not when we deal with individuals as individuals, but when certain identifiable *groups* or subcultures within the society are brought into comparison with one another *as groups or populations*. It is only when the groups are disproportionately represented in what are commonly perceived as the most desirable and the least desirable social and occupational roles in a society that the question arises concerning average differences among groups. Since much of the current thinking behind civil rights, fair employment, and equality of educational opportunity appeals to the fact that there is a disproportionate representation of different racial groups in the various levels of the educational, occupational, and socioeconomic hierarchy, we are forced to examine all the possible reasons for this inequality among racial groups in the attainments and rewards generally valued by all groups within our society. To what extent can such inequalities be attributed to unfairness in society's multiple selection processes? ("Unfair" meaning that selection is influenced by intrinsically irrelevant criteria, such as skin color, racial or national origin, etc.) And to what extent are these inequalities attributable to really relevant selection criteria which apply equally to all individuals but at the same time select disproportionately between some racial groups because there exist, in fact, real average differences among the groups—differences in the population distributions of those characteristics which are indisputably relevant to educational and occupational performance? This is certainly one of the most important questions confronting our nation today. The answer, which can be found only through unfettered research, has enormous consequences for the welfare of all, particularly of minorities whose plight is now in the foreground of public attention. A preordained, doctrinaire stance with regard to this issue hinders the

> *" 'No holds barred' is the best formula for scientific inquiry."*

achievement of a scientific understanding of the problem. To rule out of court, so to speak, any reasonable hypotheses on purely ideological grounds is to argue that static ignorance is preferable to increasing our knowledge of reality. I strongly disagree with those who believe in searching for the truth by scientific means only under certain circumstances and eschew this course in favor of ignorance under other circumstances, or who believe that the results of inquiry on some subjects cannot be entrusted to the public but should be kept the guarded possession of a scientific elite. Such attitudes, in my opinion, represent a danger to free inquiry and, consequently, in the long run, work to the disadvantage of society's general welfare. "No holds barred" is the best formula for scientific inquiry. One does not decree beforehand which phenomena cannot be studied or which questions cannot be answered.

Genetic Aspects of Racial Differences

No one, to my knowledge, questions the role of environmental factors, including influences from past history, in determining at least some of the variance between racial groups in standard measures of intelligence, school performance, and occupational status. The current literature on the culturally disadvantaged abounds with discussion—some of it factual, some of it fanciful—of how a host of environmental factors depresses cognitive development and performance. I recently co-edited a book which is largely concerned with the environmental aspects of disadvantaged minorities. But the possible importance of genetic factors in racial behavioral differences has been greatly ignored, almost to the point of being a tabooed subject, just as were the topics of venereal disease and birth control a generation or so ago.

My discussions with a number of geneticists concerning the question of a genetic basis of differences among races in mental abilities have revealed to me a number of rather consistently agreed-upon points which can be summarized in general terms as follows: Any groups which have been geographically or socially isolated from one another for many generations are practically certain to differ in their gene pools, and consequently are likely to show differences in any phenotypic characteristics having high heritability. This is practically axiomatic, according to the geneticists with whom I have spoken. Races are said to be "breeding populations," which is to say that matings within the group have a much higher probability than matings outside the group. Races are more technically viewed by geneticists as populations having different distributions of gene frequencies. These genetic differences are manifested in virtually every anatomical, physiological, and biochemical comparison one can make between representative samples of identifiable racial groups. There is no reason to suppose that the brain should be exempt from this generalization. (Racial differences in the relative frequencies of various blood constituents have probably been the most thoroughly studied so far.)

But what about behavior? If it can be measured and shown to have a genetic component, it would be regarded, from a genetic standpoint, as no different from other human characteristics. There seems to be little question that racial differences in genetically conditioned behavioral characteristics, such as mental

> *"The possible importance of genetic factors in racial behavioral differences has been greatly ignored."*

abilities, should exist, just as physical differences. The real questions, geneticists tell me, are not whether there are or are not genetic racial differences that affect behavior, because there undoubtedly are. The proper questions to ask, from a scientific standpoint, are: What is the direction of the difference? What is the magnitude of the difference? And what is the significance of the difference—medically, socially, educationally, or from whatever standpoint that may be relevant to the characteristic in question? A difference is important only within a specific context. For example, one's blood type in the ABO system is unimportant until one needs a transfusion. And some genetic differences are apparently of no importance with respect to any context as far as anyone has been able to discover—for example, differences in the size and shape of ear lobes. The idea that all genetic differences have arisen or persisted only as a result of natural selection, by conferring some survival or adaptive benefit on their possessors, is no longer generally held. There appear to be many genetic differences, or polymorphisms, which confer no discernible advantages to survival.

Negro Intelligence and Scholastic Performance

Negroes in the United States are disproportionately represented among groups identified as culturally or educationally disadvantaged. This, plus the fact that Negroes constitute by far the largest racial minority in the United States, has for many years focused attention on Negro intelligence. It is a subject with a now vast literature which has been quite recently reviewed by R.M. Dreger and K.S. Miller and by Audrey M. Shuey, whose 578-page review is the most comprehensive, covering 382 studies. The basic data are well known: on the average, Negroes test about 1 standard deviation (15 IQ points) below the average of the white population in IQ, and this finding is fairly uniform across the 81 different tests of intellectual ability used in the studies reviewed by Shuey. This magnitude of difference gives a median overlap of 15 percent, meaning that 15 percent of the Negro population exceeds the white average. In terms of proportions of variance, if the numbers of Negroes and whites were equal, the differences *between* racial groups would account for 23 percent of the total variance, but—an important point—the differences *within* groups would account for 77 percent of the total variance. When gross socioeconomic level is controlled, the average difference reduces to about 11 IQ points, which is about the same spread as the average difference between siblings in the same family. So-called "culture-free" or "culture-fair" tests tend to give Negroes slightly lower scores, on the average, than more conventional IQ tests such as the Stanford-Binet and Wechsler scale. Also, as a group, Negroes perform somewhat more poorly on those subtests which tap abstract abilities. The majority of studies show that Negroes perform relatively better on verbal than on

"Groups which have been . . . isolated . . . are practically certain to differ in their gene pools."

non-verbal intelligence tests.

In tests of scholastic achievement, also, judging from the massive data of the James S. Coleman study, Negroes score about 1 standard deviation (SD) below the average for whites and Orientals and considerably less than 1 SD below other disadvantaged minorities tested in the Coleman study—Puerto Rican, Mexican-American, and American Indian. The 1 SD decrement in Negro performance is fairly constant throughout the period from grades 1 through 12.

> *"Negroes test about . . . 15 IQ points below the average of the white population."*

Another aspect of the distribution of IQs in the Negro population is their lesser variance in comparison to the white distribution. This shows up in most of the studies reviewed by Shuey. The best single estimate is probably the estimate based on a large normative study of Stanford-Binet IQs of Negro school children in five Southeastern states, by W.A. Kennedy, V. Van De Riet, and J.C. White Jr. They found the SD of Negro children's IQs to be 12.4, as compared with 16.4 in the white normative sample. The Negro distribution thus has only about 60 percent as much variance (i.e., SD^2) as the white distribution.

The Implication of Genetics

There is an increasing realization among students of the psychology of the disadvantaged that the discrepancy in their average performance cannot be completely or directly attributed to discrimination or inequalities in education. It seems not unreasonable, in view of the fact that intelligence variation has a large genetic component, to hypothesize that genetic factors may play a part in this picture. But such an hypothesis is anathema to many social scientists. The idea that the lower average intelligence and scholastic performance of Negroes could involve, not only environmental, but also genetic, factors has indeed been strongly denounced. But it has been neither contradicted nor discredited by evidence.

The fact that a reasonable hypothesis has not been rigorously proved does not mean that it should be summarily dismissed. It only means that we need more appropriate research for putting it to the test. I believe such definitive research is entirely possible but has not yet been done. So all we are left with are various lines of evidence, no one of which is definitive alone, but which, viewed all together, make it a not unreasonable hypothesis that genetic factors are strongly implicated in the average Negro-white intelligence difference. The preponderance of the evidence is, in my opinion, less consistent with a strictly environmental hypothesis than with a genetic hypothesis, which, of course, does not exclude the influence of environment or its interaction with genetic factors.

We can be accused of superficiality in our thinking about this issue, I believe, if we simply dismiss a genetic hypothesis without having seriously thought about the relevance of typical findings such as the following:

Failure to Equate Negroes and Whites in IQ and Scholastic Ability. No one has yet produced any evidence based on a properly controlled study to show that representative samples of Negro and white children can be equalized in intellectual ability through statistical control of environment and education. . . .

Inadequacies of Purely Environmental Explanations. Strictly environmental explanations of group differences tend to have an ad hoc quality. They are usually plausible for the situation they are devised to explain, but often they have little generality across situations, and new ad hoc hypotheses have to be continually devised. Pointing to environmental differences between groups is never sufficient in itself to infer a causal relationship to group differences in intelligence. To take just one example of this tendency of social scientists to attribute lower intelligence and scholastic ability to almost any environmental difference that seems handy, we can look at the evidence regarding the effects of "father absence." Since the father is absent in a significantly larger proportion of Negro than of white families, the factor of "father absence" has been frequently pointed to in the literature on the disadvantaged as one of the causes of Negroes' lower performance on IQ tests and in scholastic achievement. Yet the two largest studies directed at obtaining evidence on this very point—the only studies I have seen that are methodologically adequate—both conclude that the factor of "father absence" versus "father presence" makes no independent contribution to variance in intelligence or scholastic achievement. The sample sizes were so large in both of these studies that even a very slight degree of correlation between father absence and the measures of cognitive performance would have shown up as statistically significant. James Coleman concluded: "Absence of a father in the home did not have the anticipated effect on ability scores. Overall, pupils without fathers performed at approximately the same level as those with fathers—although there was some variation between groups" (groups referring to geographical regions of the U.S.). And A.B. Wilson concluded from his survey of a California school district: "Neither our own data nor the preponderance of evidence from other research studies indicate that father presence or absence, *per se*, is related to school achievement. While broken homes reflect the existence of social and personal problems, and have some consequence for the development of personality, broken homes do not have any systematic effect on the overall level of school success."

> *"Genetic factors may play a part in [intelligence variation]."*

Negroes and American Indians

The nationwide Coleman study included assessments of a dozen environmental variables and socioeconomic indices which are generally thought to be major sources of environmental influence in determining individual and group differences in scholastic performance—such factors as: reading material in the home, cultural amenities in the home, structural integrity of the home, foreign language in the home, preschool attendance, parents' education, parents' educational desires for child, parents' interest in child's school work, time spent on homework, child's self-concept (self-esteem), and so on. These factors are all correlated—in the expected direction—with scholastic performance within each of the racial or ethnic groups studied by Coleman. Yet, interestingly enough, they are not systematically correlated with differences *between* groups. For example, by far the most environmentally disadvantaged groups in the Coleman study are the American Indians. On every environmental index they average *lower* than the Negro samples, and overall their environmental rating is about as far below the Negro average as the Negro rating is below the white average. (As pointed out by Robert E. Kuttner, American Indians are much more disadvantaged than Negroes, or any other minority groups in the United States, on a host of other factors not assessed by Coleman, such as income, unemployment, standards of health care, life expectancy, and infant mortality.) Yet the American Indian ability and achievement test scores average about half a standard deviation higher than the scores of Negroes. The differences were in favor of the Indian children on each of the four tests used by Coleman: non-verbal intelligence, verbal intelligence, reading comprehension, and math achievement. If the environmental factors assessed by Coleman are the major determinants of Negro-white differences that many social scientists have claimed they are, it is hard to see why such factors should act in reverse fashion in determining differences between Negroes and Indians, especially in view of the fact that *within* each group the factors are significantly correlated in the expected direction with achievement. . . .

The Magnitude of Adult Negro-White Differences

The largest sampling of Negro and white intelligence test scores resulted from the administration of the Armed Forces Qualification Test (AFQT) to a national sample of over 10 million men between the ages of 18 and 26. As of 1966, the overall failure rate for Negroes was 68 percent as compared with 19 percent for whites. (The failure cut-off score that yields these percentages is roughly equivalent to a Stanford-Binet IQ of 86.) Daniel Patrick Moynihan has estimated that during the same period in which the AFQT was administered to these large representative samples of Negro and white male youths, approximately one-half of Negro families could be considered as middle-class or above by the usual socioeconomic criteria. So even if we assumed that all of the lower 50 percent of Negroes on the SES [socioeconomic status] scale failed the AFQT, it would still mean that at least 36 percent of the middle SES Negroes failed the test, a failure rate almost twice as high as that of the white population for all levels of SES.

Do such findings raise any question as to the plausibility of theories that postulate exclusively environmental factors as sufficient causes for the observed differences?

Intelligence Is Highly Heritable

by Richard J. Herrnstein

About the author: *Richard J. Herrnstein, who died in September 1994, held the Edgar Pierce chair in psychology at Harvard University. He is the author of several articles about IQ and is the coauthor of* The Bell Curve.

The problem with nature and nurture is to decide which—inheritance or environment—is primary, for the I.Q. is exclusively the result of neither one alone. Advocates of environment—the clear majority of those who express themselves publicly on the subject—must explain why I.Q.'s usually stay about the same during most people's lives and also why high or low I.Q.'s tend to run in families. Those facts could easily be construed as signs of a genetic basis for the I.Q. The usual environmentalist answer argues that I.Q.'s remain the same to the extent that environments remain the same. If you are lucky enough to be wellborn, then your I.Q. will show the benefits of nurturing, which, in turn, gives you an advantage in the competition for success. If, on the other hand, you are blighted with poor surroundings, your mental growth will be stunted and you are likely to be stuck at the bottom of the social ladder. By this view, parents bequeath to their children not so much the genes for intelligence as the environment that will promote or retard it.

In one plausible stroke the environmentalist arguments seem to explain, therefore, not only the stability of the I.Q. but also the similarity between parents and children. The case is further strengthened by arguing that early training fixes the I.Q. more firmly than anything we know how to do later. And then to cap it off, the environmentalist may claim that the arbitrary social barriers in our society trap the underprivileged in their surroundings while guarding the overprivileged in theirs. Anyone who accepts this series of arguments is unshaken by Arthur R. Jensen's reminder that compensatory education has failed in the United States, for the answer seems to be ready and waiting. To someone who believes in the environmental theory, the failure of compensatory education is not disproof of his theory, but rather a sign that we need more and better special training earlier in a person's life.

Excerpted from Richard J. Herrnstein, "I.Q.," *Atlantic Monthly*, September 1971. Reprinted by permission of Susan Herrnstein.

Testing the Environment Theory

To be sure, it seems obvious that poor and unattractive surroundings will stunt a child's mental growth. To question it seems callous. But even if it is plausible, how do we know it is true? By what evidence do we test the environmentalist doctrine? The simplest possible assessment of the inherited factor in I.Q. is with identical twins, for only environmental differences can turn up between people with identical genes. In an article recently published in the periodical *Behavior Genetics*, Professor Jensen surveys four major studies of identical twins who were reared in separate homes. Most of the twins had been separated by the age of six months, and almost all by the age of two years. The twins were Caucasians, living in England, Denmark, and the United States—all told, 122 pairs of them. The overall I.Q. of the 244 individuals was about 97, slightly lower than the standard 100. Identical twins tend to have slightly depressed I.Q.'s, perhaps owing to the prenatal hazards of twindom. The 244 individuals spanned the range of I.Q.'s from 63 to 132, a range that brackets most of humanity—or to be more precise, 97 percent of the general population on whom intelligence tests have been standardized.

The 85 Percent Correlation

Being identical twins, the pairs shared identical genetic endowments, but their environments could have been as different as those of random pairs of children in the society at large. Nevertheless, their I.Q.'s correlated by about 85 percent, which is more than usual between ordinary siblings or even fraternal twins growing up together with their own families. It is, in fact, almost as big as the correlations between the heights and weights of these twins, which were 94 percent and 88 percent respectively. Even environmentalists would expect separately raised twins to look alike, but these results show that the I.Q.'s match almost as well. Of course if the environment alone set the I.Q., the correlations should have been much smaller than 85 percent. It would, however, be rash to leap to the conclusion that the 85 percent correlation is purely genetic, for when twins are placed into separate homes, they might well be placed into similar environments. The children had been separated not for the edification of psychologists studying the I.Q., but for the weighty reasons that break families up—illness, poverty, death, parental incapacity, and so on—and the accidents of separation may not have yielded well-designed experiments. Some of the pairs were no doubt raised by different branches of the same family, perhaps assuring them considerable environmental similarity anyway. In such cases, the correlation of 85 percent would not be purely genetic, but at least partly environmental. Fortunately for our state of knowledge, one of

> *"Twins raised apart differ on the average by about seven points in I.Q."*

the four studies examined by Jensen included ratings of the foster homes in terms of the breadwinner's occupation. Six categories sufficed: higher professional, lower professional, clerical, skilled, semiskilled, unskilled. Now, with this classification of homes, we know a little about whether the twins were raised in homes with a similar cultural ambience. To the extent that the environment in a home reflects the breadwinner's occupation, the answer is unequivocally negative, for there was literally no general correlation in the occupational levels of the homes into which the pairs were separated. At

> *"School performance responds to the environment substantially more than does the I.Q."*

least for this one study—which happened to be the largest of the four—the high correlation in I.Q. resulted from something besides a social-class correlation in the foster homes, most likely the shared inheritance.

Twins raised apart differ on the average by about seven points in I.Q. Two people chosen at random from the general population differ by seventeen points. Only four of the 122 pairs of twins differed by as much as seventeen points. Ordinary siblings raised in the same household differ by twelve points. Only nineteen of the 122 twin pairs differed by as much as that. And finally, fraternal twins raised in the same home differ by an average of eleven points, which was equaled or exceeded by only twenty-three of the 122 pairs. In other words, more than four times out of five the difference between identical twins raised apart fell short of the average difference between fraternal twins raised together by their own parents. At the same time, those separated twins were not so similar in schoolwork. Identical twins raised together resemble each other in both I.Q. and school grades. When twins are separated, their I.Q.'s remain quite close, but their grades diverge. It seems that school performance responds to the environment substantially more than does the I.Q., although neither one is solely the outcome of either nature or nurture.

Jensen and I.Q.

The comparison between I.Q. and grades was one theme of Jensen's controversial earlier article, "How Much Can We Boost I.Q. and Scholastic Achievement?", which appeared in the winter of 1969 in the *Harvard Educational Review.* Jensen answered the title's rhetorical question about I.Q. with a scholarly and circumspect form of "not very much." The article is cautious and detailed, far from extreme in position or tone. Not only its facts but even most of its conclusions are familiar to experts. The failure of compensatory education was the occasion for the article, which served especially well in assembling many scattered but pertinent items. Jensen echoes most experts on the subject of the I.Q. by concluding that substantially more can be ascribed to inheritance than environment. Since the importance of inheritance seems to say something about racial differences in I.Q. that most well-disposed people do not want to

41

hear, it has been argued that Jensen should not have written on the subject at all or that the *Harvard Educational Review* should not have, as it did, invited him to write on it.

Some of Jensen's critics have argued that because environment and inheritance are intertwined, it is impossible to tease them apart. The criticism may seem persuasive to laymen, for nature and nurture are indeed intertwined, and in just the way that makes teasing them apart most difficult. For intelligence—unlike, for example, skin color—the main agents of both nature and nurture are likely to be one's parents. One inherits skin color from one's parents, but the relevant environment does not come directly from them but from sun, wind, age, and so on. For skin color, resemblance to parents signifies (albeit not infallibly) inheritance; for intelligence, resemblance is ambiguous. Nevertheless analysis is possible even with I.Q., as Jensen and his predecessors have shown. The most useful data for the purpose are the correlations between I.Q. and kinship, as exemplified by the twin studies, which set genetic similarity high and environmental similarity low. Foster children in the same home define the other extreme of kinship and environment. If environment had no bearing at all on intelligence, then the I.Q.'s of such unrelated children should correlate slightly at most (and only to the extent caused by a special factor to be mentioned shortly). In contrast, if environment were all, then the correlation should approach the value for natural siblings. Actually, the I.Q.'s of foster children in the same home correlate by about 24 percent (less than half the value for natural siblings). However, even the correlation of 24 percent cannot be credited entirely to the children's

> *"The more closely related by blood two people are, the greater the correlation between their I.Q.'s."*

shared environment. Bear in mind that adoption agencies try to place "comparable" children in the same home, which means that there is more than just their common surroundings making them alike. Suppose, for example, that adoption agencies tried to put children with similar hair color in any given family. They could check on the natural parents, and perhaps even on the grandparents, and make a reasonable guess about the baby's eventual hair color. The foster children in a given home would then often have similar hair color; they would be unrelated by blood, but the similarity would be more genetic than environmental. By trying for a congenial match between foster child and foster parents—in appearance and in mental ability—adoption agencies make the role of environment look more important than it probably is.

Family and I.Q. Correlation

In between foster siblings and identical twins come the more familiar relations, and these too have been scrutinized. If intelligence were purely genetic, the I.Q.'s of second cousins would correlate by 14 percent and that of first

cousins by 18 percent (the reasons for those peculiar percentages are well beyond the scope of this viewpoint, so they are offered without proof). Instead of
14 percent and 18 percent, the actual correlations are 16 percent and 26 percent—too large for genetic influences alone, but in the right range. Uncle's (or
aunt's) I.Q. should, by the genes alone, correlate with nephew's (or niece's) by
a value of 31 percent; the actual value
is 34 percent. The correlation between grandparent and grandchild
should, on genetic grounds alone,
also be 31 percent, whereas the actual
correlation is 27 percent, again a

> *"If intelligence were entirely genetic, then racial differences would be genetic."*

small discrepancy. And finally for this brief survey, the predicted correlation
between parent and child, by genes alone, is 49 percent, whereas the actual correlation is 50 percent using the parents' adult I.Q.'s and 56 percent using the
parents' childhood I.Q.'s—in either case too small a difference to quibble
about. Parents and their children correlate about as well whether the children
are raised at home or by a foster family, which underscores the relative unim-
portance of the environment.

The foregoing figures are lifted directly out of Jensen's famous article, figures
that he himself culled from the literature of intelligence testing. The measurements say that (1) the more closely related by blood two people are, the greater
the correlation between their I.Q.'s and (2) the correlations fall in the right
range from the purely genetic standpoint. By evaluating the total evidence, and
by a procedure too technical to explain here, Jensen concluded (as have most of
the other experts in the field) that the genetic factor is worth about 80 percent
and that only 20 percent is left to everything else—the social, cultural, and
physical environment, plus illness, prenatal factors, and what have you.

The Racial Issue

Jensen's two papers leave little doubt about the heritability of I.Q. among North
American and Western European whites, whom most data on the subject de-
scribe. In fact, there is little dispute on this score, even among those who object
vigorously to this work. It is the relation between heritability and racial differences that raises the hackles. Given the well-established, roughly fifteen-point
black-white difference in I.Q., the argument is whether the difference arises in the
environment or the genes. If intelligence were entirely genetic, then racial differences would be genetic simply because they could be due to nothing else. Conversely, if the genes were irrelevant, then the racial difference would have to be
due to the environment, again because there would be no alternative. As it is, I.Q.
reflects both a person's genes and his environment. The racial issue really poses
the nature-nurture question all over again, but this time for a particular finding—
the higher scores of whites over blacks on I.Q. tests.

In general—not just for the racial issue—the question of nature and nurture boils down to the study of variation. Granted that I.Q.'s vary among people, to what extent does the variation correlate with the differences in their surroundings on the one hand and with the differences in their genetic makeup on the other? No one disputes the existence of all three kinds of variation—in I.Q., environment, and inheritance—only their interconnections. In effect, the environmentalist is saying that among a group of people, the various I.Q.'s reflect the various surroundings more or less without regard to the genes. In contrast, the nativist is saying the reverse—that different I.Q.'s reflect different genetic endowments rather than different environments. The study of quantitative genetics contrives to answer such riddles, and so a brief didactic excursion is in order. But instead of starting the lesson with I.Q., let us consider a trait which we are not emotionally committed to to begin with.

Determining Heritability

Suppose we wanted to know the heritability of skin color. We would not need science to tell us that dark or fair complexions run in certain families or larger groups. Nor must we be told that nongenetic elements also enter in, as when a person is tan from the sun or pale with illness or yellow from jaundice or red with rage or blue with cold. The task of quantitative genetics is to come up with a number that says how large a role inheritance plays in the total amount of variation in skin color that we see in a particular group of people at a particular time. If the number is large, then skin color is largely heritable; if very small, then the heritability is negligible. If the number is large, then there will be marked family resemblances; if small, then members of given families will be no more alike than unrelated people. To convey such information, the number must reflect which group of people we choose to study. Consider first the United States, with its racial and ethnic diversity. Much skin variation here is related to ancestry, whether black, white, yellow, red, or Mediterranean, Nordic, Alpine, or some blend. Family resemblances in skin color are quite strong in America, so the heritability should come out large. Now contrast this with an isolated village in Norway, full of Scandinavians with generations of pale-skinned ancestors. In the Norwegian town, whatever little variation there is in skin color is likely to be environmental, due to the circumstances of life rather than to the accident of inheri-

"Different I.Q.'s reflect different genetic endowments rather than different environments."

tance. As regards skin color, children will be no more like their parents than their nonrelatives, so heritability should come out low.

The hardest thing to grasp about heritability is that it says something about a trait in a population as a whole, not about the relation between particular parents and their offspring. Skin color turns out to be more heritable in the United States than in Norway, even though the physiological mechanisms of inheritance are surely the same. In the Norwegian town, a swarthy father and mother (who probably got that way from exposure to the weather) are likely to have children as fair-skinned as their neighbors. In the American town, however, it is more likely that the swarthiness of swarthy parents is genetic and will be passed on to the children. Although heritability is not the strictly physiological concept that laymen imagine it to be, it is uniquely useful for talking about the nature-nurture question, for it tells us whether traits run in families within a broader population of individuals.

> *"Heritability . . . says something about a trait in a population as a whole."*

The technical measure of heritability is a number between 0 and 1.0 that states how much of the variation in a trait is due to genetic factors. How it is calculated need not detain us here. It is enough to know that a heritability of .5 means (omitting some technical complexities) that the variation is due half to genetic factors and half to other factors; a heritability of .2 means that only a fifth of the variation is genetic, and so on. Some actual heritabilities of traits in animals may be helpful. In piebald Holstein cattle, for example, the amount of white in the fur has a heritability of about .95, a value so high that it is almost right to say the environment plays no role here. In contrast, milk yield has a heritability of only .3. White in the fur, therefore, breeds more true than milk production. In pigs, the thickness of body fat has a heritability of .55, while the litter size has a heritability of only .15.

The High Heritability of Intelligence

Now back to I.Q. and the racial issue. Using the procedures of quantitative genetics, Jensen (and most other experts) estimates that I.Q. has a heritability between .80 and .85, but this is based almost entirely on data from whites. We may, therefore, say that 80 to 85 percent of the variation in I.Q. among whites is due to the genes. Because we do not know the heritability for I.Q. among blacks, we cannot make a comparable statement for them. But let us simply assume, for the sake of discussion, that .8 is the heritability for whites and blacks taken together. What could we say about the racial difference in I.Q. then? The answer is that we could still say nothing positive about it. Recall that the concept of heritability applies to a population as a whole. All we could say is that the differences between people, on the average and without regard to color, are 80 percent inherited. But within this broad generality, particular differences could and would be more or less inherited. Take, for example, the differences in I.Q. between identical twins. Even with the average heritability equal to .8, all twin differences have to be totally environmental, since their genes cannot differ. Or conversely, consider the differences between foster children in a given foster family. Because they are growing up in the same home, their I.Q. differences could easily be relatively more genetic than those of people taken at random. When this line of reasoning is applied to a racial (or ethnic) difference in

I.Q., the only proper conclusion is that we do not know whether it is more genetic, less genetic, or precisely as genetic as implied by a heritability of .8.

Jensen notes that we lack a good estimate of the heritability of intelligence among blacks. Although there are scraps of evidence for a genetic component in the black-white difference, the overwhelming case is for believing that American blacks have been at an environmental disadvantage. To the extent that variations in the American social environment can promote or retard I.Q., blacks have probably been held back. But a neutral commentator (a rarity these days) would have to say that the case is simply not settled, given our present stage of knowledge. To advance this knowledge would not be easy, but it could certainly be done with sufficient ingenuity and hard work. To anyone who is curious about the question and who feels competent to try to answer it, it is at least irritating to be told that the answer is either unknowable or better not known, and both enjoinders are often heard. And there is, of course, a still more fundamental issue at stake, which should concern even those who are neither curious about nor competent to study racial differences in I.Q. It is whether inquiry shall (again) be shut off because someone thinks society is best left in ignorance.

> *"Intelligence is . . .*
> *highly heritable."*

Setting aside the racial issue, the conclusion about intelligence is that, like other important though not necessarily vital traits, it is highly heritable. It is not vital in the sense that it may vary broadly without markedly affecting survival, although it no doubt affects one's life-style. Does it do us any practical good to know how heritable intelligence is? We are not, for example, on the verge of Galton's vision of eugenics, even though we now have the mental test that he thought was the crucial prerequisite. For good or ill, and for some time to come, we are stuck with mating patterns as people determine them for themselves. No sensible person would want to entrust state-run human breeding to those who control today's states. There are, however, practical corollaries of this knowledge, more humble than eugenics, but ever more salient as the growing complexity of human society makes acute the shortage of high-grade intellect.

Regression Toward the Mean

Heritability is first and foremost the measure of breeding true, useful for predicting how much of some trait the average offspring in a given family will have. For example, to predict the I.Q. of the average offspring in a family:

1. Average the parents' I.Q.'s.
2. Subtract 100 from the result.
3. Multiply the result of (2) by .8 (the heritability).
4. Add the result of (3) to 100.

Thus, given a mother and father each with I.Q.'s of 120, their average child will have an I.Q. of 116. Some of their children will be brighter and some duller, but the larger the family, the more nearly will the average converge onto 116. With parents averaging an I.Q. of 80, the average child will have an I.Q. of 84. The formula predicts something the experts call "regression toward the mean," the tendency for children to be closer to the general population average (in this case, I.Q. 100) than their parents. And in fact, *very bright* parents have children who tend to be merely *bright*, while *very dull* parents tend to have them merely *dull*. The amount of regression for a trait depends on the heritability—with high heritability, the regression is smaller than with low. Also, for a given trait the regression is greater at the extremes of a population than at its center. In other words, ordinary parents are more like their children (on the average) than extraordinary ones

> *"The single most important environmental influence on I.Q. [is] . . . something prenatal."*

(whether extraordinarily high or low). All of these characteristics of the "generation gap" follow directly and completely from the simple formula given above. Thus, when the parents average 120, the regression effect is only four I.Q. points, but if they averaged 150, the regression effect would be ten points. In comparison, height, with its heritability of .95, would show smaller regression effects than I.Q., since the multiplier in step 3 of the formula is closer to 1.0. But even so, very tall parents tend to have children who are merely tall, and very short parents tend to have them merely short. As long as the heritability of a trait falls short of 1.0, there is some regression effect.

Environmental Influence on I.Q.

Intelligence may be drifting up or down for environmental reasons from generation to generation, notwithstanding the high heritability. Height, for example, is said to be increasing—presumably because of diet and medicine—even with its .95 heritability. We can easily tell whether there has been a change in height, for the measures are absolute, and there is the tangible evidence of clothing, furniture, coffins, and the skeletons themselves. For intelligence, however, we have no absolute scales, only relative ones, and the tangible remains of intelligence defy interpretation. But if height has changed, why not intelligence? After all, one could argue, the I.Q. has a heritability of only .8, measurably lower than that of height, so it should be even more amenable to the influence of the environment. That, to be sure, is correct in principle, but the practical problem is to find the right things in the environment to change—the things that will nourish the intellect as well as diet does height. The usual assumption, that education and culture are crucial, is running into evidence that the physical environment—for example, early diet—might be more important. In fact, the twin studies that Jensen surveyed showed that the single most important environmental influence on I.Q. was not education or social environment, but something prenatal, as shown by the fact that the twin heavier at birth usually grew up with the higher I.Q.

Suppose we do find an environmental handle on I.Q.—something, let us say, in the gestating mother's diet. What then? Presumably society would try to give everyone access to the favorable factor, within the limits of its resources. Intelligence would increase accordingly. But that would not end our troubles with I.Q. Recall that heritability is a measure of relative variation. Right now, about 80 percent of the variation in I.Q. derives from the genes. If we make the relevant environment much more uniform (by making it as good as we can for everyone), then an even larger proportion of the variation in I.Q. will be attributable to the genes. The average person would be smarter, but intelligence would run in families even more obviously and with less regression toward the mean than we see today. It is likely that the mere fact of heritability in I.Q. is socially and politically important, and the more so the higher the heritability.

Environment Plays an Important Role in IQ Development

by Walter Lippmann

About the author: *Walter Lippmann (1889–1974) was a journalist and critic who received a special Pulitzer Prize citation in 1958 for news analysis. This viewpoint was one of a series of six articles on IQ testing that he wrote for the* New Republic *in 1922.*

The first argument in favor of the view that the capacity for intelligence is hereditary is an argument by analogy. There is a good deal of evidence that idiocy and certain forms of degeneracy are transmitted from parents to offspring. There are, for example, a number of notorious families—the Kallikaks, the Jukes, the Hill Folk, the Nams, the Zeros, and the Ishmaelites—who have a long and persistent record of degeneracy. Whether these bad family histories are the result of a bad social start or of defective germplasm is not entirely clear, but the weight of evidence is in favor of the view that there is a taint in the blood. Yet even in these sensational cases, in fact just because they are so sensational and exceptional, it is important to remember that the proof is not conclusive.

The Inheritance of Degeneracy

There is, for example, some doubt as to the Kallikaks. It will be recalled that during the Revolutionary War, a young soldier, known under the pseudonym of Martin Kallikak, had an illegitimate feeble-minded son by a feeble-minded girl. The descendants of this union have been criminals and degenerates. But after the war was over, Martin married respectably. The descendants of this union have been successful people. This is a powerful evidence, but it would, as Professor James McKeen Cattell points out, be more powerful, and more interesting scientifically, if the wife of the respectable marriage had been feeble-minded, and the

Walter Lippmann, "Tests of Hereditary Intelligence," *New Republic*, November 22, 1922.

girl in the tavern had been a healthy, normal person. Then only would it have been possible to say with complete confidence that this was a pure case of biological rather than of social heredity.

Assuming, however, that the inheritance of degeneracy is established, we may turn to the other end of the scale. Here we find studies of the persistence of talent in superior families. Sir Francis Galton, for example, found "that the son of a distinguished judge had about one chance in four of becoming himself distinguished, while the son of a man picked out at random from the general population had only about one chance in four thousand of becoming similarly distinguished." Professor Cattell, in a study of the families of 1,000 leading American scientists, remarks in this connection: "Galton finds in the judges of England a notable proof of hereditary genius. It would be found to be much less in the judges of the United States. It could probably be shown by the same methods to be even stronger in the families conducting the leading publishing and banking houses of England and Germany." And in another place he remarks that "my data show that a boy born in Massachusetts or Connecticut has been fifty times as likely to become a scientific man as a boy born along the Southeastern seaboard from Georgia to Louisiana."

> *"Children of favored classes test higher on the whole than other children."*

It is not necessary for our purpose to come to any conclusion as to the inheritance of capacity. The evidence is altogether insufficient for any conclusion, and the only possible attitude is an open mind. We are, moreover, not concerned with the question of whether intelligence is hereditary. We are concerned only with the claim of the intelligence tester that *he reveals and measures* hereditary intelligence. These are quite separate propositions, but they are constantly confused by the testers. For these gentlemen seem to think that if Galton's conclusion about judges and the tale of the Kallikaks are accepted, then two things follow: first, that by analogy all the graduations of intelligence are fixed in heredity, and second, that the tests measure these different grades of heredity intelligence. Neither conclusion follows necessarily. The facts of heredity cannot be proved by analogy; the facts of heredity are what they are. The question of whether the intelligence test measures heredity is a wholly different matter. It is the only question which concerns us here.

Social Status and IQ

We may start then with the admitted fact that children of favored classes test higher on the whole than other children. Binet [IQ] tests made in Paris, Berlin, Brussels, Breslau, Rome, Petrograd, Moscow, in England, and in America agree on this point. In California, Professor Lewis M. Terman divided 492 children into five social classes and obtained the following correlation between the median intelligence quotient and social status:

Social Group	Median IQ
Very Inferior	85
Inferior	93
Average	99.5
Superior	107
Very Superior	106

On the face of it, this table would seem to indicate, if it indicates anything, a considerable connection between intelligence and environment. Mr. Terman denies this, and argues that "if home environment really has any considerable effect upon the IQ we should expect this effect to become more marked, the longer the influence has continued. That is, the correlation of IQ with social status should increase with age." But since his data show that at three age levels (5–8 years) and (9–11 years) and (12–15 years) the coefficient of correlation with social status declines (it is .43, .41, and .29 respectively), Mr. Terman concludes that "in the main, native qualities of intellect and character, rather than chance [*sic*] determine the social class to which a family belongs." He even pleads with us to accept this conclusion: "After all does not common observation teach us that etc. etc." and "from what is already known about heredity should we not naturally expect" and so forth and so forth.

Now I propose to put aside entirely all that Mr. Terman's common observation and natural expectations teach him. I should like only to examine his argument that if home environment counted much, its effect ought to become more and more marked as the child grew older.

A Child's Changing Environment

It is difficult to see why Mr. Terman should expect this to happen. To the infant, the home environment is the whole environment. When the child goes to school, the influences of the home are merged in the larger environment of school and playground. Gradually, the child's environment expands until it takes in a city, and the larger invisible environment of books and talk and movies and newspapers. Surely Mr. Terman is making a very strange assumption when he argues that as the child spends less and less time at home the influence of home environment ought to become more and more marked. His figures, showing that the correlation between social status and intelligence declines from .43 before eight years of age to .29 at

"The public school is an agency for equalizing the opportunities of the privileged and the unprivileged."

twelve years of age, are hardly an argument for hereditary differences in the endowment of social classes. They are a rather strong argument, on the contrary, for the traditional American theory that the public school is an agency for equalizing the opportunities of the privileged and the unprivileged.

51

But Mr. Terman could by a shrewder use of his own data have made a better case. It was not necessary for him to use an argument which comes down to saying that the less contact the child has with the home the more influential the home ought to be. That is simply the gross logical fallacy of expecting increasing effects from a diminishing cause. Mr. Terman would have made a more interesting point if he had asked why the influence of social status on intelligence persists so long af-

> *"The earlier the influence the more potent it would be, the later the influence the less significant."*

ter the parents and the home have usually ceased to play a significant part in the child's intellectual development. Instead of being surprised that the correlation has declined from .43 at eight to .29 at twelve, he should have asked why there is any correlation left at twelve. That would have posed a question which the traditional eulogist of the little red schoolhouse could not answer offhand. If the question had been put that way, no one could dogmatically have denied that differences of heredity in social classes may be a contributing factor. But curiously, it is the mental tester himself who incidentally furnishes the most powerful defense of the orthodox belief that in the mass differences of ability are the result of education rather than of heredity.

The Rate of Mental Growth

The intelligence tester has found that the rate of mental growth declines as the child matures. It is faster in infancy than in adolescence, and the adult intelligence is supposed to be fully developed somewhere between sixteen and nineteen years of age. The growth of intelligence slows up gradually until it stops entirely. I do not know whether this is true or not, but the intelligence testers believe it. From this belief it follows that there is "a decreasing significance of a given amount of retardation in the upper years." Alfred Binet, in fact, suggested the rough rule that under ten years of age a retardation of two years usually means feeble-mindedness, while for older children feeble-mindedness is not indicated unless there is a retardation of at least three years.

This being the case, the earlier the influence the more potent it would be, the later the influence the less significant. The influences which bore upon the child when his intelligence was making its greatest growth would leave a profounder impression than those which bore upon him when his growth was more nearly completed. Now in early childhood you have both the period of the greatest growth and the most inclusive and direct influence of the home environment. Is it surprising that the effects of superior and inferior environments persist, though in diminishing degree, as the child emerges from the home?

The Influence of Environment

It is possible, of course, to deny that the early environment has any important influence on the growth of intelligence. Men like eugenicist Lothrop Stoddard and Professor William McDougall do deny it, and so does Mr. Terman. But on the basis of the mental tests they have no right to an opinion. Mr. Terman's observations begin at four years of age. He publishes no data on infancy and he is, therefore, generalizing about the hereditary factor after four years of immensely significant development have already taken place. On his own showing as to the high importance of the earlier years, he is hardly justified in ignoring them. He cannot simply lump together the net result of natural endowment and infantile education and ascribe it to the germplasm.

In doing just that, he is obeying the will to believe, not the methods of science. How far he is carried may be judged from this instance which Mr. Terman cites as showing the negligible influence of environment. He tested twenty children in an orphanage and found only three who were fully normal. "The orphanage in question," he then remarks, "is a reasonably good one and affords an environment which is about as stimulating to normal mental development as average home life among the middle classes." Think of it. Mr. Terman first discovers what a "normal mental development" is by testing children who have grown up in an adult environment of parents, aunts, and uncles. He then applies this foot rule to children who are growing up in the abnormal environment of an institution and finds that they are not normal. He then puts the blame for abnormality on the germplasm of the orphans.

There Is No Evidence That IQ Differences Between Races Are Genetic

by Richard C. Lewontin

About the author: *Richard C. Lewontin is the Alexander Agassiz Professor of Zoology and a professor of biology at Harvard University. He is the author of many articles concerning intelligence and IQ.*

In the spring of 1653, Pope Innocent X condemned a pernicious heresy which espoused the doctrines of "total depravity, irresistible grace, lack of free will, predestination and limited atonement." That heresy was Jansenism and its author was Cornelius Jansen, Bishop of Ypres.

In the winter of 1968, the same doctrine appeared in the *Harvard Educational Review*. That doctrine is now called "Jensenism" by the *New York Times* magazine and its author is Arthur R. Jensen, professor of educational psychology at the University of California at Berkeley. It is a doctrine as erroneous in the twentieth century as it was in the seventeenth. I shall try to play the Innocent.

Jensen's article, "How Much Can We Boost IQ and Scholastic Achievement?" created such a furor that the *Review* reprinted it along with critiques by psychologists, theorists of education, and a population geneticist under the title "Environment, Heredity and Intelligence.". . . I shall try, in this viewpoint, to display Professor Jensen's argument, to show how the structure of his argument is designed to make his point, and to reveal what appear to be deeply embedded assumptions derived from a particular world view, leading him to erroneous conclusions. . . .

Jensen's Position on IQ

Jensen's argument consists essentially of an elaboration on two incontrovertible facts, a causative explanation and a programmatic conclusion. The two facts are that black people perform, on the average, more poorly than whites on standard IQ tests, and that special programs of compensatory education so far tried have not had much success in removing this difference. His causative explanation for these facts is that IQ is highly heritable, with most of the variation among individuals arising from genetic rather than environmental sources. His programmatic conclusion is that there is no use in trying to remove the difference in IQ by education since it arises chiefly from genetic causes and the best thing that can be done for black children is to capitalize on those skills for which they are biologically adapted. Such a conclusion is so clearly at variance with the present egalitarian consensus and so clearly smacks of a racist elitism, whatever its merit or motivation, that a very careful analysis of the argument is in order.

"Jensen's article puts the blame for the failure of his science not on the scientists but on the children."

The article begins with the pronouncement: "Compensatory education has been tried and it apparently has failed." A documentation of that failure and a definition of compensatory education are left to the end of the article for good logical and pedagogical reasons. Having caught our attention by whacking us over the head with a two-by-four, Jensen then asks:

> What has gone wrong? In other fields, when bridges do not stand, when aircraft do not fly, when machines do not work, when treatments do not cure, despite all the conscientious efforts on the part of many persons to make them do so, one begins to question the basic assumptions, principles, theories, and hypotheses that guide one's efforts. Is it time to follow suit in education?

Who can help but answer that last rhetorical question with a resounding "Yes"? What thoughtful and intelligent person can avoid being struck by the intellectual and empirical bankruptcy of educational psychology as it is practiced in our mass educational systems? The innocent reader will immediately fall into close sympathy with Professor Jensen, who, it seems, is about to dissect educational psychology and show it up as a prescientific jumble without theoretic coherence or prescriptive competence. But the innocent reader will be wrong. For the rest of Jensen's article puts the blame for the failure of his science not on the scientists but on the children. According to him, it is not that his science and its practitioners have failed utterly to understand human motivation, behavior, and development, but simply that the damn kids are ineducable. . . .

Heritability

To understand the main genetical argument of Jensen, we must dwell, as he does, on the concept of heritability. We cannot speak of a trait being molded by heredity, as opposed to environment. Every character of an organism is the result of a unique interaction between the inherited genetic information and the sequence of environments through which the organism has passed during its development. For some traits, the variations in environment have little effect, so that once the genotype [the genetic makeup of an organism] is known, the eventual form of the organism is pretty well specified. For other traits, specification of the genetic make-up may be a very poor predictor of the eventual phenotype [the appearance of an organism resulting from the interaction of genotype and environment] because even the smallest environmental effects may affect the trait greatly. But for all traits, there is a many-many relationship between gene and character and between environment and character. Only by a specification of both the genotype and the environmental sequence can the character be predicted. Nevertheless, traits do vary in the degree of their genetic determination; this degree can be expressed, among other ways, by their heritabilities. . . .

The estimation of heritability of a trait in a population depends on measuring individuals of known degrees of relationship to each other and comparing the observed correlation in the trait between relatives with the theoretical correlation from genetic theory. There are two difficulties that arise in such a procedure. First, the exact theoretical correlation between relatives, except for identical twins, cannot be specified unless there is detailed knowledge of the mode of inheritance of the character. A first-order approximation is possible, however, based upon some simplifying assumptions, and it is unusual for this approximation to be badly off.

A much more serious difficulty arises because relatives are correlated, not only in their heredities, but also in their environments. Two siblings are much more alike in the sequence of environments in which they developed than are two cousins or two unrelated persons. As a result, there will be an overestimate of the heritability of a character, arising from the added correlation between relatives from environmental similarities. There is no easy way to get around this bias in general, so that great weight must be put on peculiar situations in which the ordinary environmental correlations are disturbed. That is why so much emphasis is placed, in human genetics, on the handful of cases of identical twins raised apart from birth, and the much more numerous cases of totally unrelated children raised in the same family. Neither of these cases is completely reliable, however, since twins separated from birth are nevertheless likely to be raised in families belonging to the same socioeconomic, racial, religious, and ethnic categories, while unrelated children raised in the same family may easily be treated rather more differently than biological siblings. Despite these difficulties, the weight of evidence from a variety of correlations between relatives puts the heritability of IQ in various human populations between .6 and .8. For reasons of his argument, Jensen prefers the higher value but it is not worth quibbling over. Volumes

> *"Geneticists . . . have failed to note the extraordinary conclusions that are drawn from [Jensen's] reasonable premises."*

could be written on the evaluation of heritability estimates for IQ, and one can find a number of faults with Jensen's treatment of the published data. However, it is irrelevant to questions of race and intelligence and to questions of the failure of compensatory education, whether the heritability of IQ is .4 or .8, so I shall accept Jensen's rather high estimate without serious argument.

Extraordinary Conclusions

The description I have given of heritability, its application to a specific population in a specific set of environments, and the difficulties in its accurate estimation are all discussed by Jensen. While the emphasis he gives to various points differs from mine, and his estimate of heritability is on the high side, he appears to have said in one way or another just about everything that a judicious man can say. The very judiciousness of his argument has been disarming to geneticists especially, and they have failed to note the extraordinary conclusions that are drawn from these reasonable premises. Indeed, the logical and empirical hiatus between the conclusions and the premises is especially striking and thought-provoking in view of Jensen's apparent understanding of the technical issues.

> *"Is it not then likely that the [IQ] difference [between blacks and whites] is genetic? No. It is neither likely nor unlikely. There is no evidence."*

The first conclusion concerns the cause of the difference between the IQ distributions of blacks and whites. On the average, over a number of studies, blacks have a distribution of IQ scores whose mean is about 15 points—about 1 standard deviation—below whites. Taking into account the lower variance of scores among blacks than among whites, this difference means that about 11 percent of blacks have IQ scores above the mean white score (as compared with 50 percent of whites) while 18 percent of whites score below the mean black score (again, as compared to 50 percent of blacks). If, according to Jensen, "gross socioeconomic factors" are equalized between the tested groups, the difference in means is reduced to 11 points. It is hard to know what to say about overlap between the groups after this correction, since the standard deviations of such equalized populations will be lower. From these and related observations, and the estimate of .8 for the heritability of IQ (in white populations, no reliable estimate existing for blacks), Jensen concludes that

> all we are left with are various lines of evidence, no one of which is definitive alone, but which, viewed altogether, make it a not unreasonable hypothesis that genetic factors are strongly implicated in the average Negro-white intelligence difference. The preponderance of evidence is, in my opinion, less consistent with a strictly environmental hypothesis than with a genetic hypothesis, which, of course, does not exclude the influence of environment on its interaction with genetic factors.

Anyone not familiar with the standard litany of academic disclaimers ("not unreasonable hypothesis," "does not exclude," "in my opinion") will, taking this statement at face value, find nothing to disagree with since it says nothing. To contrast a "strictly environmental hypothesis" with "a genetic hypothesis which . . . does not exclude the influence of the environment" is to be guilty of the utmost triviality. If that is the only conclusion he means to come to, Jensen has just wasted a great deal of space in the *Harvard Educational Review*. But of course, like all cant, the special language of the social scientist needs to be translated into common English. What Jensen is saying is: "It is pretty clear, although not absolutely proved, that most of the difference in IQ between blacks and whites is genetical." This, at least, is not a trivial conclusion. Indeed, it may even be true. However, the evidence offered by Jensen is irrelevant.

Is It Likely?

How can that be? We have admitted the high heritability of IQ and the reality of the difference between the black and the white distributions. Moreover, we have seen that adjustment for gross socioeconomic level still leaves a large difference. Is it not then likely that the difference is genetic? No. It is neither likely nor unlikely. There is no evidence. The fundamental error of Jensen's argument is to confuse heritability of a character within a population with heritability of the difference between two populations. Indeed, between two populations, the concept of heritability of their difference is meaningless. This is because a variance based upon two measurements has only one degree of freedom and so cannot be partitioned into genetic and environmental components. The genetic basis of the difference between two populations bears no logical or empirical relation to the heritability within populations and cannot be inferred from it, as I will show in a simple but realistic example. In addition, the notion that eliminating what appear a priori to be major environmental variables will serve to eliminate a large part of the environmentally caused difference between the populations is biologically naïve. In the context of IQ testing, it assumes that educational psychologists know what the major sources of environmental difference between black and white performance are. Thus, Jensen compares blacks with American Indians whom he regards as far more environmentally disadvantaged. But a priori judgments of the importance of different aspects of the environment are valueless, as every ecologist and plant physiologist knows. My example will speak to that point as well.

> *"Between two populations, the concept of heritability of their difference is meaningless."*

Let us take two completely inbred lines of corn. Because they are completely inbred by self-fertilization, there is no genetic variation in either line, but the two lines will be genetically different from each other. Let us now plant seeds of these two inbred lines in flowerpots with ordinary potting soil, one seed of each line to a pot. After they have germinated and grown for a few weeks we will measure the height of each plant. We will discover variation in height from plant to plant. Because each line is completely inbred, the variation in height within lines must be entirely environmental, a result of variation in potting conditions from pot to pot. Then the heritability of plant height in both lines is 0.0. But there will be an average difference in plant height between lines that arises entirely from the fact that the two lines are genetically different. Thus the difference between lines is entirely genetical even though the heritability of height is 0!

> *"The genetic basis of the difference between two populations bears no logical or empirical relation to the heritability within populations and cannot be inferred from it."*

Genetical and Environmental Differences

Now let us do the opposite experiment. We will take two handsful from a sack containing seed of an open-pollinated variety of corn. Such a variety has lots of genetic variation in it. Instead of using potting soil, however, we will grow the seed in vermiculite watered with a carefully made up nutrient, Knop's solution, used by plant physiologists for controlled growth experiments. One batch of seed will be grown on complete Knop's solution, but the other will have the concentration of nitrates cut in half and, in addition, we will leave out the minute trace of zinc salt that is part of the necessary trace elements (30 parts per billion). After several weeks we will measure the plants. Now we will find variation within seed lots which is entirely genetical since no environmental variation within lots was allowed. Thus heritability will be 1.0. However, there will be a radical difference between seed lots which is ascribable entirely to the difference in nutrient levels. Thus, we have a case where heritability within populations is complete, yet the difference between populations is entirely environmental!

But let us carry our experiment to the end. Suppose we do not know about the difference in the nutrient solutions because it was really the carelessness of our assistant that was involved. We call in a friend who is a very careful chemist and ask him to look into the matter for us. He analyzes the nutrient solutions and discovers the obvious—only half as much nitrates in the case of the stunted plants. So we add the missing nitrates and do the experiment again. This time, our second batch of plants will grow a little larger but not much, and we will conclude that the difference between the lots is genetic since equalizing the large difference in nitrate level had so little effect. But, of course, we would be wrong, for it is the missing trace of zinc that is the real culprit. Finally, it should be pointed out that it took many years before the importance of minute trace elements in plant physiology was worked out because ordinary laboratory glassware will leach out enough of many trace elements to let plants grow normally.

59

Should educational psychologists study plant physiology?

Having disposed, I hope, of Jensen's conclusion that the high heritability of IQ and the lack of effect of correction for gross socioeconomic class are presumptive evidence for the genetic basis of the difference between blacks and whites, I will turn to his second erroneous conclusion. The article under discussion began with the observation, which he documents, that compensatory education for the disadvantaged (blacks, chiefly) has failed. The explanation offered for the failure is that IQ has a high heritability and that therefore the difference between the races is also mostly genetical. Given that the racial difference is genetical, then environmental change and educational effort cannot make much difference and cannot close the gap very much between blacks and whites. I have already argued that there is no evidence one way or the other about the genetics of interracial IQ differences. To understand Jensen's second error, however, we will suppose that the difference is indeed genetical. Let it be entirely genetical. Does this mean that compensatory education, having failed, must fail? The supposition that it must arises from a misapprehension about the fixity of genetically determined traits. It was thought at one time that genetic disorders, because they were genetic, were incurable. Yet we now know that inborn errors of metabolism are indeed curable if their biochemistry is sufficiently well understood and if deficient metabolic products can be supplied exogenously. Yet in the normal range of environments, these inborn errors manifest themselves irrespective of the usual environmental variables. That is, even though no environment in the normal range has an effect on the character, there may be special environments, created in response to our knowledge of the underlying biology of a character, which are effective in altering it.

Environmental Possibilities Are Not Exhausted

But we do not need recourse to abnormalities of development to see this point. Jensen says that "there is no reason to believe that the IQs of deprived children, given an environment of abundance, would rise to a higher level than the already privileged children's IQs." It is empirically wrong to argue that, if the richest environment experience we can conceive does not raise IQ substantially, we have exhausted the environmental possibilities. In the seventeenth century, the infant mortality rates were many times their present level at all socioeconomic levels. Using what was then the normal range of environments, the infant mortality rate of the highest socioeconomic class would have been regarded as the limit below which one could not reasonably expect to reduce the death rate. But changes in sanitation, public health, and disease control—changes which are commonplace to us now but would have seemed incredible to a man of the seventeenth century—have reduced the

> *"There is no evidence one way or the other about the genetics of interracial IQ differences."*

infant mortality rates of disadvantaged urban Americans well below those of even the richest members of seventeenth-century society. The argument that compensatory education is hopeless is equivalent to saying that changing the form of the seventeenth-century gutter would not have a pronounced effect on public sanitation. What compensatory education will be able to accomplish when the study of human behavior finally emerges from its prescientific era is anyone's guess. It

> *"The real issue is what the goals of our society will be."*

will be most extraordinary if it stands as the sole exception to the rule that technological progress exceeds by manyfold what even the most optimistic might have imagined.

The real issue in compensatory education does not lie in the heritability of IQ or in the possible limits of educational technology. On the reasonable assumption that ways of significantly altering mental capacities can be developed if it is important enough to do so, the real issue is what the goals of our society will be. Do we want to foster a society in which the "race of life" is "to get ahead of somebody" and in which true merit, be it genetically or environmentally determined, will be the criterion of men's earthly reward? Or do we want a society in which every man can aspire to the fullest measure of psychic and material fulfillment that social activity can produce? Professor Jensen has made it fairly clear to me what sort of society he wants.

I oppose him.

The Theory of Hereditary IQ Has Not Been Proven

by Leon J. Kamin

About the author: *Leon J. Kamin is a professor of psychology at Northeastern University in Boston. He is the author of* The Science and Politics of I.Q., *from which this viewpoint is taken, and numerous articles on IQ and genetics.*

I have attempted—with one exception soon to be noted—to review the major sources of evidence that have been asserted to support the view that I.Q. is heritable. The data have repeatedly demonstrated profound environmental effects on I.Q. scores in circumstances where the genes cannot be implicated. The apparent genetic effects, upon analysis, have invariably been confounded with environmental factors that have been slighted or ignored. The studies of separated MZ [monozygotic, or identical] twins have ignored the correlated environments of the twins, as well as artifacts produced by the confounding of age with I.Q. and by unconscious experimenter bias. The apparent genetic orderliness of summaries of kinship correlations reflects systematic bias and arbitrary selection of data. There is in fact much that is not known, and what is known is no more consistent with a genetic than an environmental interpretation. The kinship data seem not to have been examined for relations inconsistent with an hereditarian position, and suggestive evidence for several such relations has been indicated. The hereditarian interpretation of studies of adopted children ignores the complex problems posed by the unique characteristics of adoptive families. To consider these problems is to reverse the apparent meaning of these studies. Those studies that do not support a genetic interpretation have disappeared from contemporary reference lists. The purported demonstrations of intrauterine effects and of inbreeding depression are, to say the least, unconvincing.

To assert that there is *no* genetic determination of I.Q. would be a strong, and scientifically meaningless, statement. We cannot prove the null hypothesis, nor should we be asked to do so. The question is whether there exist data of merit and validity that require us to reject the null hypothesis. There should be no mistake here. The burden of proof falls upon those who wish to assert the implausible proposition that the way in which a child answers questions devised by a mental tester is determined by an unseen genotype. That burden is not lessened by the repeated assertions of the testers over the past 70 years. Where the data are at best ambiguous, and where environment is clearly shown to have effect, the assumption of genetic determination of I.Q. variation in any degree is unwarranted. The prudent conclusion seems clear. There are no data sufficient for us to reject the hypothesis that differences in the way in which people answer the questions asked by testers are determined by their palpably different life experiences.

That conclusion is silent with respect to another possible question. There may well be genetically determined differences among people in their cognitive and intellectual "capacities." To demonstrate this, psychologists would have to develop test instruments that provide adequate measures of such capacities. They have not as yet done this; they have only developed I.Q. tests. This viewpoint has been about—and only about—the heritability of I.Q. test scores.

There is, to say the least, no guarantee that adequate measurements of "cognitive capacities" would produce a rank-ordering of people similar to that produced by existing I.Q. tests. The experience of most teachers is sufficient to suggest otherwise. The existing I.Q. tests, as they were designed to do, predict on a better than chance basis who will do well in the kinds of school training programs we now employ. They also predict, to some extent, who will "do well" in our economy, and in our job structure. That tells us nothing about the heritability of I.Q., or of success. The simpler interpretation is that those who have been trained to answer the kinds of questions asked by I.Q. tests have been trained to succeed in our society. To be so trained requires both the opportunity and the willingness to accept the training regimen. To assert that those without opportunity or willingness have defective genes is not a conclusion of science. The social function of such an assertion is transparently obvious. The successful are very likely to believe it, including successful professors.

> *"[The existing I.Q. tests tell] us nothing about the heritability of I.Q., or of success."*

A Long History

The notion that I.Q. is heritable has been with us for so long that it is difficult for us to step back and appreciate fully the assumptions involved in that conclusion. The World War I Army Alpha test contained such multiple choice items as "The Brooklyn Nationals are called the Giants . . . Orioles . . . Superbas . . . Indians," and "Revolvers are made by Swift and Co. . . . Smith and Wesson . . .

W.L. Douglas . . . B.T. Babbitt." The Italian or Hebrew immigrant who could not answer such questions was thereby shown to have defective genes. The Stanford-Binet asked 14-year-olds to explain the following: "My neighbor has been having queer visitors. First a doctor came to his house, then a lawyer, then a minister. What do you think happened there?" Professor Lewis M. Terman explained that a satisfactory answer must normally involve a death: "The doctor came to attend a sick person, the lawyer to make his will, and the minister to preach the funeral." There were, however, "other ingenious interpretations which pass as satisfactory." For example, "A man got hurt in an accident; the doctor came to make him well, the lawyer to see about damages, and then he died and the preacher came for the funeral." The following answer was failed by Professor Terman. "Somebody was sick; the lawyer wanted his money and the minister came to see how he was." Professor Terman's high-quality genes evidently made him better disposed toward the good intentions of lawyers than did the genes of his failing respondent. To Professor Terman, it seemed more logical that a minister at the house next door is there to preach a funeral rather than to inquire after the welfare of an ill parishioner.

> *"Items in I.Q. tests are . . . largely learned in school."*

To the degree that items in I.Q. tests are not so monstrously arbitrary as those we have just cited, they largely consist of arithmetical and vocabulary materials, together with skills of logical analysis, which are largely learned in school. Those who cannot answer have not learned what in theory the school teachers wished to teach them. They are usually the same people who have failed to learn that lawyers do not want the money of their clients and are primarily useful to help one bequeath one's fortune. From this—and the fact that this failure to learn what one should seems to run in families—we are asked to conclude that a low I.Q. score indicates a genetic defect. The tests in fact seem to measure only whether one has learned, and believed, what Professor Terman and his colleagues have learned and believed. To the degree that one has, one may reasonably look forward to enjoying the kind of success that Professor Terman enjoyed. The assumption that one who has not learned these things was prevented from doing so by his bad blood is both gratuitous and self-serving.

Folly and Malice

The worst contemporary blood, if one regards the I.Q. as a mirror held up to the genotype, is black blood. The average I.Q. score of blacks is lower than that of whites. That fact, together with a very great score overlap between the black and white populations, has been documented in an enormous research literature. To some scholars, at least, racial differences in I.Q. have constituted a further demonstration of the I.Q.'s genetic basis. The dreary and at times revolting literature on race differences has not been reviewed in this viewpoint. There is no need to force oneself through it. There is no adequate evidence for the heritability of I.Q. within the white population. To attribute racial differences to genetic factors, granted the overwhelming cultural-environmental differences between races, is to compound folly with malice. That compounding characterized the mental testers of World War I, and it has not vanished.

The interpretation of I.Q. data seems never to be free both of policy implications and of ideological overtones. Professor Arthur R. Jensen began his survey of the I.Q. literature with the conclusion that "Compensatory education has been tried and it apparently has failed." The apparent failure was seen to be the inevitable consequence of demonstrated genetical truths. Professor Richard J. Herrnstein has described how he was "submerged for twenty years in the depths of environmentalistic behaviorism." The ascent to the higher spheres of I.Q. testing was noted by the *New York Times,* which cited him as acknowledging that his "conclusions, if true, amount to a death sentence for the ideal of egalitarianism, a powerful influence in contemporary Western society." The psychology of the mental testers, we are told, has doomed compensatory education and has killed egalitarianism. That is unqualifiedly bad news—for the underprivileged, for teachers, for egalitarians, and for behaviorists. Professor Herrnstein has said of American behaviorism, "The promises go back almost fifty years, to behaviorism's founder, John B. Watson, and are coming still." The promises go back much longer than 50 years, but they have seldom been expressed more forcefully or eloquently than by Watson. There is no psychology student in America who has not been exposed to a part, a small part, of Watson's dictum about the rearing of a dozen babies. To most students, it has been held out as the *reductio ad absurdum* [the absurd extreme] of a mindless environmentalism run rampant. The full passage, however, contains more than promises. There is considerable analysis, and a full and moving recognition that the promises of behaviorism applied to human affairs cannot be realized without social and political reform. The celebrated passage followed a lengthy and sophisticated discussion of the relation between inheritance of structure and inheritance of function. The passage in its full context restores to us a psychological tradition richer and truer for our time and place than the strait-jacketed ideology of the mental testers:

> *"To attribute racial differences to genetic factors . . . is to compound folly with malice."*

> Our conclusion, then, is that we have no real evidence of the inheritance of traits. I would feel perfectly confident in the ultimate favorable outcome of careful upbringing of a *healthy well-formed baby* born of a long line of crooks, murderers and thieves, and prostitutes. Who has any evidence to the contrary? . . . One cannot use statistics gained from observations in charitable institutions and orphan asylums. All one needs to do to discount such statistics is to go there and work for a while, and I say this without trying to belittle the work of such organizations.

65

Chapter 1

I should like to go one step further now and say, "Give me a dozen healthy infants, well-formed, and my own specified world to bring them up in and I'll
guarantee to take anyone at random and train him to become any type of spe-
cialist I might select—doctor, lawyer, artist, merchant-chief and, yes, even
beggar-man and thief, regardless of his talents, penchants, tendencies, abilities, vocations, and race of his ancestors." I am going beyond my facts and I
admit it, but so have the advocates of the contrary and they have been doing it
for many thousands of years. Please note that when this experiment is made I
am to be allowed to specify the way the children are to be brought up and the
type of world they have to live in.

. . . Where there are structural defects . . . there is social inferiority—competition on equal grounds is denied. The same is true when "inferior" races are
brought up along with "superior" races. We have no sure evidence of inferiority in the negro race. Yet, educate a white child and a negro child in the same
school—bring them up in the same family (theoretically without difference)
and when society begins to exert its crushing might, the negro cannot compete.

The truth is society does not like to face facts. Pride of race has been strong,
hence our Mayflower ancestry—our Daughters of the Revolution. We like to
boast of our ancestry. It sets us apart. . . . Again, on the other hand, the belief
in the inheritance of tendencies and traits saves us from blame in the training
of our young.

Chapter 2

Do IQ Tests Measure Intelligence?

CURRENT CONTROVERSIES

IQ Tests and Intelligence: An Overview

by Joe Chidley

About the author: *Joe Chidley is a columnist for the weekly Canadian magazine* Maclean's.

The Bell Curve's most controversial thesis lies in its handling of the thorny issue of intelligence and race. Authors Richard J. Herrnstein and Charles Murray claim that blacks, on average, are less intelligent than whites, citing as evidence the fact that African-Americans typically score about 15 points lower than white Americans on standard IQ tests. Asians—at least those from Japan, China "and perhaps Korea"—are smarter than whites, typically scoring about three points higher on IQ tests. And then the crux of their argument: the authors contend that between 40 and 80 per cent of cognitive ability is genetic, and therefore heritable. That, they maintain, means that blacks score lower on IQ tests, on average, at least in part because they are born that way—that is, they are born "dull." And try as one might, the authors argue, efforts to improve cognitive ability through better education or better living conditions will always have limited returns because of the genetic factor. But the scientific community remains sharply divided on the heredity of intelligence—especially when it is linked to race. "To geneticists, classifications based on skin color give us groupings that are biologically meaningless," wrote David Suzuki in a *Toronto Star* column criticizing *The Bell Curve*. "For a trait as complex as intelligence, there is lots of room to manipulate environmental conditions that affect it."

Not surprisingly, J. Philippe Rushton, a psychologist at the University of Western Ontario, is among Herrnstein and Murray's supporters. After all, in his book, *Race, Evolution and Behavior*, Rushton states even more emphatically the alleged link between race and intelligence. Of *The Bell Curve*, he says: "I think it's a superb book, and superb scholarship. It has the potential to alter the way we look at human beings."

Excerpted from Joe Chidley, "The Brain Strain," *Maclean's*, November 28, 1994. Reprinted with permission.

Questioning the Assumptions

To others, however, that very potential is worrisome, to say the least. And while it is difficult for the lay reader to argue with the data *The Bell Curve* compiles from a wide array of sources, its underlying assumptions have been widely questioned. Among the more compelling—and contentious—issues raised:

• *Can intelligence be measured?* Central to Herrnstein and Murray's argument is their belief in an entity known as *g*, for "general intelligence." That is a "unitary mental factor," the product of statistical analyses of IQ test scores made by former British army officer Charles Spearman in 1904. Tests of IQ, like any standardized test of academic achievement, measure general intelligence to some degree and, the authors say, the scores match "whatever it is that people mean when they use the world *intelligent* or *smart* in ordinary language."

They claim that *g* and the validity of IQ tests are issues that are now "beyond significant technical dispute" among psychometricians—hardly surprising given that psychometricians, by definition, are people in the business of measuring cognitive ability as if it were quantifiable. As Herrnstein and Murray acknowledge, however, some dissent remains. Howard Gardner, a Harvard psychologist whom *The Bell Curve* authors dub "a radical," dismisses the concept of *g* and argues instead that there are many types of intelligence—linguistic, musical, logical-mathematical, spatial, bodily kinesthetic, and so-called personal intelligence based on social skills. Gardner's theory seems more consistent with actual human experience: how does one measure the "intelligence" of Michael Jordan's magical manoeuvres on the basketball court, of Charlie Parker's inspired improvisations on the saxophone?

• *What is the influence of socioeconomic factors on IQ scores?* Herrnstein and Murray spend more than half their book arguing that socioeconomic performance and intelligence *are* linked—people who score better on IQ tests, they say, tend to do better in life, both socially and financially.

At this point, a chicken-and-egg argument presents itself. Rather than IQ leading to socioeconomic success or failure, it could also be the case that IQ is a measure of a group's so-

> *"[Herrnstein and Murray] claim that g and the validity of IQ tests are issues that are now 'beyond significant technical dispute.'. . . However, some dissent remains."*

cioeconomic history—that is, an ethnic group may score low because the tests measure ability to function in a political or economic system that excludes it from full participation. Catholics in Northern Ireland, for instance, have scored lower than Protestants. In South Africa, blacks have scored lower than the mixed-race "Colored," who scored lower than whites—a scale that seems to follow the three groups' relative status under apartheid. In passing, Herrnstein and Murray mention that blacks in the South generally score lower than blacks in the northern states. Is that coincidence? Or do the IQ tests, as many critics argue, simply validate socioeconomic inequalities—and in this case demonstrate that northern blacks have integrated more fully into white American society? What effect does a history of slavery, racism and poverty have on self-esteem? And what effect does self-esteem have on motivation in a test situation? In other words, it is impossible to "factor out" socioeconomic history in any comparison of racial differences.

The Effect of Culture on Intelligence

• *What effect does culture have on intelligence?* Herrnstein and Murray say that IQ tests today have no significant cultural biases. But other critics, such as outspoken Philadelphia cultural historian Camille Paglia, author of *Sexual Personae*, contend that background has deeper implications. "What they're calling IQ is Apollonian logic—cause and effect—that the West invented," she says. "It's Eurocentric. It produced all of modern technology and science. Anyone who wants to enter into the command machinery of the world, as I hope many aspiring African-Americans do, must learn that style. It is a very narrow style—like chess. But to identify that narrow thing with all human intelligence is madness. It is folly."

Even if everything Herrnstein and Murray claim were true, so what? The authors frequently caution readers not to draw real-life conclusions from their statistical analyses. "We cannot think of a legitimate argument why any encounter between individual whites and blacks need be affected by the knowledge that an aggregate ethnic difference in measured intelligence is genetic instead of environmental," they write. That might seem disingenuous—what is the point of arguing for broad racial differences if they have no meaning to individuals?

IQ Tests Measure Intelligence

by Geoffrey Cowley

About the author: *Geoffrey Cowley is a senior writer for* Newsweek.

If you've followed the news since the 1970s, you've no doubt heard the case against intelligence testing. IQ tests are biased, the argument goes, for they favor privileged whites over blacks and the poor. They're unreliable, because someone who scores badly one year may do better the next. And they're ultimately worthless, for they don't predict what a person will actually achieve in life. Richard Herrnstein and Charles Murray defy that wisdom in *The Bell Curve*, and they're drawing a predictable response. The *New York Times Magazine* asks whether they've "gone too far" by positing race- and class-based differences in IQ. A *Harper's* editor, writing in the *New Republic*, places Herrnstein and Murray within an "eccentric and impassioned sect," whose view of IQ and inequality is out of touch with "mainstream scientific thinking." A columnist for *New York Magazine* notes that "the phrenologists thought they were onto something, too."

The rush of hot words is hardly surprising, in light of the book's grim findings and its baldly elitist policy prescriptions. But as the shouting begins, it's worth noting that the science behind *The Bell Curve* is overwhelmingly mainstream. As psychologist Mark Snyderman and political scientist Stanley Rothman discovered in a 1984 survey, social scientists have already reached a broad consensus on most points in the so-called IQ debate. They may disagree about the extent to which racial differences are genetically based, and they may argue about the prospects for narrowing them. But most agree that IQ tests measure something real and substantially heritable. And the evidence is overwhelming that IQ affects what people accomplish in school and the workplace. In short, cognitive inequality is not a political preference. It's a simple fact of life.

Mental testing has a checkered past. The tests of the 19th century were notoriously goofy, concerned more with the shapes of people's skulls than with anything happening inside. But by the turn of the 20th century, psychologists had started measuring people's aptitudes for reasoning and problem solving, and in 1904 the British psychologist Charles Spearman made a critical discovery. He found that people who did well on one mental test did well on others, regardless of their content. He reasoned that different tests must draw on the same global capacity, and dubbed that capacity *g*, for general intelligence.

Some psychologists have since rejected the concept of *g*, saying it undervalues special talents and overemphasizes logical thinking. Harvard's Howard Gardner, for example, parses intelligence into seven different realms, ranging from "logical-mathematical" to "bodily-kinesthetic." But most of the 661 scholars in the Snyderman survey endorsed a simple *g*-based model of mental ability. No one claims that

> *"IQ at 4 is a good predictor of IQ at 18."*

g is the only thing that matters in life, or even in mental testing. Dozens of tests are now published every year. Some (like the SAT) focus on acquired knowledge, others on skills for particular jobs. But straight IQ tests, such as the Wechsler Intelligence Survey, all draw heavily on *g*.

The Wechsler, in its adult version, includes 11 subtests and takes about an hour and a half. After recalling strings of numbers, assembling puzzles, arranging cartoon panels and wrestling with various abstractions, the test taker gets a score ranking his overall standing among other people his age. The average score is set at 100, and everyone is rated accordingly. Expressed in this currency, IQs for a whole population can be arrayed on a single graph. Roughly two-thirds of all Americans fall between 85 and 115, in the fat midsection of the bell-shaped curve, and 95 percent score between 70 and 130.

IQ scores wouldn't mean much if they changed dramatically from year to year, but they're surprisingly stable over a lifetime. IQ at 4 is a good predictor of IQ at 18 (the link is nearly as strong as the one between childhood and adult height), and fluctuations are usually negligible after the age of 8. For reasons no one fully understands, average ability can shift slightly as generations pass. Throughout the developed world, raw IQ scores have risen by about 3 points every decade since the early part of the century, meaning that a performance that drew a score of 100 in the 1930s would rate only 85 today. Unfortunately, no one has discovered a regimen for raising *g* at will.

Genetic Factors

Fixed or not, mental ability is obviously a biological phenomenon. Researchers have recently found that differences in IQ correspond to physiological differences, such as the rate of glucose metabolism in the brain. And there's no question that heredity is a significant source of individual differences in IQ. Fully 94 percent of the experts surveyed by Snyderman and Rothman agreed with that claim. "The heritability of IQ differences isn't a matter of opinion," says University of Virginia psychologist Sandra Scarr. "It's a question of fact that's been pretty well resolved."

The evidence is compelling, but understanding it requires a grasp of correlations. By computing a value known as the correlation coefficient, a scientist can measure the degree of association between any two phenomena that are plausibly linked. The correlation between unrelated variables is 0, while phenomena that vary in perfect lockstep have a correlation of 1. A correlation of .4 would tell you that 40 percent of the variation in one thing is matched by variation in another, while 60 percent of it is not. Within families, the pattern among test scores is striking. Studies find no IQ correlation among grown adoptive siblings. But the typical correlations are roughly .35 for half siblings (who share a quarter of their genes), .47 for full siblings (who share half of their genes) and .86 for identical twins (who share all their genes).

So how much of the variation in IQ is linked to genetic factors and how much to environmental ones? The best way to get a direct estimate is to look at people who share all their genes but grow up in separate settings. In 1990, in the best single study to date, researchers led by University of Minnesota psychologist Thomas Bouchard published data on 100 sets of middle-aged twins who had been raised apart. These twins exhibited IQ correlations of .7, suggesting that genetic factors account for fully 70 percent of the variation in IQ.

Obviously, that figure leaves ample room for other influences. No one denies that the difference between a punishing environment and an adequate one can be substantial. When children raised in the Tennessee mountains emerged from premodern living conditions in the 1930s, their average IQ rose by 10 points. But it doesn't follow that the nongenetic influences on IQ are just sitting there waiting to be tapped. Scarr, the University of Virginia psychologist, has found that adoptees placed with educated city dwellers score no better on IQ tests than kids placed with farm couples with eighth-grade educations. "As long as the environment is adequate," she says, "the differences don't seem to have much effect."

> *"Mental ability corresponds strongly to almost any measure of worldly success."*

Worldly Success

IQ aside, qualities like motivation and diligence obviously help determine what a person achieves. People with low IQs sometimes accomplish great things—Muhammad Ali made the big time with an IQ of 78—but rare exceptions don't invalidate a rule. The fact is, mental ability corresponds strongly to almost any measure of worldly success. Studies dating back to the 1940s have consistently found that kids with higher IQs complete more years of school than those with lower IQs—even when they grow up in the same households. The same pattern emerges from studies of income and occupational status.

Can IQ be used to predict bad things as well as good ones? Until now, researchers haven't focused much on the role of mental ability in social problems, such as poverty and crime, but *The Bell Curve* offers compelling new data on that front. Most of it comes from the National Longitudinal Survey of Youth (NLSY), a study that has tracked the lives of 12,000 young people since 1979, when they were 14 to 22 years old. The NLSY records everything from earnings to arrests among people whose IQs and backgrounds have been thoroughly documented. The NLSY participants come from various racial and ethnic groups. But to keep the number of variables to a minimum, Herrnstein and Murray looked first at how IQ affects the social experience of whites. Their analysis suggests that although growing up poor is a disadvantage in life, growing up with low mental ability is a far greater one.

> *"The questions on IQ tests provide equally reliable readings of blacks' and whites' abilities."*

Consider the patterns for poverty, illegitimacy and incarceration. Poverty, in the NLSY sample, is eight times more common among whites from poor backgrounds than among those who grew up in privilege—yet it's *15* times more common at the low end of the IQ spectrum. Illegitimacy is twice as common among the poorest whites as among the most prosperous, but it's *eight* times as common among the dullest (IQ under 75) as it is among the brightest (IQ over 125). And males in the bottom half of the IQ distribution are nearly 10 times as likely as those in the top half to find themselves in jail.

Race Gap

If the analysis stopped there, the findings probably wouldn't excite much controversy. But Herrnstein and Murray pursue the same line of analysis into the painful realm of racial differences. Much of what they report is not new. It's well established, if not well known, that average IQ scores differ markedly among racial groups. Blacks, like whites, span the whole spectrum of ability. But whereas whites average 102 points on the Wechsler test, blacks average 87. That gap has changed little in recent decades, despite the overall rise in both groups' performance, and it's not simply an artifact of culturally biased tests. That issue was largely resolved in 1980 by Berkeley psychologist Arthur Jensen. Jensen is still notorious for an article he wrote in 1969, arguing that the disappointing results of programs like Head Start were due partly to racial differences in IQ. His lectures were disrupted for years afterward, and his name became publicly synonymous with racism. But Jensen's scientific output continued to shape the field. In a massive 1980 review titled *Bias in Mental Testing*, he showed that the questions on IQ tests provide equally reliable readings of blacks' and whites' abilities. He also showed that scores had the same predictive power for people of both races. In 1982, a panel assembled by the National Academy of Sciences reviewed the evidence and reached the same conclusion.

If the tests aren't to blame, why does the gap persist? Social scientists still differ sharply on that question. Poverty is not an adequate explanation, for the black-white IQ gap is as wide among the prosperous as it is among the poor. Some scholars, like University of Michigan psychologist Richard Nisbett, argue that the disparity could simply reflect differences in the ways children are socialized. Writing in the *New Republic*, Nisbett cites a North Carolina study that found working-class whites more intent than blacks on preparing their children to read. In light of such social differences, he concludes, any talk of a genetic basis for the IQ gap is "utterly unfounded." Jensen, by contrast, suspects a large genetic component. The gap between black and white performance is not restricted to literacy measures, he says. It's evident even on such culturally neutral (but highly *g*-loaded) tasks as repeating number sequences backward or reacting quickly to a flashing light.

Jensen's view, as it happens, is more mainstream than Nisbett's. Roughly two-thirds of those responding to the Snyderman survey identified themselves as liberals. Yet 53 percent agreed that the black-white gap involves genetic as well as environmental factors. Only 17 percent favored strictly environmental explanations.

Herrnstein and Murray say they're less concerned with the causes of the IQ gap than they are with its arguable consequences. Are Black America's social problems strictly the legacy of racism, they wonder, or do they also reflect differences in mental ability? To answer that question, Herrnstein and Murray chart out the overall black-white disparities in areas like education, income and crime. Then they perform the same exercise using only blacks and whites of equal IQ. Overall, blacks in the NLSY are less than half as likely as whites to have college degrees by the age of 29. Yet among blacks and whites with IQs of 114, there is no disparity at all. The results aren't always so striking, but matching blacks and whites for IQ wipes out half or more of the disparities in poverty, welfare dependency and arrest rates.

> *"IQ tests measure something hugely important in life."*

Social scientists traffic in correlations, and these are strong ones. Correlations are of course different from causes; low IQ does not *cause* crime or illegitimacy. While Herrnstein and Murray clearly understand that vital distinction, it's easily lost in their torrent of numbers. There is no longer any question, however, that IQ tests measure something hugely important in life. It's also clear that whatever mental ability is made of—dense neural circuitry, highly charged synapses or sheer brain mass—we didn't all get equal shares.

IQ Tests Are Useful

by Daniel Seligman

About the author: *Daniel Seligman is a former senior editor at* Fortune, *a financial magazine, and the author of* A Question of Intelligence: The IQ Debate in America, *from which the following viewpoint is excerpted.*

The case for IQ testing is simple, straightforward, and unpopular. It rests on the well-established proposition that in many different situations, decision makers can make better judgments if they have test data to help them. In the American school system, still the principal consumer of formal IQ tests, testing makes it easier to identify underachievers, to ascertain who needs remedial treatment, to decide who gets to skip a grade. In other contexts, quasi-IQ tests like the Scholastic Aptitude Tests (SATs), the Labor Department's General Aptitude Test Battery, and the Armed Services' Vocational Aptitude Battery help decision makers decide which candidates represent the best bets and which should be turned away. Listening to some of the expressed concerns about IQ tests creating classes of winners and losers in America, you could get the impression that the tests are given mainly to decide who ends up with bragging rights in the intelligence derby. In fact, the tests are given because a lot of different decision makers find them useful.

An Aid to Understanding

IQ research, an exercise centered on analysis of the test scores, is even less popular than testing itself. The case for performing this research begins with the fact that the research data have always been fascinating. The infinity of correlations extracted from these data have enormous explanatory power. They help us understand why some people get ahead and others do not. They help us understand the nature of race, sex, and age differences in thinking. They illuminate the powerful tug of the genes on individual differences in intelligence. They leave us thinking that to an extraordinary extent, the occupational hierarchy in the United States is an IQ hierarchy. They demonstrate the connection between mental ability and productiveness, especially but not only in the "brainpower jobs" like computer programming; the data also make it plain that even in low-level jobs, general intelligence is positively correlated with performance.

To be sure, the data also remind us of the limits of IQ's predictive powers. None of those correlations are close to 1.0. [A coefficient of 1.0 is a perfect positive correlation; an increase in one set of figures is matched by a proportional increase in the other set.] The .50 correlation between IQ and income, for example, tells us that smart people start out with an edge in life but are a long way from being guaranteed winners. Your high IQ can be more than offset by your laziness, bad luck, ill health, or abrasive personality. Squaring that .50 correlation and converting it into a "coefficient of determination," we learn that only about 25 percent of the variability in income is traceable to IQ differences. [A correlation coefficient measures the extent that two variables tend to rise or fall together. If there is a causal connection, it is not measured by a correlation coefficient but by the square of the correlation coefficient, called the coefficient of determination.] Still, a casino with a 25 percent edge at the gaming tables would regularly take its patrons (assuming it had any) to the cleaners; and the squared correlation is large enough to guarantee that high-IQ people will be enormously overrepresented among the affluent. . . .

Education and IQ Research

In a rational world, American educators would be paying a lot of attention to IQ research. The version of intelligence measured by IQ tests is something close to being synonymous with "learning ability." (When the Snyderman-Rothman scholars were asked to identify the most important elements of intelligence, 96 percent named "capacity to acquire knowledge.) [The Snyderman-Rothman scholars are 66 experts whose opinions concerning intelligence were published in 1988 by Mark Snyderman and Stanley Rothman.] Since Americans have been chronically unhappy with what their children learn in school, you would think that they would want to know a lot more about the link between IQ and education. The link is a much-studied subject, with obvious implications for educational policy. The central question raised by the studies is: What kinds of teaching are best for students at different IQ levels? You would think that the giant research bureaucracy in the U.S. Department of Education would be evidencing a continuing interest in such questions. Instead it has fled from them. Several years ago, I contacted a helpful assistant to the secretary (then William Bennett) and asked what data the department had on the relationship between IQ and academic achievement. He wrote back telling me that the answer was

> *"Decision makers can make better judgments if they have test data to help them."*

essentially none. He added: "Insofar as intelligence is considered a fixed limit on achievement, it may not be viewed as a high priority study," a statement I translate to mean that the department does not wish to have formal knowledge of data suggesting some students have limits.

How can this be? One can only assume that the broad unpopularity of IQ research has made it impossible for the department's political leadership to focus on it.

Research on differences in mental ability is feared for another reason: the putative link between equal ability and equal rights. You sometimes hear formulations implying that the equal rights constitutionally guaranteed to Americans are somehow dependent on a consensus judgment that all people (and all ethnic groups) are truly equal in ability. Statements of this belief are often accompanied by professed concerns about democratic America lapsing into totalitarian modes of thought. Hitler stigmatized non-Aryans as inferior, then proceeded to deprive them of all human rights, and therefore—the argument goes—it is pernicious even to take note of group differences in ability.

> *"Testing makes it easier to identify underachievers, to ascertain who needs remedial treatment, to decide who gets to skip a grade."*

That argument itself is pernicious. It is absurd to equate an individual's or group's below-average test scores with "inferiority." I know of no scholars involved in research on group differences who would put forward any such inhumane formulation, publicly or privately; it is only *critics* of the research who keep trying to make that equation, presumably in the hope that they are thereby helping to suppress discussion of IQ differentials.

Equal Rights Versus Equal Ability

In addition to being pernicious, the argument rests on a stunning non sequitur. Equality of rights in the United States does not depend on a belief in equal ability. Whatever Jefferson did or did not believe about all men literally being created equal, the equal protection guaranteed by the Fourteenth Amendment to the Constitution was put in place in order to protect a population—the newly liberated slaves—that was widely understood to be illiterate and uneducated.

Even if equal rights had come into the Constitution by some other route, it would be a bad idea to link the idea of equal protection to the idea of equal abilities, for reasons stated forcefully by Nobel laureate F.A. Hayek in *The Constitution of Liberty*. "Nothing . . . is more damaging to the demand for equal treatment," Hayek wrote, "than to base it on so obviously untrue an assumption as that of the factual equality of all men." He added:

> To rest the case for equal treatment of national or racial minorities on the assertion that they do not differ from other men is implicitly to admit that factual inequality would justify unequal treatment; and the proof that some differences do, in fact, exist would not be long in forthcoming. It is of the essence of the demand for equality before the law that people should be treated alike in spite of the fact that they are different.

Some egalitarian Americans have another, quite different reason for disliking the data generated by IQ research. Their problem is that they *want* to treat people differently. They quite reasonably identify the below-par social and economic performance of American minorities as a corrosive social problem. But their explanation of the problem begins and ends with discrimination, and their solution centers on affirmative action. They are inflexibly uninterested in the message that much, perhaps most, of that subpar performance is predicted by minorities' subpar IQ scores.

One extraordinary example of resistance to this message occurs in a 1989 volume called *A Common Destiny: Blacks and American Society*, produced by a distinguished panel of scholars for the National Research Council (an arm of the American Academy of Sciences). The volume is more than six hundred pages long. It has brought together an avalanche of valuable data on the culture, education, housing, health, and economic performance of American blacks and concludes, not surprisingly, that "by almost all the . . . indicators, blacks remain substantially behind whites." But in explaining this lag, the scholars never get beyond discrimination. Reviewing the book in the *Public Interest*, Richard J. Herrnstein of Harvard found astonishing the authors' unwillingness to look further, the more so in that other National Research Council studies had identified "tested aptitude" as a major factor in material success. Said Herrnstein: "No individual trait predicts as much about one's personal destiny in America as test scores. Given the hypothetical choice of being black with an IQ of 120 or white with an IQ of 80, one should choose the former to get ahead in America now or in the readily visible future." How could this enormous project have gone forward over a span of more than five years without evidencing any interest in the IQ data? You have to tell yourself that psychological resistance to the data must have been overpowering.

> *"The tests are given because a lot of different decision makers find them useful."*

The War on Testing

Egalitarian pressures guarantee that tests of mental ability travel a rocky road in the United States these days. The tests tend to generate lawsuits on behalf of groups that score low, and the suits have often prevailed. Herewith three reports from the war on testing:

• In the California public-school system, it was until recently impermissible to give IQ tests to black children. Other children could be tested, but not blacks. This astonishing arrangement resulted from a class-action lawsuit tried in 1977–78. The suit complained that IQ testing resulted in disproportionate numbers of black children being placed in EMR classes (for the "educable mentally retarded") and that the placements stigmatized the kids and deprived them of equal educational opportunity. The state responded that (a) the tests were unbiased and (b) the EMR classes were helping children who needed help. But Federal District Judge Robert F. Peckham found for the plaintiffs. He ordered that

IQ tests no longer be administered to black children for any reason—*even if the parents requested the tests.*

In September 1992, Judge Peckham relented in part, in response to a lawsuit brought by black parents who wanted their kids tested. His modified ruling said they could be tested provided that test results were never used to place the children in EMR classes or their equivalent.

> *"Much, perhaps most, of . . . subpar performance is predicted by minorities' subpar IQ scores."*

• In New York State, the legislature decreed in 1987 that SAT scores could no longer be the sole basis for awarding state scholarship prizes. The new arrangement required that high school grades be used along with SATs. The legislature imposed this requirement in the wake of a lawsuit complaining that the SAT must be biased because men had been outscoring women—by something like 60 points for the verbal and math tests combined. The suit was brought by a coalition of feminist and antitesting activists whose cause was taken up by the legislature.

Neither the judge who heard the suit nor the legislators who passed the law had a theory to explain how bias was translating into a 60-point gap. Both basically ignored the explanation provided by the College Board, which administers the SAT. The Board's explanation: Women's scores were lower on average than those for men not because the test was biased but because the women taking it were more likely than men to come from minority and low-SES [socioeconomic status] families. When you adjust for socioeconomic status, the verbal gap disappears, and the math gap shrinks to 20 or 25 points.

Test Bias or True Ability Revealed?

To be sure, that leaves us still looking at a small gap. Does it mean that the SATs are just a little bit biased? A more likely interpretation of the SES-adjusted figures is that they represent the interaction of two research findings. Finding number 1: At any given level of IQ, women will do better at verbal tests, men better at quantitative tests. Finding number 2: With more variable IQs, men are overrepresented at the extremes of the distribution curve. In an above-average group like the teenagers taking the SATs, you would expect men to be overrepresented at the top. (They would also be overrepresented in any group of teenage retardates.) So they overcome the male disadvantage on the verbal tests and hang on easily to their edge at math.

You will possibly not be surprised to learn that no pressure groups in New York have been pushing this analysis of SAT tests. The field has been swept by those screaming "bias."

• Throughout the United States, state employment services have been increasingly restricted in their efforts to send over the best workers when employers call for help. In deciding who is best qualified, the state services used to rely primarily on a test supplied by the U.S. Employment Service (USES): the General Aptitude Test Battery (GATB). The test, heavily *g* [general intelligence] loaded, predicts job performance with a high level of accuracy. In the 1970s, the tests came under increasing criticism because blacks on average scored lower than Hispanics and Hispanics scored lower than whites; these disparities triggered claims of test bias and threats of litigation. Eager to preserve testing but leery of going into court, the USES agreed in 1981 to a compromise: It would instruct the state agencies to provide separate rankings for black and white workers. Each race would have its own set of scores and percentile rankings.

In the spring of 1990, an anonymous government official mailed off the racial conversion tables to Robert Holland, associate editor of the *Richmond Times-Dispatch*, and he hastened to publish examples of how they worked. Suppose, for example, that a white worker, a Hispanic worker, and a black worker took the test for a toolmaker's job. Suppose that all three had a raw score on the test of 300. In that case, the black job candidate would be placed in the seventy-ninth percentile, the Hispanic, in the sixty-second percentile, and the white toolmaker, in the thirty-ninth percentile. Needless to say, the black worker would get the job interview; indeed, he would have gotten it with a raw score well under 300. The "race-norming" arrangement guaranteed that black, Hispanic, and white job applicants would each get the same proportionate number of referrals. It did not, of course, guarantee that the employer would get the best applicants.

Race-norming was outlawed by the Civil Rights Act of 1991. But instead of returning to a system of simply referring applicants with the highest GATB scores, USES has announced plans to come up with a new test.

Familiar Themes

Stories like these could be multiplied endlessly. I take it that multiplication would be superfluous, as all three stories echo themes that will look familiar to any casual reader of the daily papers. The three situations described above have several things in common.

First, all involve massive, ideologically driven denials of reality. Rejecting the possibility that groups might actually differ in mental ability, all three of the stories depict a society determined to prove that test-score differences can only reflect test bias.

"No individual trait predicts as much about one's personal destiny in America as test scores."

These denials impose substantial costs on society—also on a certain number of identifiable individuals. One victim who first surfaced in 1987 was Mary Amaya, a mother in California, who was bothered by her son's educational progress and became infuriated upon being told that he could not be tested because he was black. Thousands of other unnamed and unknown children have also been hurt by the California ban on testing. The results of the ban were described by Rogers Elliott, a Dartmouth-based lawyer and psychologist who wrote a book (*Litigating Intelligence*) that dealt at length with the California suit. Writing in 1987, Elliott observed: "Many, perhaps half, of all children removed from EMR classes in California have been placed in regular classrooms—which means that they have been returned to the environments in which they had failed in the first place. . . . Since the early 1970s, thousands of children have never been placed in EMR who would have been so placed before that time." It is hard to believe those kids are better off.

> *"The first effect of eliminating formal tests is to replace them with informal or less precise or egregiously prejudiced arrangements."*

The Amaya story continued to make headlines early in the 1990s. When Mary Amaya demanded that her son be tested, she was told that this was impossible so long as he was considered to be black. State education officials proposed blandly that Mrs. Amaya, who is of Mexican descent, identify the child as Hispanic, which would make it legal for him to take an IQ test. She turned down this proposal, saying she did not want the boy to be in the position of repudiating his black father, and along with other black parents brought suit against the state for the right of their children to take IQ tests.

Do IQ Tests Have a Future?

It was this suit that led to Judge Peckham's retreat in September 1992. But even after his new ruling, it is unclear whether IQ tests have a future in California schools. The state's education commissioner has been unrelentingly hostile to the tests, and they are now banned in the Los Angeles and San Francisco school districts. It is hard to believe the state's kids will be better off as a result.

Nor is it credible that the campaign against GATB is helping American competitiveness or supporting the "search for excellence" in American business. Nobody knows how to figure the cost of the campaign, but one message built into it is that excellence is not, after all, a top priority.

It is hard to think of benefits that offset these costs. When testing is eliminated, you do not ordinarily eliminate the need to make distinctions among people—poorly performing students who might need remedial help, SAT scholarship prospects, or machinists hoping to catch on at General Electric. The first effect of eliminating formal tests is to replace them with informal or less precise or egregiously prejudiced arrangements: job interviews, for example, or teacher grades. Can anybody really anticipate that New York State has eliminated prejudice with its new criteria for determining who will win the valuable (up to $10,000) and prestigious Empire State scholarships? A guaranteed result of bringing school grades into the equation and downgrading the role of SAT scores is pressure on teachers to inflate the grades of the SAT test takers.

A Radical Meritocracy

After two decades of massive affirmative-action programs in government and just about all large corporations, many Americans find it hard even to imagine any sizable organization not committed to racial preference. It happens, however, that one extremely large and quite prominent organization does well without it; furthermore, minorities do very well in the organization—the U.S. military. For many years the armed services have been more than 20 percent black.

The military has been described as a "radical meritocracy." Anyone wishing to enlist in the armed services must first take the vocational aptitude test battery, several sections of which function as an IQ test equivalent. By law, the services are required to screen out prospects in the lowest 10 percent of testees, roughly those below IQ 80. Individuals accepted as recruits instantly find themselves in a regime where only "merit" matters. Said Charles Moskos in an article in the *New Republic*: "Basic training is the leveling experience par excellence. The mandatory short haircuts, the common uniform, the rigors of eight weeks of infantry training, all help to reduce pre-existing civilian advantage. For many youths from impoverished backgrounds, successful completion of basic training is the first occasion on which they can outshine those coming from privileged backgrounds." The armed services offer the spectacle, all too rare in American life, of blacks exercising authority over whites without generating resistance and resentment—because everybody knows the authority was earned.

It is a regime entirely without discrimination and almost entirely without reverse discrimination. (The "almost" in that sentence refers to the fact that women and minority-group members seem to get preference for promotions in situations where the distinction between candidates is effectively too close to call.) White recruits are more likely to end up in highly technical fields; black recruits are more likely to end up in clerical work or the supply services. But thousands of blacks—beginning with the 7,500 or so commissioned officers and the 80,000-odd noncoms—have found that the armed services offer opportunities superior to those available in the civilian economy. And not only in conventional career terms. As Moskos observed in the *New Republic*, the army is integrated in ways that Harvard cannot begin to emulate. Visiting an army dining facility, he was struck by "the easy mixing of races" and noted: "Black and white soldiers eat together in seemingly random fashion. The bantering that goes on across the tables seems to have no particular racial direction. What a contrast with the self-imposed segregation found in most college dining halls today."

> *"IQ tests represent a constant challenge to egalitarian social policies."*

A Challenge to Affirmative Action

IQ tests represent a constant challenge to egalitarian social policies. Where the policies assume equal ability, the tests play the role of hated whistle-blowers.

83

This is notoriously true where IQ tests confront affirmative action. One of affirmative action's sustaining ideas is the proposition that minority "underrepresentation" in the labor force, and especially in the better, higher-paying jobs, is an expression of irrational bias. This idea is instantly in trouble when confronted with IQ test data, which insistently remind you of (a) lower average scores for minorities and (b) the link between test scores and job performance. It is an understatement to say that black-white IQ studies have "policy implications." A more reasonable formulation would be that the studies represent a profound and insistent challenge to affirmative action.

What of the argument that group-ability differences should not be studied or discussed—that public parading of the differences can be traumatic to

> *"One major message of the IQ data is that groups are different."*

low-scoring groups? The argument seems never to be accompanied by evidence of trauma. But even if such evidence were producible, I do not see how we could (a) systematically suppress evidence of group differences while (b) systematically implementing policies of group preference. My own view is that the preferential policies make the studies not only inescapable but far more sensitive than they would otherwise be. If our public policy demanded not preference but the treatment of blacks as individuals—in employment, college admissions, and everything else—then the relevance of the group data would be instantly undermined.

Policy Implications of IQ Tests

It is worth recalling that many well-known group differences are not at all sensitive. Poor whites, for example, score appreciably lower than middle-class whites. I have never heard anybody argue that this detail should be suppressed as too painful for the poor. But if public policy were suddenly to require employment and educational preferences for the poor—and to construe their low rates of progress as evidence of continuing bias—then the group's average performance would be a contentious and inescapable issue.

One major message of the IQ data is that groups are different. A major policy implication of the data, I would argue, is that people should not be treated as members of groups but as individuals.

IQ Scores Explain Behavior

by James Q. Wilson

About the author: *James Q. Wilson is the James A. Collins Professor of Management and Public Policy at the University of California at Los Angeles. He is the coauthor of* Crime and Human Nature.

Serious readers will ask four main questions about *The Bell Curve*. Is it true that intelligence explains so much behavior? How can IQ produce this effect? If it does, is there anything we should do differently in public policy? And will this nexus affect race relations?

My answer to the first question is unequivocally yes. I first became aware of the significance of low IQ as a predictor of ordinary criminality when I collaborated with the late Richard Herrnstein in writing *Crime and Human Nature*. Since we published that book in 1985, evidence showing that delinquents and other offenders have a lower measured intelligence, especially on the verbal component of the tests, has continued to accumulate. Now Herrnstein and Charles Murray have shown that there are strong correlations between IQ and occupation level, school attainment, worker productivity, and possibly even political participation. These correlations exist within a given racial group (say, whites) and after matching people on the basis of their social class. (Controlling for social class means that the IQ-outcome link is even stronger than many of *The Bell Curve*'s graphs reveal, since IQ also partially determines a person's social class.) Herrnstein and Murray present their evidence abundantly, cautiously, and in painstaking detail. Though quibbles are possible, I find it very unlikely that their answers to this question will be confuted.

How IQ Affects Behavior

The second question seems to present a tougher challenge. How can IQ affect things that don't seem to involve much thinking, like stealing a radio, conceiving a child out of wedlock, or doing a poor job as a bricklayer? The answer, I

James Q. Wilson, "Acting Smart," *National Review*, December 5, 1994; © 1994 by National Review, Inc., 150 E. 35th St., New York, NY 10016. Reprinted by permission.

think, is that even the simplest tasks require the mind to recall and process an enormous amount of information; even the most powerful temptations evoke from us very different degrees of vividness in imagining future consequences. We forget this when we adopt the language of "instinct," "social forces," "economic incentives." Though all of these factors are important, all are mediated by the human mind in complex ways. On average, bright people are more likely than not-so-bright ones to recall past experiences and use them to shape present actions, to foresee vividly the future consequences of actions, and to internalize rules of thumb for everything from how to lay a straight line of bricks to how to prevent an unwanted pregnancy. There are many exceptions—bright people who give way to every temptation, not-so-bright people who follow the Ten Commandments scrupulously. But on average, IQ makes a difference across a wide range of human behaviors. How wide a range we have yet to learn.

My answer to the third question is, "It depends." To be exact, the public-policy implications depend on two things. One is how much of the variance in unhappy conditions—criminality, poverty, low worker productivity, and the like—can be explained by differences in intelligence. We know with certainty that IQ cannot explain all of the variance, because rates of crime, poverty, and illegitimacy change dramatically without corresponding changes in intelligence. But even allowing for these changes, the statistical techniques that Herrnstein and Murray use do not, for technical reasons, permit a good estimate of how much of the difference between two groups (say, white women on welfare and white women not on welfare) can be attributed to IQ differences.

> *"Delinquents and other offenders have a lower measured intelligence."*

The other point is that we do not know how policy measures designed to change the things that can be changed interact with IQ. For example, suppose having a low verbal IQ makes a young girl more likely to become a teenage mother, get on welfare, and remain poor. Knowing that we can't change IQ very much (as we have learned from virtually every study of pre-school education that has ever been done), we decide to change other things: we provide girls with sex education and contraception, enroll them in classes that teach them how to resist peer pressure, and develop apprenticeship programs that enable them to get jobs that do not require a lot of brain power. Such programs may work well with girls of ordinary talents, but how well will they work with girls of below-par talents? Or to put the same thing in other words, how heavily must we invest money and effort in a program to make up for whatever cognitive deficits the participants bring to it? Except for some isolated cases, we don't know the answer to that question. In those instances where one kind of investment (in pre-school education) has been shown to have enduring beneficial effects on behavior, the investment usually has been quite heavy—much heavier than in the standard Head Start project and, in many cases, lasting much longer.

Herrnstein and Murray agree with almost every other scholar that human behavior is the result of a complex interaction between nature and nurture. But they also remind us of a point that many laymen and some scholars forget: it is often just as hard to change nurture as it is to change nature, or even harder. Don't suppose for a moment that believing in the great importance of environmental factors facilitates planned social change. One example: almost everybody agrees that childhood experiences affect the risk of becoming a juvenile delinquent, a teenage mother, a school dropout. Now ask yourself: How do you change cold, discordant, abusive, neglectful parents into decent, loving, caring ones?

The Effect on Race Relations

The answer to the fourth question is: Knowledge of the connection between intelligence and behavior shouldn't have any effect on race relations, but it probably will. In principle—and especially in the light of the principles on which the United States was founded—a person's group membership ought to have no effect on the assessment we make of that person. Yesterday the reader was dealing with a variety of individuals who were white, Oriental, or black. Today he reads *The Bell Curve*. Tomorrow, should his behavior toward these people change in any way? No. They are the same individuals, with the same strengths and weaknesses, that they were yesterday.

That, alas, is not always the way the world works. Some people, eager to have a generalizable reason for their dislike of a particular person, will impute to that person the average IQ of his ethnic group as learned from Herrnstein and Murray. We call that racism. It is wrong. But it will happen. Some other people, eager to deny the reality of group (or even individual) differences, will want to deny the accuracy of *The Bell Curve* by assailing the motives of the authors. We call that an *ad hominem* argument. It is wrong. But it will happen.

In an ideal world, the book Herrnstein and Murray have written would pass into public consciousness with scarcely a ripple. "Of course," readers would say, "we know that people differ in intelligence and we know, from having watched them in school, on the job, and in the neighborhood that this difference will make a difference in how they behave." And then they would add: "But we are Americans, and in America it is your individual talents and inclinations, and only those, that count. So we don't have to change anything we are doing as individuals."

> *"There are strong correlations between IQ and occupation level, school attainment, worker productivity, and possibly even political participation."*

But this is not an ideal world, and so some conservative racists and some liberal multiculturalists (who are racists of a different kind) will make the wrong kind of fuss about this penetrating and magisterial book. Shame on them.

IQ Scores Predict Performance

by Peter Brimelow

About the author: *Peter Brimelow is a senior editor at* Forbes, *a biweekly business magazine.*

"My political aspiration," the American Enterprise Institute's Charles Murray says, "is the restoration of the Jeffersonian republic."

Murray's critics may read his aspirations differently—and a good deal less charitably. Since 1989 there has been fascinated speculation about his collaboration with Harvard's Richard J. Herrnstein (who died of lung cancer in September 1994). Herrnstein was one of the most honored academic psychologists in the country. Murray is one of the most influential social scientists, whose work has been accepted by conservatives and liberals alike.

Now these formidable talents were jointly taking on the most feared taboo of modern times: the links among intelligence, heredity and some of the puzzling but apparently unstoppable pathologies raging in American society—such as crime, family breakup, the emergence of the underclass.

The Bell Curve's New Research

Finally, their long-awaited book *The Bell Curve: Intelligence and Class Structure in American Life* has appeared. It's massive, meticulous, minutely detailed, clear. Reading it gives you the odd sensation of trying to swim in a perfectly translucent but immensely viscous liquid.

Like Darwin's *Origin of Species*—the intellectual event with which it is being seriously compared—*The Bell Curve* offers a new synthesis of research, some of which has been mounting insistently for years, and a hypothesis of far-reaching explanatory power.

But what about the Declaration of Independence—"All men are created equal"?

The ideal of equality was central to the American and the French revolutions.

But is it to be taken as a literal statement about abilities?

Some would say yes, that, given the same opportunities, most people are pretty much alike.

But the reality is that guaranteeing equal opportunity does not produce equality of results. Some people are more disciplined than others, work harder—and, yes—are more intelligent. Some of the traits that make for worldly success can be acquired, but some are genetic, programmed in. Out of an erroneous, if well-meaning, overemphasis on egalitarianism, Herrnstein and Murray argue, we downplay the programmed-in part.

> *"The reality is that guaranteeing equal opportunity does not produce equality of results."*

Psychometrics, the measurement of mental traits including intelligence, was a rapidly developing science earlier this century. But then came the savagery of Nazism. The pendulum swung. Any talk of inherent differences became taboo.

Since the 1970s, as Herrnstein and Murray note, public repression of psychometrics reached its climax. Scientific popularizers like Leon Kamin and Stephen Jay Gould were able to proclaim not merely that intelligence was 100% determined by environment and a meaningless concept anyway but that any argument to the contrary was racist.

Herrnstein, tragically, is gone. But Murray still has a lot to lose. His 1984 book *Losing Ground* argued that Great Society programs had largely failed to help the poor and were actually stimulating illegitimacy. When it came out *Losing Ground* was bitterly assailed, but it has recently been enjoying a curious vindication as welfare reform becomes an ever hotter issue. Newspapers like the *New York Times* and the *Chicago Tribune* have noted his new acceptability. Even President Clinton mentioned Murray's work favorably in an interview with NBC's Tom Brokaw.

But isn't heredity discredited? Isn't intelligence a meaningless concept?

No, the authors argue forcefully. And they have many allies. The most extraordinary aspect of this extraordinary episode of intellectual regression is that psychometric research has continued, quietly, in ivory towers. And since the 1970s every major objection to its findings has been rebutted.

The bizarre result: Surveys by psychologist Mark Snyderman and Smith College political scientist Stanley Rothman, published in their *IQ Controversy: The Media and Public Policy*, found a gulf between the consensus among experts in the field (cognitive scientists, behavioral geneticists) and the consensus among the "media elite" (key editors and journalists).

Basically, the experts believe that human intelligence
- can be measured;
- matters, a lot;
- differs by heredity (40% to 80% of IQ variation).

The media elite believe, and report, the opposite.

Chapter 2

Intelligence Predicts Performance

So what? It's a theoretical issue—what's it got to do with practical problems like crime and drugs?

A lot, Herrnstein and Murray argue. They believe that intelligence is highly predictive of how people will do in the world.

Consider two issues that have preoccupied the U.S. media: poverty and inequality.

• *Poverty.* For several decades the proportion of Americans living in poverty fell. It went from over half the population in 1939 to less than 15% in the late 1960s. Then—ironically, just as the Great Society programs to abolish poverty were kicking in—the decline stopped. Poverty has stayed stubbornly static for more than 20 years.

To avoid having their argument sidetracked by the race issue, Herrnstein and Murray looked at poverty among non-Hispanic whites. Their finding: A white individual's intelligence now predicts the likelihood of his being poor far better than whether or not he was born into poverty.

Among whites born into average socioeconomic conditions, but with IQs below 85, the probability of poverty in adulthood reached 26%—inner-city proportions. Conversely, among whites born into the very worst poverty, but with average intelligence, the probability of poverty in adulthood was only one in ten. About two-thirds of America's poverty-level population is white. Of that group, nearly two-thirds have IQs below 96.

Ironically, more equal opportunity means that differences in intelligence matter more than they once did. Born poor but smart, a child has a good—though not, of course, guaranteed—chance of rising in the world. Born middle class but dumb, he has a significant chance of descending in the world.

That was always somewhat true in the U.S.—shirtsleeves to shirtsleeves in three generations—but never to the degree it is today.

That's offensive—Murray and Herrnstein are saying that the poor deserve to be poor!

That's not at all what they say. But they do suggest that a good deal of poverty may be getting down to an intractable core, caused by personal traits rather than bad luck or lack of opportunity.

> **"Intelligence is highly predictive of how people will do in the world."**

Which does not mean nothing can be done about poverty. Even most sub-75 IQ whites, after all, are still not poor. That's where environment comes in. Whites of below-average IQ who come from stable families are less likely to be in poverty than those born to unstable families. This suggests that people of below-average IQ are poverty-prone but are by no means destined for poverty. Note carefully: Herrnstein and Murray don't claim that IQ is the only thing that matters. A good home environment, nutrition, motivation, all still count. Unfortunately, Herrnstein and Murray demonstrate massively, these characteristics today are less likely to be present in families with low-IQ parents than in families with high-IQ parents.

• *Income Inequality.* The economy is placing an increasing premium on skills. This process began well before the much-reviled Reagan Decade of Greed. There is more competition for brainpower and skills than for strong backs. And significantly, even within the "high-IQ professions," such as accountants, lawyers, physicians, Herrnstein and Murray show that individuals with superior IQ scores tend to earn significantly more.

> *"A white individual's intelligence now predicts the likelihood of his being poor far better than whether or not he was born into poverty."*

Which suggests that income inequality cannot be eliminated simply by stuffing more schooling down the throats of those who, up until now, have been able to avoid it. The students must actually be able to use that schooling as well.

But why would this be happening now?

Apart from the economy's increasing premium on skills, education has become a much more efficient sorting mechanism.

Education and Intelligence

In 1920, Herrnstein and Murray note, only about 2% of 23-year-olds had college degrees. By 1990 the proportion had reached 30%. And the relationship between intelligence and college had become much closer. In the 1920s only one in seven of American youths with 110-plus IQs went directly to college. By 1990 it was four in seven. For the very highest IQs, college had become almost universal.

And the sorting continued within the college population. In the 1950s, for whatever reason—maybe it was the newly completed interstate highway system—a national market in higher education suddenly emerged. Admissions standards at Harvard and other elite colleges jumped dramatically, and decisively, as they spread their geographical nets more widely. And the average IQ of students at these elite colleges drew away from the average of college students overall, even though that had increased, too.

This, perhaps, would have pleased the Founding Fathers. And that's not counting sex. Despite reports to the contrary, love is not blind. Studies dating back to the 1940s show that the IQs of spouses correlate powerfully, almost as closely as that of siblings. More recent evidence suggests this "assortative mating" may be intensifying, as college graduates increasingly marry each other—rather than the boy or girl back home or someone met in church. No surprise, since the intelligent of both sexes are increasingly corralled together, on campuses and afterward in the "high-IQ professions."

The results are startling. The children of a typical Harvard-Radcliffe Class of '30 marriage, Herrnstein and Murray estimate, would have a mean IQ of 114; a third would be below 110—not even college material, by some definitions. But the children of a Harvard-Radcliffe Class of '64 marriage, after the admissions revolution, would have an estimated mean IQ of 124. Only 6% would fall below 110.

The Cognitive Elite

The American upper class, Herrnstein and Murray conclude, is becoming an upper caste. Society is stratifying according to cognitive ability. A "cognitive elite" is emerging at the top.

Americans can take a lot of pride in much of what this book describes. In one sense *The Bell Curve* is a description of how thoroughly the U.S. has realized the Founding Fathers' vision of equal opportunity for all.

Just look around. Who are the new American elite? They are, at least in part, drawn from every class, race and ethnic background. The old domination of the so-called WASP [White Anglo-Saxon Protestant] class is over. Where once it was common to find mediocre people occupying high places by reason of birth, today it is much less so. The poor farm boy, the laundryman's children do not inevitably languish in their parents' social situation but have the opportunity to rise in the world.

If you doubt the American dream, read this book. Your eyes will be opened.

Isn't that great?

Well, yes, Herrnstein and Murray say, but. . . .

The "but" is that the sorting process may be ending. Herrnstein and Murray argue that the "cognitive elite" may be increasingly isolated from the rest of society.

And the problems of the lower reaches of society, increasingly unleavened with intelligence, may become more chronic. Herrnstein and Murray, confining themselves first to the non-Hispanic white population, show that lower IQ is now more powerful than the socioeconomic status of parents in predicting an adult individual's likelihood of poverty, welfare dependency, dropping out of high school, unemployment, workplace injury (even when adjusted for type of occupation), divorce, illegitimacy and criminality.

> *"Born poor but smart, a child has a good—though not, of course, guaranteed—chance of rising in the world."*

Still, intelligence can't be that important. Look at all those rich businessmen in Kansas City with IQs of 106!

This comment was made recently by a prominent New York academic. But it just shows that, like many people, he hasn't thought through the way intelligence works in society.

The Bell Curve

Intelligence is distributed according to what statisticians call a "normal" (or "bell") curve. Most people are around the average of 100. Over two-thirds of the population are between 85 and 115. Very small numbers of people compose the extremes, or "tails." Five percent have IQs below 75. And 5% have IQs above 125.

This last is the group Herrnstein and Murray roughly define as the "cognitive elite." They estimate it at about 12.5 million Americans—out of a total population of nearly 260 million.

Two points [are] clear:

• Numbers fall off rapidly going up the IQ scale. Whatever snotty academics may think, Herrnstein and Murray report, the IQ of top executives is typically high—above the 115 average for college graduates.

But even if that rich Kansas City businessman really did have a 106 IQ, he would still be above 60% of the population.

• Life gets rarefied rapidly in the right tail. Paradoxically, the special cocoons in which society's winners live often confuse them about the critical role of intelligence. They see that success among their peers is not highly correlated with test scores. A chief executive realizes that he has many people working for him who are IQ-smarter than he or she is. It's almost a cliché today to say, "I'm where I am because I have a lot of people smarter than I am working for me." But people who say that forget that they themselves are probably well out there on the bell curve—their associates just happen to be a bit further out.

> *"Born middle class but dumb, [a child] has a significant chance of descending in the world."*

Basketball players might say that height doesn't matter much—if you're over 7 feet tall.

Come on, everyone knows tests don't predict academic or job performance.

Everyone may "know" this, but it's not true. Tests actually work well. This is not to say that the highest-scoring person will necessarily be the best performer on the job. Performance correlates with test scores: It is not commensurate with them. So, overall, the best performers will be recruited from the pool of higher test scorers.

But what about cultural bias?

The argument that intelligence testing reflects white European cultural values was always shaky. Tests do predict performance (approximately) for everyone. And East Asians tend to outperform whites. Herrnstein and Murray estimate the mean East Asian IQ to be about three points above whites'. Is anyone arguing that the tests are biased against Caucasians?

Moreover, IQ appears to be reflected by an objective measure: neurologic processing speed, as measured in recent laboratory experiments that involve hitting buttons when lights flash.

The Environmental Factor

But even if heredity is important, surely that environmental factor is enough to swamp it?

Not quite. Unlike the dominant intelligence-is-environment orthodoxy, the hereditarian position, as reported by Herrnstein and Murray, is actually very moderate: Everyone acknowledges that environment plays a role (20% to 60%) in determining intelligence.

But remember: We're talking about environment controlling 20% to 60% of the *variation*. The average variation between randomly selected individuals is 17 points. Equalizing environment, assuming a midpoint environmental influence of 40%, would still leave an average gap of nearly 10 points.

But haven't IQs increased over the years?

It's an apparently unkillable myth that IQ researchers once claimed that Jews and other immigrant groups in the 1900s were "feebleminded." They weren't, and the testers never claimed it. But, yes, there has been a significant worldwide upward drift in average scores over the century—the so-called Flynn effect. One explanation: improvements in nutrition. Average height has increased similarly. As with IQ improvement, the increase in height is concentrated among individuals at the lower end of the range. Neither giants nor geniuses seem more common, but there are fewer dwarfs and dullards. Wide and systematic variations, however, remain.

Don't compensatory programs like Head Start make a difference?

Not much, the authors say. Periodically there are optimistic press stories, but under careful scrutiny even the most expensive and ambitious programs have turned out to have little lasting effect, particularly on IQ.

What about Thomas Sowell? He's argued in his 1994 book Race and Culture: A World View *that improving environments will eventually overcome group IQ differences.*

Characteristically, *Forbes*'s pugnacious columnist, an economist at the Hoover Institution, has a position in the IQ debate that is distinctly his own. He agrees with Herrnstein and Murray that tests do predict individual performance and that ignoring their results is destructive for tester and testee alike. But he also thinks that environment determines much (although not all) cognitive ability. So he predicts that low-scoring groups will eventually improve with better social conditions.

> *"A good deal of poverty may be getting down to an intractable core, caused by personal traits rather than bad luck or lack of opportunity."*

Murray's response: Sowell's concept of "environment" must invoke extraordinarily subtle and pervasive cultural factors to explain why groups can live side by side for generations and still score differently. Sowell himself says it offers little opportunity for quick intervention and improvement. As a practical matter, Sowell and *The Bell Curve*'s authors are not so far apart as they might seem.

IQ isn't everything. The tests can't capture creativity, special talents . . .

Quite right, says Murray. He's a keen but not brilliant chess player, and says he wouldn't like to think his competitive rank reflects his IQ. (Which he says he doesn't know, but seems pleased with anyway.) Chess ability is correlated with, but is not at all commensurate with, general intelligence.

More generally, Murray argues, there's no reason any individual should regard an IQ score as a death sentence: Intelligence is only one of many factors contributing to success. Good personal habits, an ability to defer gratification, discipline, all these factors matter. Even without high IQ, individuals obviously can and do lead productive and satisfying lives.

So, what's the point of discussing IQ? There's nothing we can do about it.

Social Policy's Effect on IQ

In fact, *The Bell Curve* argues, social policy is already doing a lot about it—in a damaging and dangerous way.

• Welfare: "The technically precise description of America's fertility policy," the authors write, "is that it subsidizes births among poor women, who are also disproportionately at the low end of the intelligence distribution." They propose making birth control devices and information more widely available to poor people.

• Education: The impressive thing about America's education system, Herrnstein and Murray suggest, is not that 55% of sub-75 IQ whites drop out of high school—but that 45% graduate. The idea that everyone should complete high school is very new: As late as 1940, fewer than half of American 17-year-olds did so. However, that apparent progress among the less bright may have incurred a very high price. *The Bell Curve* demonstrates in a particularly closely argued passage that it has been achieved by focusing on the less able, a "dumbing down" that has resulted in sharply poorer performance among the most gifted children.

In 1993 over nine-tenths of federal aid to schools went to the "disadvantaged," meaning those with learning problems. Earmarked for the gifted: one-tenth of 1%. Herrnstein and Murray suggest a national scholarship program, to be awarded solely on merit.

• Adoption: Adopted children tend to do better than their natural siblings. Heredity still counts: They still tend to underperform their adoptive families. But this is an intervention that works—yet adoption is increasingly discouraged, particularly across racial lines.

• Affirmative action: There are high-IQ individuals of all races. But, exactly as Thomas Sowell has argued, young blacks and young people of other minority groups are the victims of college admissions officials blindly trying to fill quotas. This means they throw bright members of some minority groups into extremely competitive situations that neither they nor most whites can stand. Result: burnout.

Thus the average Harvard black student had an SAT score 95 points below the average Harvard white student—not because there aren't brilliant black kids but because Harvard overwhelms the quality of the black pool with its quota-based admission policies. This has the perverse effect of creating the illusion that minority kids cannot keep up.

Here's the rub: Some minority students over their heads at Harvard might do very well at other elite schools. The average black score at Harvard is about the same as the white average at Columbia, a fine school by any standard. By contrast, Asians appear to be held to a higher standard than everyone else at almost all the top schools.

> *"Lower IQ is now more powerful than the socio-economic status of parents in predicting an adult individual's likelihood of poverty [or] welfare dependency."*

"Whatever else this book does," said Herrnstein, showing his deep faith in the power of ideas, "it will destroy affirmative action in the universities." This may be hoping for too much. But remember that Murray's ideas about welfare were thought radical ten years ago.

This IQ stuff is too awful to think about.

Americans are optimists. They don't want to believe there are problems to which there are no solutions. The idea that IQ is destiny suggests a preordained universe that is uncongenial to us.

Changing Society

Ah, but there are things we can do, the authors say. What do they recommend?

Return to a society with "a place for everyone"—simpler rules, more neighborhood control, more direct incentives for virtue and disincentives for vice. A society where once again the cop on the beat is everyone's friend, where fortunate neighbors help unfortunate neighbors. A society that understands marriage is not just an inconvenient artifact but an institution that evolved to promote the care and nurture of children.

Thus, Herrnstein and Murray argue, people who disparage marriage and conventional morality are doing particular damage to the less intelligent portion of the population. Murphy Brown may be able to cope with being a single mother and even give her kid a good upbringing. But a poor woman with a relatively low IQ is less able to.

Herrnstein and Murray are not libertarian dreamers. They are critical of many past policies—state-sponsored segregation, for example. And they assume that government redistribution of income is here to stay. Indeed, in a society where the market puts increasing premiums on cognitive skills, they think that government should restore some balance by making routine jobs more attractive. Thus they express interest in such income-supplementing programs as Milton Friedman's negative income tax.

But—they insist—the reality of human differences must be recognized. "What good can come of understanding the relationship of intelligence to social structure and public policy?" the authors write in their preface. "Little good can come without it."

IQ Tests Are Not Accurate Measures of Intelligence

by Leonard Lieberman

About the author: *Leonard Lieberman is a professor of anthropology at Central Michigan University in Mount Pleasant and the author of several articles on race. He is writing a book on the controversy over IQ and race in the twentieth century.*

> "Race" and "IQ" are terms which seemingly possess a clear and well-defined meaning for millions of people . . . but in fact correspond to no verifiable reality, and have, indeed, been made the bases for social and political action of the most heinous kinds.
>
> *Race and IQ*, edited by Ashley Montagu

By the title "IQs 'R Us" I do not mean that IQ tests are toys; rather that they have been used as weapons against African Americans, Jews, Southern and Eastern Europeans, and the poor from the early decades of this century. *The Bell Curve*, coauthored by Richard Herrnstein and Charles Murray, continues this tradition in regard to the poor and African Americans.

The coauthors make several claims. They claim that, first, IQ tests measure intelligence; second, that those of the African American race have IQ scores that average 10 to 15 points lower than those for European Americans; third, a large proportion of differences in mean IQ between Blacks and Whites is due to a genetic component; and fourth, environment or social programs can do little to improve IQs, because heredity is so strong. I will present studies that contradict the authors' hereditarian position.

Measuring Intelligence

Do IQ tests measure intelligence? Although some mental testers are satisfied in saying that intelligence is whatever IQ tests measure, others do not agree. Mark Snyderman and Stanley Rothman asked 66 experts and nonexperts from 17 mostly academic psychological subdisciplines involved in mental measure-

Leonard Lieberman, "IQs R Us," *American Behavioral Scientist*, vol. 39, no. 1, September/October 1995, pp. 25-34; © 1995 Sage Publications, Inc. Reprinted by permission of Sage Publications, Inc.

ment of education whether they agreed that there is "consensus among psychologists and educators as to the kinds of behaviors that are labelled 'intelligent.'" Respondents "were inclined" to agree (somewhat or strongly) 53%, compared to 39.5% disagree. Although 53% is a majority, it is no consensus.

Yale psychologist Robert Sternberg says there are different kinds of intelligence that are as important as those on conventional tests. An example is a study of housewives who did poorly in pencil-and-paper calculations but were efficient comparison shoppers in the supermarket. Harvard psychologist Howard Gardner writes that innovativeness is not a dimension

> *"There are dimensions of life chances poorly predicted by IQ tests."*

significantly included in IQ tests. What IQ tests do measure is reflected in their predictive validity through correlations: .80 with scholastic achievement, .50 to .70 with occupational status, .35 with income, and .20 to .25 with actual performance on the job. IQ tests are said to measure what is called "g," or Level II intelligence, or cognitive ability. Thus "g" has to do with problem solving, abstract reasoning, generalizing from specifics, and perceiving abstract relationships. These skills are closely related to scholastic achievement, but because they correlate less strongly with actual performance on the job, and with income, there are dimensions of life chances poorly predicted by IQ tests.

Racial Differences in Intelligence

In the context of evolutionary biology, we have evolved to manipulate and survive in a variety of changing situations, and test taking relates to that process only in the narrower scholastic sense measured by IQ tests devised for modern industrial society. In the historical sense, an ethnic group may have a lower mean IQ score because the test reflects skills at participating in a society that prevents the ethnic group from participating fully. Examples are endless: Catholics in Northern Ireland score lower than Protestants; Blacks in South Africa score lower than "colored" people, who score lower than Whites under apartheid; Blacks in the U.S. South score lower than Blacks in the North; Jews entering Ellis Island in the early 1900s scored lower than Jews today. Put differently, as J. Blaine Hudson argues, "Racial differences in average IQ scores are simply one measure of the impact of racism and racial inequality."

What is the significance of the fact that Anglos, people of European descent, score higher, on the average, than African Americans or Chicanos? In addition to the above, there are two additional answers. First, the claim that African Americans and Anglo-Americans differ in measured intelligence by 10 or 15 points is based on group mean scores and does not meet the standard requirement of effectively controlling for the most obvious variable of all, environment. Of course socioeconomic status has been controlled in numerous studies, but this is done by using a few indicators such as occupational status and education as if they had the same meaning in all ethnic cultures. To understand the limitations of these indicators of socioeconomic status, examine the stronger set of indicators used by Jane Mercer (to be discussed below), which get at some of the crucial qualities of family environment in two ethnic cultures.

Second, the tests are written by Anglos, for Anglos, drawing upon Anglo-American culture. If the tests were written by members of a different culture, the results might be different. R. Williams developed an intelligence test called the Black Intelligence Test of Cultural Homogeneity (Bitch 100). It is a vocabulary test of 100 words selected from *The Dictionary of Afro-American Slang*. It was tested on 100 Black and 100 White St. Louis, Missouri, high school students. The Black group averaged 36 points higher than the White group. Williams did not conclude that White students were less intelligent or had fewer "smart genes." Rather, he concluded, "A culture-specific test clearly shows the ability of the population for which the test was intended." Although test makers claim that they have now constructed culture-free or culture-fair tests, their understanding of cultural differences is narrow.

> *"Racial differences in average IQ scores are simply one measure of the impact of racism and racial inequality."*

Claims in support of the culture fairness of IQ tests, in relation to the 15-point IQ gap between Blacks and Whites, are justified by Arthur R. Jensen on the basis of abstractness. That term refers to the idea that Blacks do more poorly on portions of tests that are more abstract. Stephen J. Ceci asked whether scholars would agree on which items require abstract reasoning and which do not. In 1981 two of his colleagues queried 20 students to rank-order a number of items said to favor Whites and a number that favored neither Blacks nor Whites. They found no consensus on the degree of abstractness. In a second study, Ceci and N. Nightingale queried a group of eminent scholars, including many with a Nobel prize in physics, literature, or chemistry. They were asked to rate 32 questions and problems as to degree of abstractness. The questions were associated with the largest degree of Black-White differences on the Wechsler test. The scholars disagreed with those from other fields, and even within a specific field there was frequent lack of agreement. Ceci concludes that the lack of consensus undermines the claim for abstractness as "the basis for reported racial differences."

Heredity and Environment

As to the high degree of genetic determination, the dispute here is *not* over the power of our genes. Our heredity gives this species extraordinary mental and linguistic potential. But also let it be noted that despite our marvelous genetic potential, we would be totally speechless and we would have no measurable IQ at all if we were left from birth in isolation deprived of other humans who nurtured and talked to us. It takes both biology and a human sociocultural environment to make another human. Genes cannot express themselves in phenotypic intelligence without interaction with the individual organism and the external environment. Therefore it is not possible to imply a direct measure of heredity. The claims of high heritability are based on studies of identical twins reared separately. However, a significant number of the separated twins were reared in very similar environments. Some had contact with each other. The most recent claim to have overcome this problem is the 1990 Minnesota study of twins. But this project has not published full details about the timing and degree of separation, and it uses limited measures of environmental differences.

Herrnstein and Murray base their claims of heritability on twin studies. They then utilize these figures to explain Black-White differences in IQ scores while at the same time denying that they do so by using these words:

> Scholars accept that IQ is substantially heritable, somewhere between 40 and 80 percent. . . . Yet this information tells us nothing for sure about the origin of the differences between races in measured intelligence.

Yet a paragraph later they refer to "available data" and

> further stipulate that one standard deviation (fifteen IQ points) separates American blacks and whites and that a fifth of a standard deviation (three IQ points) separates East Asians and whites. Finally, we assume that IQ is 60 percent heritable (a middle ground estimate).

The authors go on to argue that the required magnitude of environmental differences required to explain this difference would have to be of an implausible magnitude. In rejecting an environmental explanation the authors are, in effect, attributing the IQ difference between races to a very high component of heritability. The coauthors want it both ways: Heritability "tells us nothing for sure about the origin of the differences between races," yet it explains a large proportion of the differences because environment does not explain it. They are desperately seeking deniability of what they nonetheless assert.

> *"We would have no measurable IQ at all if we were left from birth in isolation deprived of other humans who nurtured and talked to us."*

The Effect of European Ancestry on African Americans

It is possible to test the coauthors' claims that so-called races as biological entities differ significantly from each other in intelligence due to heredity. If the coauthors, Herrnstein and Murray, are correct, then African Americans who have more European and less African ancestry should have higher IQs. This proposition was tested by psychologist Sandra Scarr. Restated, the proposition was that the higher the degree of European ancestry, the higher should be the IQ of African Americans. They gave an IQ test to a sample of 350 African Americans in the Philadelphia area. They estimated each person's degree of African and European ancestry from blood samples in which they could identify serum proteins indicating 12 hereditary traits that were more likely to have either African or European ancestry. These results were supported by degree of skin color and were similar for siblings.

> *"Genetic differences in intelligence between so-called races are not supported."*

To make this population more vivid, picture in your mind 350 African Americans looking like celebrities arranged in a continuum from Colin Powell and Lena Horne, to Oprah Winfrey and Jesse Jackson, to Clarence Thomas and Martin Luther King Jr. This is not a bell curve, it is a continuum. All along this continuum there would be considerable variation in physical appearance. I could perform the same mental exercise showing a variety of physical traits among Jewish Americans, Mexican Americans, Native Americans, Euro-Americans, and so on.

According to Scarr and Richard Weinberg:

> The results were unequivocal. Blacks who had a large number of European ancestors did no better or worse on the tests than blacks of almost total African ancestry. These studies dispute the hypothesis that IQ differences between blacks and whites are in large part the result of genetic differences.

In the language of correlations, they found zero correlations between degrees of European/African ancestry and test scores. Herrnstein and Murray do not refer to this study in their very long and detailed book.

These results do not show that individuals are all the same in whatever IQ tests measure, but they do show that genetic differences in intelligence between so-called races are not supported by this careful study. These results are all the more impressive because the first author, Scarr, is a hereditarian. She believes, along with Herrnstein and Murray, that heredity strongly influences intelligence, but her results show that "intelligence" test scores do not vary with degree of African or European ancestry.

No Homogeneous Races

The study by Scarr and Weinberg also illustrates that when various researchers measure a population and call it a race, it is not a so-called biologically homogeneous race. There are none. In the long span of evolutionary history, due to past and present migrations, there have been extensive matings between peoples. Selective perception and racial stereotypes magnify the differences, and simultaneously fail to accept them as different aspects of our common humanity.

This is all the more apparent given the definition of race used by Herrnstein and Murray. On page 271 they ask, "What does it mean to be 'black' in America in racial terms, when the word black (or African American) can be used for people whose ancestry is more European than African? . . . The rule we follow here is to classify people according to the way they classify themselves." Given that definition, all the studies they cite of so-called race that claim to deal with genetic differences are worthless in so far as alleged biological race is concerned because they are studying mixed populations, and all large populations contain a high degree of heterogeneity.

A related study used IQ scores of children fathered by United States servicemen and born to German women following World War II. The average IQ score of children of African American fathers was almost identical with the average score of children with Euro-American fathers (the groups were matched on age, sex, socioeconomic status, and other social variables).

Environment's Effect on IQ Scores

But what about the claim by Herrnstein and Murray that culture or environment is relatively unimportant? There is a way to test that proposition. Jane Mercer, a sociologist, has conducted a series of studies in Riverside, California, carefully measuring environment for Chicanos and African Americans as compared to middle-class European Americans. Her study included *all* Chicano and African American schoolchildren 6–14 years of age. She used the full-scale Wechsler Intelligence Scale for Children (WISC) test, and she also measured five sociocultural characteristics.

Table 1 lists these five sociocultural characteristics representing Chicano and African American environmental differences. The author assumes that the greater the number of these five characteristics that are present, the closer the family environment will be to the Anglo middle class and the higher will be the IQ scores of the children.

> *" 'Intelligence' test scores do not vary with degree of African or European ancestry."*

Table 2 shows the mean IQ scores for Chicano and African Americans at 90+ and the Anglo mean at 100. The rest of the table shows the effect of environment on IQ scores. Among children from homes with only one of these characteristics, the mean is in the low 80s. With each additional characteristic, the score rises until with all five characteristics present, the mean IQ score is equal to that of Anglos.

On the basis of the strong pattern in Table 2, Mercer concludes that

> Black children who came from family backgrounds comparable to the modal pattern for the community did just as well on the Wechsler Intelligence Scale for Children as the [White middle class] children on whom the norms were based. When sociocultural differences were held constant there were no differences in measured intelligence.

Mercer's study also demonstrates the point made earlier in this viewpoint, namely, that it is meaningless to compare means without adequately controlling for different cultural environments.

Table 1: Five Indicators of Environment as of 1970 in Riverside, California

Type of Characteristic[a]	Chicano	African American
1. Crowding	Less crowded homes (less than 1.4 per room)	Living in a family with five or fewer members
2. Mother's education expectations	Mother expects them to be educated beyond high school	Mother expects them to get some college education
3. Role model 1: education/occupation	Head of household had more than ninth-grade education and reared in an urban environment over 10,000 population	Father had an occupation rated 30 or higher on the Duncan Socioeconomic Index
4. Role model 2: language/marriage	English spoken in home all or most of time	Parents married and living together
5. Economic stability	Buying or owning home	Buying or owning home

Source: Mercer (1972).
[a] These headings are added by L. Lieberman

Table 2: Wechsler Intelligence Scale for Children's Scores, Ethnicity, and Number of Environmental Characteristics

Number of Environmental Characteristics	Chicano		African American	
	M (mean)	N (number)	M	N
	90.4	598	90.5	339
0 or only one	84.5	127	82.7	47
Two	88.1	146	87.1	100
Three	89.0	126	92.8	106
Four	95.5	174	95.5	69
Five	104.4	25	99.5	17

Source: Mercer (1972, p. 17).

It is a surprise that a paragraph in *The Bell Curve* presents Mercer's findings. But it is no surprise that Herrnstein and Murray dismiss the study by attributing the environmental differences to "variation in intelligence as ordinarily understood." And we know that Herrnstein and Murray understand variation in intelligence to be mostly due to heredity. In short, when confronted with strong evidence of the influence of environment, the coauthors say that environment is determined by heredity. There is therefore no contrary evidence the authors will accept.

Social Programs Can Help

The final claim made by Herrnstein and Murray is that environmental programs can do little, because heredity is so strong. I have already cited studies that contradict that biological determinism. I have also cited studies showing the power of the environment. Environmental intervention programs were discredited by Murray in his 1984 book *Losing Ground*, and again in 1994 in *The Bell Curve* with Herrnstein, although for environmental reasons in 1984 and for hereditary reasons in 1994.

The success of a massive social program is illustrated by the GI Bill (the Serviceman's Readjustment Act of 1944). It provided tuition, books, and living allowances to 7.8 million veterans of World War II. According to R. Wilson, in 1940 higher education was "separate and very unequal," with the best universities attended primarily by upper-middle-class White students, segregated colleges being attended mostly by Black students. In 1947 the number of veterans increased 29% at White colleges and 50% at Black colleges. College integration would come later, but the result of the increased Black enrollment was the emergence of "today's large and growing Black middle class."

Another test of social programs is the Milwaukee Project designed by Howard Garber and Richard Heber. It identified children at risk of mental retardation and sought to prevent that outcome. The at-risk children and their mothers were the experimental group. For 6 years, starting within the first 6 months of life, the children were given stimulation programs, while the mothers were given a vocational-personal rehabilitation program. The IQ gain at age 5 was around 30 points higher for the experimental group than for the controls, and 4 years later the score was still 20 points higher. The Milwaukee program improved the child's learning experience and probably the mother's ability to interact with the child. Programs that alter several aspects of the environment have more and longer lasting success.

> *"IQ scores, and school achievement, can be enhanced through better economic, educational, and family opportunities."*

After the publication of *The Bell Curve*, the Science Directorate of the American Psychological Association issued a "media advisory" that "there is a wealth of research evidence showing that early educational interventions are effective in raising performance and achievement levels for disadvantaged groups."

Although individuals differ in cognitive potential, large populations have a range of potential among their members, and the mean (average) outcome depends on the quality of the environment. IQ scores, and school achievement, can be enhanced through better economic, educational, and family opportunities. And of these I believe that in the long run, better economic opportunity is the horse that leads the cart. According to J.L. Graves Jr. and T. Place, those who wish to further test the genetic hypothesis should work toward "equalization of environmental influences." The most salient means to accomplish this, Graves and Place write, would be to "[equalize opportunity and] to eliminate the unnecessary poverty that most people . . . face." In 1970 geneticists W.F. Bodmer and L.L. Cavalli-Sforza suggested that "the question of a possible genetic base for the race-IQ difference will be almost impossible to answer satisfactorily before the environmental differences between U.S. blacks and whites have been substantially reduced." In this light, Murray's efforts to end most social programs would seem to be directed away from a genuine answer to the question of hereditary and environmental influences.

Part of the attention in the media to *The Bell Curve* is an expression of the social context in which a California referendum made it a state requirement that illegal immigrants be deprived of medical, educational, and welfare sources.

104

This occurred in the same social setting in which welfare will require work after 2 years, but will not raise the minimum wage, and in which great resources will be used to build prisons, but not to develop job opportunities that can give hope and focus and keep people out of prison.

Using Science for Political Purposes

The social issue involved in the IQ controversy is not what science can tell us, but the use of science for political purposes. The idea of low IQ as a product of heredity has been, and still is, used as a justification to blame, scapegoat, and squeeze the powerless. The late twentieth century is a period in which biological explanations are seen as science and environmental explanations are seen as wasting taxpayers' money. It is not a scientific issue, but one that is political and ethical: Should those at the bottom of society live in desperation while those at the top pay low wages, aggrandize their wealth, and export jobs out of the country?

Finally, I am aware that I have not explicitly commented on the many chapters in *The Bell Curve* dealing with the American poor of European origin. Those sections are pertinent because they illustrate the process of racialization presented by Michael Omi and Howard Winant. We may be moving toward the time when the Euro-American poor will be defined in much the same way as Blacks are today. The foundations of that were built by Herrnstein in his 1971 article on IQ, which, like *The Bell Curve*, reluctantly concludes that a hereditary meritocracy is emerging. Thus those at the top and bottom of society will be said to differ in genetic traits for intelligence. Such genetic differences are part of what has been meant by race. In 1903, W.E.B. Du Bois said that the color line would be the crucial problem of the twentieth century. If Herrnstein and Murray have their way, and social participation is denied to the less privileged, the problem of the 21st century will be the dividing line between the cognitive elite and almost everyone else.

IQ Tests Measure Learned Knowledge

by F. Allan Hanson

About the author: *F. Allan Hanson is a professor of anthropology at the University of Kansas in Lawrence and the author of* Testing Testing: Social Consequences of the Examined Life.

At some gut level, many middle- and upper-class white Americans apparently harbor the conviction that they are more intelligent than people of the lower class and ethnic minorities (especially of African descent). While its obviously racist and anti-democratic connotations are sufficient to keep this attitude under wraps most of the time, periodically works grounded in psychometrics (the branch of psychology devoted to measuring differences among people) encourage this sentiment to re-emerge with an apparent mantle of scientific respectability. The most notorious of several 1994–95 eruptions has been sparked by the publication of Richard J. Herrnstein and Charles Murray's book, *The Bell Curve*.

Herrnstein and Murray are only the latest in a 125-year-long succession of social scientists dedicated to the enterprise of postulating intellectual differences between classes and races. Important predecessors include Francis Galton, H.L. Goddard, Lewis Terman, and Arthur Jensen. Herrnstein himself articulated the main theme of *The Bell Curve* in 1973, when he predicted that the importance of inherited mental abilities for achieving high income and prestige in our society would inexorably open a social rift between an intellectually gifted ruling class and a dull underclass.

Interpreting I.Q. Test Scores

Despite a bulky 800-plus pages bulging with statistics and charts, *The Bell Curve* conveys a very simple message: The ills of society—poverty, unemployment, unmarried parenthood, crime—are causally connected to the low intelligence of the people who manifest them. From this put-down of the lower class,

F. Allan Hanson, "Testing, *The Bell Curve*, and the Social Construction of Intelligence." Reprinted from the January/February 1995 issue of TIKKUN MAGAZINE, A BI-MONTHLY JEWISH CRITIQUE OF POLITICS, CULTURE AND SOCIETY. Subscriptions are $31 per year from TIKKUN, 251 W. 100th St., 5th floor, New York, NY 10025.

Herrnstein and Murray go on to make the highly controversial claim that races differ in intelligence, and particularly that Blacks are significantly less intellectually endowed than whites.

Indisputably, intelligence test scores vary directly with socioeconomic status. If people are sorted into groups defined by $10,000 increments in annual family income, average intelligence test scores increase with each step up the income ladder. It is also true that, on average, Ashkenazi Jews score between a half and a full standard deviation (about 7 to 15 I.Q. points) higher on intelligence tests than other whites, and whites average a full standard deviation higher than Blacks.

> *"Tests are always indirect measures."*

The interpretation of these facts forms the heart of the debate over *The Bell Curve*. Herrnstein and Murray insist that they mean that upper-class people, on average, are more intelligent than lower-class people, and that this difference goes a long way in explaining the affluence of the one group and the chronic crime, dependence on welfare, unmarried parenthood, and other social problems of the other.

In fact, Herrnstein and Murray's thesis about different levels of mental ability between rich and poor, white and Black, is wholly predicated on the notion that intelligence is an independently existing human characteristic that is accurately measured by intelligence tests. But that fundamentally misconstrues the nature of intelligence tests and what they measure, throwing the entire argument of *The Bell Curve* off track. Some reflections on the nature of tests in general, and intelligence tests in particular, will make this clear.

What Tests Measure

Tests are always indirect measures. What we wish to know from a test—the target information—and what we learn directly from it—the test result—are never identical. Test results represent target information. This is particularly obvious in a lie detector test, in which the test result consists of information about certain physiological changes—in blood pressure, pulse and respiration rates, and so on—as measured by a polygraph machine. The target information is whether or not the subject is telling the truth. The assumption underlying the test is that the test result tells us something about the target information: that certain physiological perturbations, when associated with responses to certain questions, signify deception.

The moment it is recognized that a gap exists between test result and target information, it becomes clear that the relation between the two is not one-to-one. Other variables may intervene. Thus, one of the biggest debates about polygraph tests is whether it is possible to weed out "false positives"—honest individuals whose physiological responses manifest the same pattern as that associated with deception, but for other reasons.

107

There is a similar gap in intelligence testing. The point of an intelligence test is not to learn if the subject knows the meaning of the exact words found on that test, or can solve the particular mathematical problems or identify the patterns among the specific numbers and shapes that appear there. Performance on the test is assumed to represent the subject's ability to define words or solve problems of these types, and that, in turn, is taken to represent the subject's level of some largely inherited capacity called "general intelligence." Thus, the gap between test results (right and wrong answers on a particular test) and target information (general intelligence, or I.Q.) is wide indeed, and dependent upon many variables. The most important of them is learning.

Literally every answer on an intelligence test depends on what a person has learned. Vocabulary and reading comprehension questions probe how well the individual has learned to read; quantitative questions explore how much mathematics the individual has learned; questions in logic have to do with how well the person has learned to think systematically; spatial relations problems concern how well the subject has learned to visualize shapes, compare, and mentally transpose them. Of course, intelligence or aptitude tests aim to tap learning that is more broadly applicable and loosely specified than "achievement" tests such as, say, tests limited to addition and subtraction of fractions or American colonial history. It remains true, however, that any mental test, including the most general intelligence test, is inevitably limited to measuring what the test-taker has learned.

More than Innate Intelligence

Recognizing this, it becomes apparent that the score on an intelligence test indicates much more than an individual's innate intelligence. What the individual has learned may reflect inherited abilities to some degree, but other factors are critical, such as opportunities and motivation to learn. These depend on a variety of considerations such as the rewards and encouragements the individual has received for learning, personal relationships with parents and teachers, if and when the individual was exposed to subject matter that stimulated interest, and how much time and how many facilities, books, instruments, and other resources have been made available for learning.

> *"The gap between test results . . . and target information . . . is . . . dependent upon many variables. The most important of them is learning."*

Herrnstein and Murray acknowledge that intelligence is not entirely inherited; they attribute about 40 per cent of it to environmental factors. So they would be likely to chalk up what has just been said to the environmental component in intelligence. Their recognition of an environmental factor is mitigated, however, by their claim that intelligence remains stable throughout life after about age ten. Thus, they imply that the environmental impact on intelligence occurs only in relatively early childhood.

Given that tests can only measure what has been learned, it seems appropriate to reverse the direction of causality that Herrnstein and Murray propose. Far from differences in intelligence (as indicated by intelligence test scores) causing class differences, it is more likely that class membership (with all the discrepancies in opportunities to learn that that entails) causes differences in intelligence test scores.

> *"Literally every answer on an intelligence test depends on what a person has learned."*

This way of phrasing causal connection intentionally begs the question of the relation between intelligence test scores and intelligence, since that topic requires careful, separate consideration. The most basic flaw in *The Bell Curve* is its concept of intelligence as a single, independently existing human trait that is accurately measured by intelligence tests. Intelligence is better understood as an artifact of intelligence testing. This is not to say that there is no such thing as intelligence. It exists, but it has been brought into being by intelligence tests.

A Thought Experiment

Consider a thought experiment that constructs a new test and imagines its consequences. We will call our test the New Intelligence Test, or NIT. It is intended to surpass current tests by sampling more widely from the full range of cognitive ability, and particularly its practical applications in everyday life. The NIT consists of eight sections:

• A name recall scale tests ability to remember the names of persons to whom the subject has just been introduced;

• A mathematics section tests the subject's ability to solve problems of arithmetic and algebra;

• In the exposition of ideas section, the subject is given five minutes to read a complex idea—such as a page from Rousseau describing his distinction between self-love (*amour de soi*) and selfishness (*amour-propre*)—and thirty minutes to present a clear and accurate written account of it, with original examples;

• The small-talk scale evaluates subjects' ability to carry on an interesting conversation with someone they have just met;

• In the follow-the-directions scale, the subject is told once, at the speed of ordinary conversation, to do a task consisting of six distinct steps, and is evaluated on how well the task is accomplished;

• A bullshitting scale assesses skill at participating in a discussion with two other people on a topic about which the subject knows nothing;

• The adult sports scale evaluates the subject's ability to play golf or tennis, with suitable adjustments for male and female subjects;

• The presiding scale assesses ability to run a business meeting, including matters such as maintaining focus of discussion, building consensus, and finishing on time.

The test result is reported as a composite score generated from the outcomes of the NIT's eight sections.

The ability or human capacity tested by the NIT is certainly nothing inconsequential. If the appropriate studies were done, it would doubtless turn out that high NIT scores correlate positively (probably more positively than I.Q. scores) with desirable social outcomes such as success in the university, in business or professional life, high income, and election to public office. But it is also obvious that what the NIT tests is not a single quality or capacity of persons. It is rather a set of distinct qualities, which have been measured by the several sections of the NIT and combined into a single score for convenience in reporting NIT results.

But assume now that the NIT were to catch on in a big way—that it came, for example, to be widely used for college and graduate admissions and for hiring and promotion purposes by law firms, government, and corporations. In such an event, the different abilities measured by the NIT would not remain static. People would spare no effort in preparing for the test, in the hope of achieving the rewards awaiting those who excel on it. They would bone up on arithmetic and algebra, master techniques for remembering the names of strangers, hone skills of bullshitting, take golf and tennis lessons, learn how to run successful business meetings. School curricula would shift in the direction of more training in the areas covered by the NIT. (If they did not, irate parents would demand to know why their children were not being taught something useful.) Kaplan and Princeton Review would explode into the marketplace with courses that promise dramatic improvement in one's NIT scores.

Converting Test Results into a Number

All of this dedicated effort would have a palpable effect. Although the NIT obviously measures several quite different abilities, people would knit them together as they strive to improve them all in order to raise their NIT scores. Because NIT scores are reported as simple numbers, they would begin to imagine these several abilities to be one. They would name it . . . perhaps "NITwit." Given its relevance for success in life, it would be valued as a thing of great importance. People would worry about how much of it they possess; they would look for promising signs of it in their children and envy evidence of its abundance in other people's offspring.

> *"Any mental test, including the most general intelligence test, is inevitably limited to measuring what the test-taker has learned."*

Not only would a new mental category swim into the social consciousness. The empirical amount of it possessed by individuals would literally increase as, in preparing for the NIT, they got better at following directions, playing golf, expounding on ideas, engaging in small talk, and the rest of it. And, of course, as individuals increase these skills, NIT scores would go up. There would be rejoicing in the land as today's average NIT scores exceed those achieved in the past or by test-takers in other countries . . . until, perhaps, an apogee is passed and national consternation about declining NIT scores

> *"[Intelligence] exists, but it has been brought into being by intelligence tests."*

sets in. Given all these transformations and developments, it is fair to say that NITwit would become a new, singular, personal trait—an objective reality literally constructed by NIT testing. Perhaps the ultimate development (and the ultimate absurdity, but it unquestionably would happen) would be the marketing of rival tests that claim to measure NITwit faster, cheaper, or more accurately than the NIT.

The foregoing discussion of the NIT has, of course, its facetious moments. But its purpose is entirely serious. It demonstrates two fundamental characteristics of all mental testing. One is that test results inevitably reflect what test-takers have learned. The other is that, when a given test becomes sufficiently important, whatever that test tests gets reified as a single quality or thing. This has been the experience of "intelligence" in the real world. Because of intelligence tests, several different abilities (to solve mathematical problems, to comprehend texts, to compare shapes, to sort ideas or objects into classes, to define words, to remember historical events, and to do all of these things rapidly) have been welded together to form a new, unitary mental characteristic called "intelligence." People place great emphasis on it because intelligence tests serve as the basis for offering or denying educational and career opportunities and other social rewards. Precisely as with NITwit in our thought experiment, intelligence has been fashioned into an objectively real personal trait by the practice of intelligence testing.

Socioeconomic Status and I.Q.

We have distinguished two very different ways of understanding the relation between intelligence, intelligence tests, race, and social class. They agree that intelligence test scores increase as one goes up the social ladder, but disagree as to why. The sociological explanation I support is that, on average, opportunities to learn increase with higher socioeconomic status. (The Black/white difference in average intelligence test scores is then attributable to the fact that the socioeconomic status distribution of Blacks is lower than that of whites.) To say that intelligence increases with socioeconomic class is true in a sense, but it is potentially misleading because of the common tendency to think of intelligence as an independently existing human trait. On the contrary, general intelligence is nothing but a social construct produced by intelligence testing. "Intelligence" rises with socioeconomic status only because intelligence test scores do. And that is explicable not by any difference in largely innate cognitive potential between people of different classes (and races), but by different opportunities to learn.

In contrast, *The Bell Curve* and other works in its genre take intelligence test scores to be accurate measures of an independently existing human trait called general intelligence. The fact that scores are lower for certain ethnic minorities and for the lower class indicates that people in those conditions are, on average, less intelligent than others. Moreover, low intelligence is an explanatory factor for poverty, crime, welfare dependence, and other social problems that tend to cluster in the lower class, as well as for the disproportionate representation of certain ethnic minorities (especially Blacks) in the lower class.

This point of view is perverse as well as erroneous. Its endorsement of the idea that ethnic groups and social classes differ in intellectual capacity fuels a combination of smug condescension and hostility toward minorities and those who live in poverty. This has closed opportunities for millions and has driven racism, class discrimination, and eugenic programs such as immigration quotas and enforced sterilization.

Eliminating Intelligence Tests

Over the last century, each eruption of the discriminatory idea that some races and classes are less intelligent than others has been met with vigorous opposition, as have the contentions of *The Bell Curve*. It appears that this time, as in the past, after a relatively brief popular infatuation with the idea, scholarly counter-arguments will ultimately succeed in beating it back. But, if history is any indicator, in twenty years or so the issue will pop up again.

Perhaps it has not been defeated decisively because the critiques dealing with challenges to statistics and alternative explanations have not struck at its roots. Those consist not of ideas or propositions but of a social *practice*: intelligence testing. The practice of intelligence testing itself has produced both the concept of intelligence as a single thing and test results indicating that that thing systematically varies among ethnic groups and social classes. Thus, the most effective way to lay this spurious and socially disruptive issue to rest once and for all is to change the practice of intelligence testing.

> *"When a given test becomes sufficiently important, whatever that test tests gets reified as a single quality or thing."*

While it may be inconvenient to do without the efficiency and economy achieved by large-scale intelligence testing, some institutions show signs that they are beginning to wean themselves from it. Antioch, Bard, Hampshire, and Union colleges, together with some two dozen others, no longer require applicants to submit SAT or ACT scores, and Harvard Business School has dropped the GMAT (Graduate Management Aptitude Test) as an application requirement. These schools make their selections on the basis of academic records, written statements by applicants, and letters of recommendation, and they manage to operate their admissions programs effectively without intelligence tests.

A movement is afoot in the primary and secondary schools to assess children not in terms of standardized intelligence tests, but according to portfolios they develop with examples of their best work in a variety of subjects. If this becomes widespread, the conventional notion of intelligence as a single, quantifiable entity will begin to fade, as people focus on children's different talents—in such areas as music, visual art, the use of language, mathematical skills, athletics, and interpersonal relations.

> *"'Intelligence' rises with socioeconomic status only because intelligence test scores do."*

Developments of this sort would not signal the end of all testing. In addition to other evidence of accomplishments (such as portfolios), tests will doubtless continue to play a role in decisions about school promotions and graduation as well as competition among aspirants for scholarships, admission to selective colleges and training programs, or employment in desirable jobs. The tests, however, would not be designed to measure anything like "general intelligence." They would aim to assess how well individuals have succeeded in mastering knowledge or skills that have been presented to them in academic courses, technical, or artistic training programs. Different individuals would, of course, perform at different levels on these tests, and this would be taken into account along with other qualifications in deciding who will receive scarce rewards and opportunities.

Alternate Evaluations Are Already in Place

To implement practices such as these would not require sea changes in attitudes about assessment. The alternative perspective is already well established. Consider how evaluation works in a typical American college course. Depending on the discipline, students are usually graded on the basis of some combination of the following: problems or questions to be completed and handed in at regular intervals, laboratory reports, term papers, performance in discussion groups, and tests. The notion of general intelligence plays no role in the process. When students do not perform adequately and one wishes to understand why, the first questions have to do with how much interest they have in the subject matter and how much effort they put into it. If it is clear that they are interested and are trying hard, investigation turns next to their preparation. Have they developed good study habits? Do they have the requisite background for this course? Have they learned the particular modes of thinking and analysis that are used in this discipline?

Academic advisers account for the great majority of cases of unsuccessful course performance in terms of one or another of these lines of investigation. Only for the few cases that remain does the question of sheer ability or "intelligence" come up. And even then, the matter is posed in terms of the particular talents appropriate for a specific subject matter (ability to do mathematics, to draw, to interpret literature, and so on) rather than general intelligence.

If the attitudes represented in this process were to become commonplace, it is likely that we would lose the habit of thinking of general intelligence as an all-important, single trait that is distributed unequally among the population. Instead, we would evaluate quality of performance in terms of a variety of factors, only one of which is native ability in that particular area. Such a change in thinking would drastically curtail the destructive view that some people are irredeemably inferior to others by birth, and perhaps even by race. It would place primary responsibility for achievement squarely on the individual's effort and hold out the promise that, if given a fair opportunity, the degree of one's own determination is the major factor in achieving one's goals.

The model of the college classroom does not apply to larger evaluation programs in one crucial regard. It is a given that all of the students enrolled in a single course have the opportunity to receive the same instruction. This, of course, does not hold when large numbers from different localities and backgrounds are being assessed. They will have been exposed to a variety of different experiences and curricula in schools that are anything but uniform in the quality of education they provide. The question is how to achieve a fair evaluation of how well people have acquired academic, technical, artistic, or other skills when some of them have had much richer opportunities to acquire them than others. No simple answer exists. The only satisfactory long-range solution is to provide all primary- and secondary-school children with equal educational opportunities. And that will require much more than just fixing the schools. It also involves fostering supportive home and community environments.

Whether or not those ends will ever be achieved, doing away with testing for general intelligence would preclude the periodic eruption of facile explanations such as that crime, poverty, and other social problems are attributable to low intelligence. It would spare us from fighting the battle of *The Bell Curve* all over again in twenty years' time, and would help fix attention on our real challenges to eradicate race and class discrimination and to enrich environments, providing all Americans with an equal opportunity to develop their talents.

IQ Tests Do Not Measure All Kinds of Intelligence

by Howard Gardner

About the author: *Howard Gardner is a Harvard psychologist and the author of* Frames of Mind: The Theory of Multiple Intelligences.

Despite its largely technical nature, *The Bell Curve* has already secured a prominent place in American consciousness as a "big," "important," and "controversial" book. In a manner more befitting a chronicle of sex or spying, the publisher withheld it from potential critics until the date of publication. Since then it has grabbed front-page attention in influential publications, ridden the talk-show waves, and catalyzed academic conferences and dinner table controversies. With the untimely death of the senior author, psychologist Richard Herrnstein, attention has focused on his collaborator Charles Murray (described by the *New York Times Magazine* as "the most dangerous conservative in America"). But this volume clearly bears the mark of both men.

Questionable Science

The Bell Curve is a strange work. Some of the analysis and a good deal of the tone are reasonable. Yet, the science in the book was questionable when it was proposed a century ago, and it has now been completely supplanted by the development of the cognitive sciences and neurosciences. The policy recommendations of the book are also exotic, neither following from the analyses nor justified on their own terms. The book relies heavily on innuendo, some of it quite frightening in its implications. The authors wrap themselves in a mantle of courage, while coyly disavowing the extreme conclusions that their own arguments invite. The tremendous attention lavished on the book probably comes less from the science or the policy proposals than from the subliminal messages and attitudes it conveys.

Taken at face value, *The Bell Curve* proceeds in straightforward fashion. Herrnstein and Murray summarize decades of work in psychometrics and policy studies and report the results of their own extensive analyses of the National

Abridged from Howard Gardner, "Cracking Open the IQ Box." Reprinted with permission from the *American Prospect*, Winter 1995; © New Prospect, Inc.

Longitudinal Survey of Labor Market Experience of Youth, a survey that began in 1979 and has followed more than 12,000 Americans aged 14–22. They argue that studies of trends in American society have steadfastly ignored a smoking gun: the increasing influence of measured intelligence (IQ). As they see it, individuals have always differed in intelligence, at least partly because of heredity, but these differences have come to matter more because social status now depends more on individual achievement. The consequence of this trend is the bipolarization of the population, with high-IQ types achieving positions of power and prestige, low-IQ types being consigned to the ranks of the impoverished and the impotent. In the authors' view, the combined ranks of the poor, the criminal, the unemployed, the illegitimate (parents and offspring), and the uncivil harbor a preponderance of unintelligent individuals. Herrnstein and Murray are disturbed by these trends, particularly by the apparently increasing number of people who have babies but fail to become productive citizens. The authors foresee the emergence of a brutal society in which "the rich and the smart" (who are increasingly the same folks) band together to isolate and perhaps even reduce the ranks of those who besmirch the social fabric. . . .

Do Genes Explain Social Class?

In a textbook published in 1975, Herrnstein and his colleague Roger Brown argued that the measurement of intelligence has been the greatest achievement of twentieth-century scientific psychology. Psychometricians can make a numerical estimate of a person's intelligence that remains surprisingly stable after the age of five or so, and much convergent evidence suggests that the variations of this measure of intelligence in a population are determined significantly (at least 60 percent) by inheritable factors. As Herrnstein and Murray demonstrate at great length, measured intelligence correlates with success in school, ultimate job status, and the likelihood of becoming a member of the cognitively entitled establishment.

But correlation is not causation, and it is possible that staying in school causes IQ to go up (rather than vice versa) or that both IQ and schooling reflect some third causative factor, such as parental attention, nutrition, social class, or motivation. Indeed, nearly every one of Herrnstein and Murray's reported correlations can be challenged on such grounds. Yet, Herrnstein and Murray make a persuasive case that measured intelligence—or, more technically, "g," the central, general component of measured intelligence—does affect one's ultimate niche in society.

"Many authorities have challenged the notion of a single intelligence or even the concept of intelligence altogether."

But the links between genetic inheritance and IQ, and then between IQ and social class, are much too weak to draw the inference that genes determine an individual's ultimate status in society. Nearly all of the reported correlations be-

116

tween measured intelligence and societal outcomes explain at most 20 percent of the variance. In other words, over 80 percent (and perhaps over 90 percent) of the factors contributing to socioeconomic status lie beyond measured intelligence. One's ultimate niche in society is overwhelmingly determined by non-IQ factors, ranging from initial social class to luck. And since close to half of one's IQ is due to factors unrelated to heredity, well over 90 percent of one's fate does not lie in one's genes. Inherited IQ is at most a paper airplane, not a smoking gun.

> *"Other equally important kinds of intelligence, such as spatial, musical, or personal, are ignored [by IQ tests]."*

Indeed, even a sizeable portion of the data reported or alluded to in *The Bell Curve* runs directly counter to the story that the authors apparently wish to tell. They note that IQ has gone up consistently around the world during this century—15 points, as great as the current difference between blacks and whites. Certainly this spurt cannot be explained by genes! They note that when blacks move from rural southern to urban northern areas, their intelligence scores also rise; that black youngsters adopted in households of higher socioeconomic status demonstrate improved performance on aptitude and achievement tests; and that differences between the performances of black and white students have declined on tests ranging from the Scholastic Aptitude Test to the National Assessment of Educational Practice. In an extremely telling phrase, Herrnstein and Murray say that the kind of direct verbal interaction between white middle-class parents and their preschool children "amounts to excellent training for intelligence tests." On that basis, they might very well have argued for expanding Head Start, but instead they question the potential value of any effort to change what they regard as the immutable power of inherited IQ.

Psychology, Biology, and Culture

The psychometric faith in IQ testing and Herrnstein and Murray's analysis are based on assumptions that emerged a century ago, when Alfred Binet devised the first test of intelligence for children. Since 1900, biology, psychology, and anthropology have enormously advanced our understanding of the mind. But like biologists who ignore DNA or physicists who do not consider quantum mechanical effects, Herrnstein and Murray pay virtually no attention to these insights and, as a result, there is a decidedly anachronistic flavor to their entire discussion.

Intoxication with the IQ test is a professional hazard among psychometricians. I have known many psychometricians who feel that the science of testing will ultimately lay bare all the secrets of the mind. Some believe a difference of even a few points in an IQ or SAT score discloses something important about an individual's or group's intellectual merits. The world of intelligence testers is peculiarly self-contained. Like the chess player who thinks that all games (if not the world itself) are like chess, or the car salesman who speaks only of

117

horsepower, the psychometrician may come to believe that all of importance in the mind can be captured by a small number of items in the Stanford-Binet test or by one's ability to react quickly and accurately to a pattern of lights displayed on a computer screen.

Though Herrnstein deviated sharply in many particulars from his mentor B.F. Skinner, the analysis in *The Bell Curve* is Skinnerian in a fundamental sense: It is a "black box analysis." Along with most psychometricians, Herrnstein and Murray convey the impression that one's intelligence simply exists as an innate fact of life—unanalyzed and unanalyzable—as if it were hidden in a black box. Inside the box there is a single number, IQ, which determines vast social consequences.

Outside the closed world of psychometricians, however, a more empirically sensitive and scientifically compelling understanding of human intelligence has emerged in the past hundred years. Many authorities have challenged the notion of a single intelligence or even the concept of intelligence altogether. Let me mention just a few examples. (The works by Stephen Ceci and Robert Sternberg, as well as my own, discuss many more.)

Sternberg and his colleagues have studied valued kinds of intellect not measured by IQ tests, such as practical intelligence—the kind of skills and capacities valued in the workplace. They have shown that effective managers are able to pick up various tacit messages at the workplace and that this crucial practical sensitivity is largely unrelated to psychometric intelligence. Ralph Rosnow and his colleagues have developed measures of social or personal intelligence—the capacities to figure out how to operate in complex human situations—and have again demonstrated that these are unrelated to the linguistic and logical skills tapped in IQ tests.

Important new work has been carried out on the role of training in the attainment of expertise. Anders Ericsson and his colleagues have demonstrated that training, not inborn talent, accounts for much of experts' performances; the ultimate achievement of chess players or musicians depends (as your mother told you) on regular practice over many years. Ceci and others have documented the extremely high degree of expertise that can be achieved by randomly chosen individuals; for example, despite low measured intelligence, handicappers at the racetrack successfully employ astonishingly complex multiplicative models. A growing number of researchers have argued that, while IQ tests may provide a reasonable measure of certain linguistic and mathematical forms of thinking, other equally important kinds of intelligence, such as spatial, musical, or personal, are ignored (this is the subject of much of my own work). In short, the closed world of intelligence is being opened up.

> *"A high IQ cannot in itself substitute for training, expertise, motivation, and creativity."*

Accompanying this rethinking of the concept of intelligence(s), there is growing skepticism that short paper-and-pencil tests can get at important mental capacities. Just as "performance examinations" are coming to replace multiple-choice tests in schools, many scientists, among them Lauren Resnick and Jean Lave, have probed the capacities of individuals to solve problems "on the scene" rather than in a testing room, with pencil and paper. Such studies regularly confirm that one can perform at an expert level in a natural or simulated setting (such as bargaining in a market or simulating the role of a city manager) even with a low IQ while a high IQ cannot in itself substitute for training, expertise, motivation, and creativity. Rather than the pointless exercise of attempting to raise psychometric IQ (on which Herrnstein and Murray perseverate), this research challenges us to try to promote the actual behavior and skills that we want our future citizens to have. After all, if we found that better athletes happen to have larger shoe sizes, we would hardly try to enlarge the feet of the less athletic.

The Interaction of Genes and Environment

Scientific understanding of biological and cultural aspects of cognition also grows astonishingly with every passing decade. Virtually no serious natural scientist speaks about genes and environment any longer as if they were opposed. Indeed, every serious investigator accepts the importance of both biological and cultural factors and the need to understand their interactions. Genes regulate all human behavior, but no form of behavior will emerge without the appropriate environmental triggers or supports. Learning alters the way in which genes are expressed.

The development of the individual brain and mind begins in utero, and pivotal alterations in capacity and behavior come about as the result of innumerable events following conception. Hormonal effects in utero, which certainly are environmental, can cause a different profile of cognitive strengths and limitations to emerge. The loss of certain sensory capacities causes the redeployment of brain tissue to new functions; a rich environment engenders the growth of additional cortical connections as well as timely pruning of excess synapses. Compare a child who has a dozen healthy experiences each day in utero and after birth to another child who has a daily diet of a dozen injurious episodes. The cumulative advantage of a healthy prenatal environment and a stimulating postnatal environment is enormous. In the study of IQ, much has been made of studies of identical and fraternal twins. But because of the influences on cognition in utero and during infancy, even such studies cannot decisively distinguish genetic from environmental influences.

Herrnstein and Murray note that measured intelligence is only stable after age five, without drawing the obvious conclusion that the events of the first years of life, not some phlogiston-like "g," are the principal culprit. Scores of important and fascinating new findings emerge in neuroscience every year, but scarcely a word of any of this penetrates the Herrnstein and Murray black-box approach.

119

IQ Scores Do Not Predict Behavior

by William F. Allman

About the author: *William F. Allman is an assistant managing editor for* U.S. News & World Report.

For nearly a century it has been the merit badge of the mind—the intelligence quotient, or IQ. For members of the Mensa society, genius-level IQ test results have the cachet of boasting a superior brainpower. But for others, IQ is merely a curiosity, if they think about it at all.

Now, however, IQ is at the center of an explosive debate involving psychology, social policy, race relations and the very fabric of the American experience. Researchers have reached a cautious, if unsettling, consensus: IQ is real. It plays a role in what happens in people's lives. And it is in part based in the genes. But behind these seemingly simple notions lies a huge gulf in what, exactly, to make of them.

Explosive Debate

At one end of the spectrum is a book, *The Bell Curve,* by sociologist Charles Murray and the late psychologist Richard Herrnstein. They argue that Americans are separating themselves into a "cognitive elite" of high-IQ performers and a dull-witted underclass. A low IQ in the U.S. meritocracy is a strong predictor of crime, poverty and unemployment, they argue, and a high IQ increasingly is a ticket to wealth and a stable marriage. The authors contend that social policy must be overhauled to account for this: Welfare, education and affirmative action programs aimed at helping the poor should be scrapped because the recipients have limited intelligence and cannot benefit from a helping government hand.

Others, of course, have made the case that the limitations of poor persons are the very reason that they need assistance to make sure they are productive citizens. President Clinton told aides he is "outraged by the thrust of the book" and the way it might affect the national debate over social programs. Murray and Herrnstein's rejoinder is that such programs simply subsidize the growth of the lower-intelligence population, which is a socially harmful thing to do. The authors do not propose any programs to replace those that would be scrapped. Instead, they urge passage of solutions that would lessen the serious problems of the poor by making adoption easier, laws simpler and communities more nurturing.

Yet research is demonstrating that such a prescription would be based on a too-constricted—and perhaps faulty—reading about what intelligence is. IQ is but one piece of the puzzle of what makes people smart and dumb, successes and deadbeats. There are other kinds of "intelligence" that are crucial to determining a person's performance in life, this research shows. They include common

> *"IQ is but one piece of the puzzle of what makes people smart and dumb."*

sense, experience, intuition, creativity and, perhaps most important, social intelligence—that is, the smarts to work well with other people. Some of the most path-breaking researchers argue that it is these talents, not the skills measured by IQ tests, that the brain was designed by evolutionary forces to perform.

IQ and Success

Despite the tarnished image of IQ testing in the past, especially its abuse in the name of theories of racial superiority, most scholars agree that IQ is partly related to how people do in life. Having a high IQ can be a big factor in determining how well a person performs in academia, for instance. Tests like the Scholastic Assessment Test (SAT), which are geared toward measuring IQ—approximated by the g factor, for general intelligence—are a good general indication of a person's success in school. However, the relationship between grades and SAT scores becomes less strong after the freshman year in college.

IQ plays a role in job success as well. A recent survey of military specialists found that for highly technical jobs such as working with nuclear weapons or weather predictions, IQ accounts for more than 65 percent of people's success at their positions. Analysts who average the findings from dozens of smaller surveys estimate that IQ explains some 16 percent of the variation in a worker's productivity on the job. Some argue that hiring on the basis of IQ would result in billions of dollars in increased productivity.

IQ and Social Ills

On the other end of the spectrum, low IQ scores lie behind many of the nation's most pressing social ills, argue Herrnstein and Murray. They analyzed data from the government's National Longitudinal Survey of Labor Market Experience of Youth, a project that tested the IQs and tracked the lives of a sample of more than 12,000 men and women from all social classes since the 1970s. The researchers argue that low-IQ people are the most prone to poverty, unemployment, single motherhood, divorce, welfare dependency and criminal behavior.

121

While most experts agree with Herrnstein and Murray's basic argument linking IQ to social status, they are far less enthusiastic about their conclusions. "The fact that IQ is correlated with these things is old stuff," says Yale University psychologist Robert Sternberg. "But the links are very weak." Sternberg points out that, statistically, IQ can account for only a tiny part of a person's social status, his tendency to commit crimes or other behavior. On average, IQ explains less than 10 percent of the variation in behavior among a group of people. "Would you want to make your entire national policy around something that has less than a 10 percent effect?" Sternberg asks. He also notes that the link between IQ and social problems is suspect in part because IQs around the world have been going up at the same time baleful trends in crime, illegitimacy and welfare dependence have worsened.

Indeed, Murray and Herrnstein repeatedly point out in their book that IQ predicts nothing at all about any *individual's* performance and life. The results only apply to groups at large. "We don't want people to read the book and walk away thinking that IQ is the end all and be all of a human being," says Murray. "If you show me two individuals, one who has an IQ of 110 and another who has an IQ of 90, I'll say I can't tell you a damn thing about their future. But give me 3,000 or 3 million such people, and I can tell you more."

Many other factors, taken together, have far more influence on the outcome of people's lives than IQ, says

> *"On average, IQ explains less than 10 percent of the variation in behavior among a group of people."*

Sternberg. Those factors include a person's personality, motivation, experience and the impact of the social and economic world in which he was born. Sternberg acknowledges that certain professions like medicine or law favor having an above-average IQ to master the fundamental skills. But once people are in that profession, their performance at their position is unrelated to IQ. "IQ tests cannot be said to measure most of what we need to know about intelligence," he argues. "Success of practically any kind depends on much more."

Practical Intelligence

One big part of what makes people smart is what Sternberg calls "tacit knowledge." Unlike IQ, which involves the mental power to manipulate symbols, tacit knowledge is closer to "practical" intelligence, or common sense. To probe this common-sense kind of thinking, Sternberg interviewed hundreds of business people, asking about practical problems and possible solutions at work, such as what to do about a pushy boss. After further tests of other workers, he found that those who chose the best course of action on the test problems were those higher up in management—and that their performance was unrelated to their IQ or their length of time on the job. "Our studies suggest that not having common sense can hamper your career," says Sternberg. "As an employer, I'd take common sense over a few IQ points."

One recent study suggests that having a high IQ can actually hurt a person's performance under stress. Examining the behavior of officer candidates of the Washington and Oregon national guards, psychologist Fred Fiedler of the University of Washington found that when the subjects were under extreme stress, those with the highest IQs actually performed the worst. In high-stress situations, the best leaders rely on drawing on their past experiences, says Fiedler. The higher people's IQ, the more reluctant they are to go with their intuition based on experience.

> *"One of the biggest short-comings of IQ tests is how deficient they are in probing the links between intelligence and everyday activities."*

One of the biggest shortcomings of IQ tests is how deficient they are in probing the links between intelligence and everyday activities. One study showed that homemakers who performed dismally in conventional mathematics tests were quite adept at doing comparison shopping for prices at supermarkets. In another study of expert handicappers at a racetrack, Cornell psychologist Stephen Ceci found the best bettors used a complex system of algorithms to pick winning horses. The abilities of these handicappers did not correlate with their IQ.

Another major shortcoming of IQ tests is that they cannot account for that mystical quality commonly known as insight or creativity. "In any field such as art, technology, teaching and science, creativity is at least as important as IQ," Sternberg says. "It's very hard to succeed on analytical ability alone. You need to come up with new ideas." Creativity may also help in acquiring knowledge. In one recent study, students were asked to come up with stories about a dream before they read a psychology lesson on dreaming, while another group of students merely did rote copying of data before the lesson. A test immediately following the lesson showed no differences in how people comprehended the lesson, say Brandeis University psychologists Teresa Amabile and Regina Conti. When the students were quizzed a week later, however, those who had engaged in the creative exercise had retained nearly twice as much.

The prevalence of different kinds of mental talents has led Harvard University's Howard Gardner to suggest that people possess seven different kinds of intelligence: the traditional notions of intelligence, such as verbal skills, mathematical reasoning and spatial abilities, as well as smarts in music and body movement, and social skills involving the degree of mastery a person has over himself and his talent for interacting with others. Conventional IQ tests measure only a tiny sliver of these skills, argues Gardner, thereby ignoring the "genius" of artists like Pablo Picasso, Martha Graham and Igor Stravinsky.

IQ and Race

A rough consensus now exists among researchers that 40 percent to 70 percent of the variability in IQ among different people is due to the genes they inherit from their parents. From that finding, Herrnstein and Murray suggest, but do not directly posit, that there may be genetic reasons why African-Americans as a whole score 15 points below whites on IQ tests. By the same token, they note it might account for the higher scores that Asians and Jews record on average. That implied line of argument is the most explosive of their book.

Yet, experts say it is wrong to assume that because genes play a role in the variation in IQ among people, genes therefore play a role in the difference in IQ *between* ethnic or racial groups. The 15-point IQ gap between blacks and whites is a longstanding reality—and experts say that the gap is not due to testing bias. But the differences could just as likely be attributable to environmental factors such as poverty, racism and nutrition as to genes. By raising a question for which there is yet no answer, complains Harvard's Gardner, "the book is an exercise in rhetorical brinkmanship."

The IQ of a child can be substantially affected by environmental influences within the first several years of life, says psychologist Sandra Scarr of the University of Virginia. Her work suggests that improvements in IQ come, though, only with intensive intervention aimed at stimulating a child's cognitive skills. Merely putting children into a different family environment is not enough, says Scarr. In one study of African-American children who were adopted into white, upper-middle-class families, Scarr found that their IQs deviated little from the average for blacks as a whole. Still, the adopted children could have suffered a harsher time in foster homes and received poorer nutrition or neonatal care before they were adopted. The historic legacy of racism, in fact, could overwhelm most kinds of parental influence.

One more problem in trying to tie intelligence differences among races to genes, according to some critics, is that intelligence is likely to be the result of the interaction of hundreds if not thousands of different genes, each playing a tiny role in mental development. This vast genetic complexity underlying intelligence makes it very unlikely that there is a simple relationship between genes, IQ and race. The first step in understanding how genes are related to intelligence has been taken by Robert Plomin of Pennsylvania State University. In a paper published in 1994, Plomin announced preliminary results of his search for one small set of these genetic markers for IQ. Testing a sample of low-, medium- and high-IQ children, Plomin found that two particular candidates appear to show promise as correlating with IQ. One of the genes is a previously unknown gene that has no analogue in other mammals, which is a rarity. Plomin is doing further tests to see if his findings hold up.

In all, this body of research into intelligence reveals the ultimate irony in Herrnstein and Murray's book: They urge that Americans should revive communities and neighborhoods to prevent a self-perpetuating cognitive elite and an underclass from forming. Yet IQ tests do not take into account the very traits of morality, creativity and other mental talents beyond IQ that must be present to make such a community possible.

Chapter 3

Is Genetics Responsible for IQ Differences Between Races?

Genetics and IQ:
An Overview

by Tom Morganthau

About the author: *Tom Morganthau is a senior editor at* Newsweek.

The Bell Curve is a big, complex book that is based on a deeply pessimistic—
and deeply angry—view of American society. Charles Murray and his coauthor,
the late Harvard psychologist Richard Herrnstein, argue that intellectuals and
policymakers have largely overlooked the role intelligence plays in determining
wealth, poverty and social status. They say America is increasingly stratified by
intellectual ability, with a "cognitive elite" of highly educated politicians, pro-
fessionals and business leaders at the top and a growing underclass of dullards
at the bottom. Their most explosive argument is a blunt declaration that blacks
as a group are intellectually inferior to whites, which leads them to a dead-
serious attack on affirmative action. Although Murray emphatically denies that
the book panders to white resentment, *The Bell Curve* may be a mirror for our
morally exhausted times. It plays into public anxieties over crime, illegitimacy,
welfare dependency and racial friction. It feeds and confirms the sense that, as
Murray puts it, society is coming unhinged. . . .

"Overwhelming Evidence"

Murray and Herrnstein say the evidence of a black-white IQ gap is overwhelming. They think the difference helps explain why many blacks seem destined to
remain mired in poverty, and they insist that whites and blacks alike must face up
to the reality of black intellectual disadvantage. Nevertheless, they maintain that
the differences should have no bearing on the way individual whites and blacks
view each other. "We cannot think of a legitimate argument why . . . whites and
blacks need be affected by the knowledge that an aggregate difference in measured intelligence is genetic instead of environmental," they write.

This positively enrages white liberals—and it strikes black intellectuals as pi-
ous claptrap. "They're saying it's science, but it has a racist effect," said Dr.

Alvin Poussaint of Harvard Medical School. "For whites who are already pre-disposed to believe that blacks are inferior, this is going to confirm their preju-dices." Poussaint said blacks "have been hearing for a long time" that "people think they're inferior," but said the book's message was especially "hurtful" to younger African-Americans. William Julius Wilson of the University of Chicago said there was "nothing new" and "nothing to get excited about" in the Murray-Herrnstein the-sis. He also said the book "will not withstand scientific and scholarly criticism." Leon Wieseltier, literary editor of the *New Republic*, attacked *The Bell Curve* with icy sarcasm. "Having delivered African-Americans to inferiority and inequality," Wieseltier wrote, Murray "tells them to 'Have a nice day. . . .'"

> *"Who really doubts that intelligence matters—or that it is at least partly inherited?"*

Murray, an intellectual snake charmer whose greatest gift may be the knack of always seeming to be fair and always in earnest, vehemently denies he is racist. An inveterate number cruncher whose fund of social-science data seems inex-haustible, he is now the star salesman for a neoconservative policy agenda that is radical by any standard. That agenda includes a call for the outright abolition of welfare and limitations on affirmative action. "People like you must understand that people like me . . . are proposing a radically different way of thinking," he says pleasantly. "We're saying, 'OK, we understand you're very resistant to this. Think again. Don't change your mind right away. Just think again.'"

Whether *The Bell Curve* will do what he hopes—trigger a revolution in the way Americans think about social inequality—is anybody's guess. Murray knows it may be years before the 850 pages of densely detailed argument have any impact on government policy, if they ever do. The book represents eight years of collaboration between Murray and Herrnstein, who died in September 1994 at the age of 64. Despite their efforts to make statistics accessible to lay-men, they serve up a crunchy mix of data and abstruse reasoning. *The Bell Curve* is the sort of book that educated people will buy and dutifully attempt to read, but about which their primary source of opinion is likely to be journalistic commentaries like this one. So here's a summary of the book—a cheat sheet, as it were, to the controversy.

Three Arguments

The Bell Curve consists of three broadly related arguments. The first is a rein-terpretation of social class. As Murray and Herrnstein see it, the country is now mostly ruled (badly, they think) by a "cognitive elite" selected by IQ tests, the SATs and admission to elite colleges and universities. The vast cognitive mid-dle class—125 million Americans whose IQs measure between 90 and 110—comes next, but the authors waste few words discussing them. At the bottom, ominously, lies an underclass of 12.5 million Americans who largely lack the intellectual capacity to make their way up the social ladder.

This is the second argument and main theme of the book—a relentless insistence on the role of intelligence in explaining who is rich, who is poor and who is in between.

The Bell Curve takes its title from what statisticians refer to as a "normal distribution," which is a method for organizing data like IQ scores. Bell curves have "tails" on both sides. In an IQ bell curve, the right tail consists of smart people and the left tail consists of slow people. Murray and Herrnstein divide the left tail into two groups, Class IV (dull) and Class V (very dull), and they are worried about both. Together, these groups equal 25 percent of the U.S. population or 62.5 million people.

As the authors see it, social pathologies like poverty, welfare dependency, illegitimacy and crime are all strongly related to low IQ. They take it further than that, claiming that IQ is the best single explanation of why some people never get off welfare, why crime is rampant in the inner city and why some teenage girls get pregnant. They reject conventional theories about the role of environment and culture in creating dependency and crime, and they criticize liberal attempts to use government subsidies to move people out of poverty. Most of these not-so-smart people, they imply, will *never* become middle class.

None of this is likely to be front-page news—and, in fact, *The Bell Curve* rests on some crushingly obvious ideas. Who really doubts that intelligence matters—or that it is at least partly inherited? But then comes what Murray jokingly calls "the 800-pound gorilla in the corner." This is the assertion that blacks score significantly lower than whites on IQ tests and other measures of cognitive ability. In fact, there is nothing new about this statement either: educators and psychologists have known for years that the difference between the mean (or average) white IQ and the mean black IQ is 15 points—a score of 100 compared with a score of 85. This does not mean, as Murray and Herrnstein emphasize, that there are no black Americans with superior IQs. It simply means there are proportionately fewer smart blacks than smart whites.

> *"[Charles] Murray and [Richard J.] Herrnstein try to straddle the pivotal issue of whether the origin of blacks' lower IQ scores is genetic or environmental."*

But it also means black inferiority. Murray objects to that word, but it is inescapable—and so are its political consequences. If blacks as a group are inferior to whites as a group, the old dream of a truly integrated society—of blacks and whites meeting as equals—is dead. The syllogism is complicated, and Murray and Herrnstein carefully stop short of taking it to its logical conclusion. But the logic is clearly implied in the book, and here it is: IQ is more than partly inherited—it is *largely* inherited. Blacks have a lower group IQ—and if low IQ is related to crime, welfare dependency and poverty, it follows that blacks are unlikely to overcome these social pathologies. Fully a quarter of the black population of the United States has estimated IQs below 75, which is borderline retardation. So although some blacks on the right-hand tail of the bell curve will rise and prosper, IQ testing seems to show that millions of others will not.

A Genetic or Environmental Explanation

Murray and Herrnstein try to straddle the pivotal issue of whether the origin of blacks' lower IQ scores is genetic or environmental. They say they are "resolutely agnostic" on the question—then speculate that "the evidence eventually may become unequivocal that genes are also part of the story." They use test-score data to show that middle-class blacks are no closer to closing the black-white gap than lower-class blacks, a finding that also suggests a genetic explanation. But other experts strongly dispute the notion that IQ testing confirms the existence of genetic differences in intelligence between the races, and some say the book's use of IQ data is selective and

> *"Other experts strongly dispute the notion that IQ testing confirms the existence of genetic differences in intelligence between the races."*

apparently political. "We all know that IQ tests showed some racial differences, but we also know there's a difference between 'intelligence' and IQ tests," said psychologist Robert Sternberg of Yale. The fact that Murray and Herrnstein ignore this difference, Sternberg said, "is proof that the authors' [political] agenda is driving their interpretation of the statistics."

Murray and Herrnstein may be right in thinking that we are fed up with the seemingly intractable problems of the underclass, and they are right to point up the problem of black underachievement. But the solutions are more complex than they grant. And if the social fabric is unraveling, only we Americans can repair it—one small stitch, and one face-to-face encounter, at a time.

Genetics Is Not Responsible for IQ Differences Between Races

by Richard A. Weinberg, Sandra Scarr, and Irwin D. Waldman

About the authors: *Richard A. Weinberg and Irwin D. Waldman are psychologists at the University of Minnesota. Sandra Scarr is a psychologist at the University of Virginia. Scarr and Weinberg are the authors of the 1976 transracial adoption study, "IQ Test Performance of Black Children Adopted by White Families," which is updated in the following viewpoint.*

In 1976, we reported findings of the Minnesota Transracial Adoption (TRA) Study, a project designed to test the hypothesis that black and interracial (i.e., at least one black parent) children reared by white families perform on IQ and school achievement tests as well as other adoptees. We posited that these black and interracial adoptees would perform as well as other adoptees because they are growing up in "the culture of the tests and the schools"; that is, they are being exposed to more of the economic, health care, and socialization influences that promote high performance on measures of IQ and school achievement. In addition, the sample we studied included many families with both adoptees and birth children. Sources of individual differences among adoptees and birth children could be studied without fear of possible differences between the adoptive families and those with birth children. This viewpoint is a report of the IQ test performance of these families 10 years later.

Summary of Findings of Initial Study

Briefly, in 1976 we found that:

1. Adoptive parents and their biological children in the 101 participating families scored in the bright-average to superior range of age-appropriate IQ tests.
2. The 130 black and interracial adopted children scored above the white population average for the same U.S. region (median = 100) and were performing

adequately in school. In fact, we found the average IQ of the black/interracial children adopted in the first 12 months of life to be 110, some 20 points above the average IQ for black children being reared in the black community. Nevertheless, as found by other researchers, the adopted children scored on average below the birth children of these families. This was true not only for black/interracial adoptees, but also for white and Asian/Indian adoptees.

> *"Putative genetic racial differences do not account for a major portion of the IQ performance difference between racial groups."*

3. We interpreted these data to indicate that: (a) putative genetic racial differences do not account for a major portion of the IQ performance difference between racial groups, and (b) black and interracial children reared in the culture of the tests and the schools perform as well as other adopted children in similar families, as reported by other researchers.

4. The personality and social adjustment of the parents, biological offspring, and adopted children (ages 4–12) in these families was, on average, quite good.

We believe that findings from our first study have supported the malleability/plasticity of IQ test and school performance of socially classified black and interracial children. Such malleability appears to be a result of being reared in middle- to upper-middle-class environments: environments that represent the culture of these tests and schools.

Ten years later, we restudied the adopted children (average age = 17) and the birth children (average age = 20), as well as other members of their families. After an extensive search for the 101 families, we collected data on intellectual performance and academic achievement, on personality and psychopathology, and on family members' life adjustment. The objective of this longitudinal study was to see how these children were faring approximately a decade after they were initially studied. What was their current level of intellectual performance, school achievement, and personal and social adjustment? What might account for any change in performance or adjustment over that interval? We were also interested in the status of other family members and the quality of the families' adaptation to their unique circumstances. We were provided the rare opportunity to explore systematically the impact of a potentially stressful situation on families at a point in their lives when adolescent problems may emerge to disrupt their adaptation. This viewpoint is limited to an examination of the follow-up IQ and school achievement data, and the magnitude and correlates of changes over time in IQ test performance. . . .

IQ Decline and IQ Rankings

On average, all family members declined in IQ from Time 1 [1976] to Time 2 [1986]. In interpreting this decline, one must keep in mind that different IQ tests were employed at Time 1 and Time 2. Depending on their ages, family members were tested using the Stanford-Binet Form L–M, WISC [Wechsler Intelligence Scale for Children], or WAIS [Wechsler Adult Intelligence Scale] in the original study, and using the WISC–R [Revised] or WAIS–R in the follow-up study. Declines in IQ scores have been documented when individuals are retested on a revised form of an original measure, as well as when a test used at a first administration was normed earlier than a test used at a subsequent administration. For example, the decline in Full-Scale IQ score from the WAIS to the WAIS–R averaged 6.8 points across a number of studies and was 7.5 points in a sample of 72 35–44-year-olds tested as part of the standardization of the WAIS–R. This is precisely the test combination used for adoptive parents in our study.

Similarly, substantial declines would be expected when individuals are tested with the Stanford-Binet or WISC at Time 1 and with the WISC–R or WAIS–R at Time 2, the situation that characterized nearly all biological children and adoptees in our sample. Although we cannot be certain how much of the IQ decline found across all family member groups is attributable to this phenomenon, it appears safe to say that most of this decline is a product of test revision and test norm obsolescence.

Despite the decline in IQ test scores, the relative rankings of Time 2 test scores remained identical to that for Time 1 IQ scores. Adoptive fathers continued to perform slightly better, on average, than adoptive mothers, and both parent groups continued to perform better on average than their biological offspring. Biological offspring continued to rank higher in IQ scores than white adoptees, who were followed in ranking by black/interracial adoptees and Asian/Indian adoptees, respectively. Adoptees with two black parents scored lower than other family groups.

> *"Black and interracial children reared in the culture of the tests . . . perform as well as other adopted children in similar families."*

Recall, however, that the adoptees with two black parents were also adopted later, had more preadoptive placements, and lower quality placements than children with one black parent. Their biological mothers and fathers had lower educational levels than the black fathers and white mothers of the interracial adoptees. Thus, parental race subsumes a number of biological and social differences between the two groups.

IQ Comparisons

The major question addressed by the follow-up study was whether the malleability in black/interracial adoptees' Time 1 IQ test performance would be similarly manifest at Time 2. Would the beneficial effects of rearing environment on transracial adoptees' IQ continue into late adolescence and adulthood?

Although the biological offspring achieved significantly higher IQ scores at Time 2 than adoptees, there was no difference in IQ change among the groups, suggesting that the rearing environments continued to have positive effects on children in the adoptive families. Both biological offspring and adoptee groups scored in the average range of IQ based on the new norms for IQ tests.

These results are congruent with those of other recent adoption studies in demonstrating strong effects of the rearing environment on IQ, and go on to demonstrate that these effects are

> *"The rearing environments continued to have positive effects on children in the adoptive families."*

largely sustained over a 10-year period, when the adoptees are late adolescents or adults. These results also highlight the strong impact that dramatic environmental interventions can have on cognitive development. The findings here demonstrate persistent beneficial effects of being reared in the culture of the schools and the IQ tests.

That white families provide a rearing environment more closely tied to the tests and the schools can hardly be doubted. For example, E.G.J. Moore (1986) found differences in test-response style between black/interracial children adopted by white parents and those adopted by black parents. Moore also found that white adoptive mothers showed greater positive affect, encouragement, and support to their black/interracial adopted children than did the black adoptive mothers. These differences were related to the differences in IQ test performance between the two adoptee groups. James Flynn also hypothesized that increased test sophistication and enhanced educational achievement may be responsible for a substantial portion of the IQ gains shown by Americans from 1948 to 1972. It seems reasonable that such cultural factors may also account, in part, for differences in the IQ test performance of black children reared by white adoptive parents and those reared in the black community.

Differences in IQ between early- and late-adopted black/interracial adoptees, and between adoptees who had two black biological parents or one black and one white biological parent persisted at Time 2. As in our original study, the early-adopted group continued to show higher IQ test performance at Time 2, but also showed greater IQ decline, than the late-adopted group. Similar differences for Time 2 IQ were found for the black/white group as compared with the black/black group. In our original study, we pointed out that the black/white group had more favorable adoptive placement experiences, higher biological parent education, and higher adoptive fathers' education and adoptive mothers' IQ than the black/black group. This suggests that the effects and/or concomitants of early adoption, and of the selective placement and adoptive experiences associated with biological parents' race, continue into late adolescence, but are not as strong then as they are in childhood.

IQ Correlations

In our original study, we examined the correlations of black/interracial adoptees' IQ with biological parent, adoptive experience, and adoptive family variables in an effort to explicate some of the biological and social factors underlying variation in black/interracial adoptees' IQ scores. It was possible only to establish ranges of estimated variance accounted for by the two sets of variables, because the biological and social variables were confounded. At Time 2, almost all of the biological and adoptive variables that were related to Time 1 IQ were related to Time 2 IQ, though the magnitude of these correlations decreased somewhat. It was similarly impossible to disentangle biological parent characteristics of race and educational level from adoptive experience variables in the follow-up study. Biological mothers' education and race accounted for 6–16% of the variance in black/interracial adoptees' IQ scores, whereas adoptive experience variables accounted for 7–17%.

For unknown reasons, black mothers who eventually gave up their children for adoption did so later, and their children experienced more preadoptive placements of poorer quality than interracial children with white mothers. Thus, biological and social characteristics of the black/black and interracial children were confounded. Biological mothers' race remained the best single predictor of adopted child's IQ when other variables were controlled. Nonetheless, this relation may be due, in large part, to the role of unmeasured, social characteristics associated with biological mothers' race in the development of IQ.

Only a few of the biological parent, adoptive experience, and adoptive family variables were related to IQ decline. Adoptees with a white or Asian biological mother showed greater IQ decline than those with a black biological mother, suggesting that the effects of biological mothers' race on IQ are greater in childhood than in adolescence or adulthood. Adoptive fathers' education was the only adoptive family variable related to IQ decline, such that adoptive fathers' education was more strongly related to IQ in childhood than in adolescence or adulthood. This finding may be consistent with those of other studies in demonstrating decreased impact of shared environmental influences on IQ in adolescence and adulthood than in childhood. Nonetheless, other findings—such as the increase in correlations of adoptive mothers' and fathers' Time 1 IQ with adoptees' IQ from Time 1 to Time 2—suggest that shared environmental influences on IQ play at least as large a role in adolescence and adulthood as in childhood. . . .

> *"The findings here demonstrate persistent beneficial effects of being reared in the culture of the schools and the IQ tests."*

A number of the adoptive experience variables were related to IQ decline. Specifically, adoptees who had fewer and better quality preadoptive placements, and who were placed at a younger age, showed greater IQ decline. Again, this finding appears to reflect the greater relation of these adoptive factors to IQ in childhood than in late adolescence or adulthood.

Although we believe that IQ test performance represents a significant index of adjustment to adoption, we were interested in adjustment indices, such as school achievement, that possess additional "real-life" validity. At the secondary school level, the biological offspring of the adoptive families performed at about the 70th percentile on numerous indices of school achievement, in contrast to the adoptees who performed generally in the average range. The black/interracial adoptees appeared to maintain their vocabulary and reading achievement levels to the same degree as the biological offspring, showing greater decline only in math achievement. Compared to the average scores of black/interracial children reared in the black community, the adoptees' scores are high, especially given that the schools they have attended are in middle- to upper-middle-class neighborhoods. The school achievement results lend additional support for the beneficial effects of being reared in the culture of the tests and schools.

> *"The school achievement results lend additional support for the beneficial effects of being reared in the culture of the tests and schools."*

The Results Support the Environment Theory

Our original study was intended primarily to examine the effects of cross-fostering on the IQ scores of black/interracial children. The focus was on the relative effects of genetic background *and* social environment on IQ levels and variations among socially classified black children. The results of the longitudinal follow-up continue to support the view that the social environment maintains a dominant role in determining the average IQ level of black and interracial children and that both social and genetic variables contribute to individual variations among them.

It may be instructive to consider the pattern of findings that would be expected if genetic background but *not* social environment contributed to the average follow-up IQ of black/interracial adoptees. First, we would expect them to show greater IQ decline than biological offspring, because their Time 2 IQ would regress back to their biological, but not their adoptive, parents' IQ levels. Second, we would expect their Time 2 IQ to be correlated with their biological parents' education but not their adoptive parents' education or IQ. Third, we would not expect their Time 2 IQ to be correlated with adoptive experiences such as age at placement and time in adoptive home. The data did not support these hypotheses, thus suggesting the important role of social environment in adoptees' follow-up IQ.

IQ Differences Between Races Are Due to Environment

by Mickey Kaus

About the author: *Mickey Kaus is a senior editor with the* New Republic, *a weekly opinion magazine, and the author of* The End of Equality.

In *Losing Ground*, the 1984 book that made his name, Charles Murray pooh-poohed the role of race in America's social pathology. Instead, Murray blamed liberal welfare programs that trapped black and white alike in poverty. "Focusing on blacks cripples progress," he declared in a 1986 op-ed piece (entitled "Not a Matter of Race"),

> because explanations of the special problems facing blacks nearly all begin with the assumption that blacks are different from everyone else, whether because of racism (as the apologists argue) or because of inherent traits (as the racists argue).

But that was then. Now, it turns out, Murray indeed thinks blacks face problems because they "are different from everyone else," and they are different "because of inherent traits (as the racists argue)" or, at any rate, because of immutable traits. In *The Bell Curve*, Murray and the late Richard Herrnstein contend that blacks have, on average, significantly lower "cognitive ability" than whites, ability that won't be raised in "the foreseeable future." Herrnstein and Murray connect this mental disability with all sorts of pathologies (poverty, crime, illegitimacy). They also use it as the basis for some stark political extrapolations. Affirmative action, of course, must go, since "it has been based on the explicit assumption that ethnic groups do not differ in the abilities" and "that assumption is wrong." For those blacks stuck at the bottom of the bell curve, meanwhile, nothing less than a "custodial state" looms. There is "nothing they can learn that will repay the cost of the teaching." Instead, a "significant part of the population" will be made "permanent wards of the state," subdued and supported in a "high-tech and more lavish version of the Indian reservation."

The Ethnic Difference Argument

Let us call this overall argument by Herrnstein and Murray the Ethnic Difference argument. It is but one of several major arguments of *The Bell Curve*, so I should make clear what I'm *not* talking about. I'm not talking about the authors' assertion that general mental ability is in large part genetically inherited by *individuals* from their parents. As Herrnstein and Murray acknowledge, it is one thing to say that differences among individuals are explained by genetic differences; it's something else completely to say that *group* differences are the result of genetic differences rather than differences in the environments different groups face. The example Herrnstein and Murray offer is this:

> Take two handfuls of genetically identical seed corn and plant one handful in Iowa, the other in the Mojave Desert, and let nature (i.e., the environment) take its course. The seed will grow in Iowa, not in the Mojave, and the result will have nothing to do with genetic difference.

Nor is the Ethnic Difference argument implicated in the view, with which Herrnstein has long been associated, that American society is increasingly becoming stratified along lines of inherited mental ability. I have always (perhaps naively) thought this argument of Herrnstein's identified an unfortunate, but real trend. Yet it is a trend that exists quite independent of race; if it is occurring it is occurring among whites as well as blacks, and would indeed be occurring if the United States were composed of a single ethnic group. The Ethnic Difference argument, rather, asserts that blacks disproportionately occupy the lower rungs of this emerging hierarchy by virtue of innate cognitive disability, and they will continue to do so more or less permanently, with the various apocalyptic implications Herrnstein and Murray detail.

Just because many people (myself included) resist this argument as alien and repellent doesn't mean Murray and Herrnstein are wrong. But neither does it mean they are right. Many of *The Bell Curve*'s defenders seem to interpret any disgust with the book as evidence of a desire to suppress all discussion of the possibility of ethnic mental differences—to the point where criticism of the book becomes, in a perverse way, its validation. But the question isn't whether such ethnic differences in mental ability are possible (it would be odd if every group averaged the same). The question is whether Herrnstein and Murray are reliable guides when it comes to exploring this possibility.

> *"There is a good deal of evidence that the 'B-W [black-white] difference' in IQ is a function of environment rather than heredity."*

I think not. *The Bell Curve* isn't (as far as I can tell) a dishonest book, if by dishonesty you mean the falsification of data or the willful failure to recognize unhelpful evidence. But intellectual probity makes more stringent demands. One is that every assertion be examined, and reexamined, for its validity. The scholar or social critic operating in good faith constantly asks himself the question: Is this really what I think? Is it completely accurate? Or am I saying it because it sounds good or in some other way serves my own (large, small, noble, selfish) purpose? It is this test of honesty *The Bell Curve* fails, at a critical moment.

Environmental Factors in IQ

To make the pessimistic Ethnic Difference argument work, Murray and Herrnstein must demonstrate three things: 1) that there is a single, general measure of mental ability; 2) that the IQ tests which purport to measure this ability (and on which blacks score roughly fifteen points lower than whites) aren't culturally biased; and 3) that this mental ability is fixed across generations—classically, that it's "in the genes."

Let us, for purposes of this viewpoint, accept what is in fact quite controversial: that the first two claims are correct. It's pretty obvious, however, even to a lay reader, that Murray and Herrnstein run into big difficulties on step three, because it turns out there is a good deal of evidence that the "B/W [black-white] difference" in IQ is a function of environment rather than heredity. There is, for example, the convergence of black and white test scores over the

> *"The convergence of black and white test scores over the past twenty years . . . has been so fast it is 'likely' due to 'environmental changes.'"*

past twenty years, which Murray and Herrnstein agree has been so fast it is "likely" due to "environmental changes." There is the "Flynn Effect"—rapidly rising test scores worldwide. Scores on the Scholastic Aptitude Test (SAT), which Herrnstein and Murray say "is partly an intelligence test," can be increased by over sixty points with less than 100 hours of studying. French researchers have succeeded in boosting IQ twelve points by placing poor children in affluent homes. IQs were also raised almost eight points by the Abecederian Project, which offers intensive day care for five years.

I know of this evidence because it is presented in *The Bell Curve* itself, something the book's defenders regard as a majestic act of evenhandedness. That claim would be more plausible were not these pro-environment findings regarding ethnic differences subjected to a kitchen-sink barrage of objections that have the effect of minimizing their significance—while the pro-genetic evidence, such as it is, receives no such treatment.

In their discussion of the narrowing black-white gap in SAT scores, for example, Murray and Herrnstein admit that if the trend continues, black and white SAT scores would "reach equality sometime in the middle of the twenty-first century." Sounds like the environment may ultimately explain everything! But Herrnstein and Murray immediately suggest that low-IQ black parents are reproducing at a relatively faster rate, so there is "the possibility that convergence has already stalled." That may be true, but it has nothing to do with the environment versus genes issue, since even if the black and white distributions were genetically identical a differentially high low-IQ birth rate among blacks (or whites) would cause their "group" scores to drop. Murray and Herrnstein then toss out a speculative theory that "the convergence of black and white SAT scores . . . is symptomatic of what happens when education slows down toward the speed of the slowest ship in the convoy." Their scramble to debunk the black-white convergence becomes so embarrassing they insert a defensive note: "Many of you will be wondering why we have felt it necessary to qualify the good news."

A Weak Argument for Genetic Differences

And what of the evidence for thinking the difference between whites and blacks is *genetic*? Here Herrnstein and Murray feebly offer "Spearman's hypothesis," which suggests that blacks do worse on questions that tap into general mental ability. But, as the authors admit in the middle of a crucial paragraph, Spearman's hypothesis only suggests the tests aren't biased (i.e., they're really measuring general mental ability). It doesn't mean that the difference in ability the tests measure isn't caused by the environment. I urge a close inspection of this paragraph (page 303, beginning "How does . . ."). It is a wonderful example of how authors can try to conceal a hole in their argument by hiding it in a mess of near-unintelligible verbiage they fervently pray the reader won't bother to untangle. I have written similar fudge-paragraphs myself, but nothing (I hope) as bad as this one.

Even after all this huffing and puffing, the best Herrnstein and Murray can do with the evidence at hand is to declare it "highly likely" that genes have "something" to do with the racial differences. How much? "We are resolutely agnostic on that issue," they say. In other words, the genetic contribution could be 50 percent, it could be 1 percent, or .001 percent, for all they know. Or (though this is not "likely") it could be zero. A significant role for the environment, however, has been substantiated.

IQ Differences Between Races Are Due to Racism

by J. Blaine Hudson

About the author: *J. Blaine Hudson is an assistant professor of African American studies at the University of Louisville in Kentucky.*

The Bell Curve by Richard J. Herrnstein and Charles Murray revives a centuries-old controversy regarding alleged genetic differences in the respective intellectual capacities of Americans of European and African descent. The credibility of this argument rests on several interdependent assumptions related to the validity of:

- group intelligence (and other standardized) tests;
- comparisons between the average test scores of different racial groups; and
- interpreting the results of these comparisons in genetic terms.

Before proceeding with a discussion of these assumptions, some background is needed to establish both the social science and the historical context of the controversy itself.

Since the administration of earliest "intelligence" tests, particularly the Army Intelligence tests during World War I, African Americans, Hispanic Americans and Native Americans have scored consistently and significantly lower (one standard deviation lower, in statistical terms) than whites. This does not suggest that persons of color do not score in the highest score ranges or that whites do not score in the lowest, only that the average scores differ by race.

Some researchers, including Herrnstein and Murray, have interpreted these differences to mean that—just as skin and eye color, hair texture, and some anatomical features (e.g., shape of head, nose, lips) are genetically transmitted "racial" characteristics—different levels of ability to perform certain mental tasks must somehow be genetically transmitted as well.

However, the vast preponderance of social science and genetic research over several generations indicates that this conclusion, when examined closely, is inherently illogical and baseless—and that differences in test score patterns re-

Excerpted from J. Blaine Hudson, "Scientific Racism: The Politics of Tests, Race, and Genetics," *Black Scholar*, Winter 1995, pp. 3-9. Reprinted by permission of the *Black Scholar*.

flect differences in how racial groups are educated and/or treated.

Unfortunately, this is not merely a question of objective science. The belief in the intellectual inferiority of persons of color is a core assumption of ideological racism—a useful, consoling and remarkably resilient myth and, despite being proven wrong repeatedly, a great many Americans consider this "received wisdom" to be intuitively "right." Consequently, from the standpoint of social science, the issue is not the existence of score differences between racial groups, which are unquestioned, but what, if anything, such differences mean—and the extent to which one of the oldest and most dehumanizing racial stereotypes in Western culture can be supported with empirical evidence.

Because of the persistence, pervasiveness and potency of this myth, and the insidious purposes it has served over time, it is crucial both to demonstrate that the argument advanced in *The Bell Curve* is wrong and to "deconstruct" the stereotype as well.

Tests and Scores Interpretations

The tests used to measure "intelligence," "aptitude," and "achievement" are themselves problematic. Some cultural bias is virtually inescapable in the choice of language, connotations and shadings of meaning. There are also related problems with how tests are developed, e.g., whether test items which discriminate between racial or gender groups are retained or discarded—and how tests are normed, e.g., whether test scoring norms based on the performance of white, middle-class, and typically northeastern or midwestern groups are appropriate for other races, classes and regions.

Beyond these considerations, the "constructs" measured by such tests are often murky or misleading. For example, human consciousness, personality and intelligence result from a complex and on-going series of interactions between each individual and his/her environment. Although these "qualities" have physical basis in the human body, we cannot see or touch them directly—only infer their presence and attempt to define their "nature" based on their effects. However, definitions vary widely. With respect to intelligence, if there is no general agreement on a definition, how might it be measured? How can we be certain that, in striving to measure intelligence, we are not measuring "something else"? In practice, we usually resort to a circular definition—that those who perform well on tests defined as intelligence tests are, by definition, "intelligent."

> *"Differences in test score patterns reflect differences in how racial groups are educated and/or treated."*

Aptitude Tests as Institutional Racism

Aptitude tests assume that the potential to learn or do "something" in the future can be measured in the present. Consequently, if this is true, scores on such tests should predict future performance with a high degree of accuracy. However, such tests (e.g., [Scholastic Aptitude Test] SAT, [American College Test] ACT) do not predict performance well at all, accounting, at best, for about 25 percent of the variation in actual performance. Notwithstanding this major limitation, because their score distribution patterns by race parallel those of IQ tests, these instruments serve as extremely

"The belief in the intellectual inferiority of persons of color is a core assumption of ideological racism."

effective "gate keepers." Such tests exclude those who score poorly, usually persons of color and the poor, from the opportunity to perform in educational institutions and/or the work force.

For example, simply using the national mean on a "scholastic aptitude" test as a college admission cut-off will arbitrarily exclude 84 percent of the prospective African American applicant pool—compared to only 50 percent of the white applicant pool. In a pure meritocracy, this might be defensible if the tests predicted performance accurately. However, as the long history of compensatory/developmental educational programs has demonstrated, students of color will consistently out-perform the predictions of these tests if afforded an opportunity to do so. Consequently, the use of these tests as admissions criteria is a clear example of institutional or structural racism.

Achievement tests measure what has been learned prior to the date of testing, not intelligence or aptitude per se. Thus, performance on such tests, including basic skills tests in reading and mathematics, can be interpreted in an inherently simple and straightforward manner—i.e., those who have been taught and have learned "more" will typically score higher than those who have been taught and have learned "less."

In theory, IQ, aptitude and achievement tests are different. In reality, however, virtually all tests are or have attributes of "achievement" tests because they both rely on and measure the prior acquisition of content knowledge, literacy and/or numeric skills. Yet what individuals have learned (or "achieved") is a reflection, not only of their capacity to learn, but of what they have been taught in formal educational settings and what they have absorbed from their life experiences in general. Consequently, score differences on what are, in fact, achievement tests are far more likely to reflect differences in the quality of schooling and life experiences—than to reflect differences in the inherited intellectual capacities—of those who took the tests.

Research Design and Research Bias

In a society with a long history of racism, scholarly researchers are as likely to be racist as any other group and must subject their own racial (and class and gender) biases to constant scrutiny. Otherwise, they risk distorting their research designs and interpretations—often unconsciously—to prove what they believe, or wish to believe, rather than to illuminate objective "truth."

Furthermore, social science research designs, however pristine and elegant, must be informed both by history and a grasp of contemporary social reality—and a bit of common sense. A classic example is research on the relationship between race, poverty and crime. Criminal behavior is largely a function of poverty, not race. However, if this historical/social relationship is ignored, researchers can easily create the impression that African Americans (who are disproportionately poor) are innately more "criminal."

Similarly, elaborate and impenetrable statistical analyses can produce mountains of meaningless data unless the "right" questions are asked and the people or phenomena under study are understood properly. Where research comparisons between racial and ethnic groups are concerned—even to the point of confusing, intentionally or unintentionally, race and ethnicity—these precautions are seldom taken.

The Logic of Test Score Comparisons

Even if tests measure what they purport to measure, can valid comparisons be made between the average scores of different individuals? Within the same racial group? Between different racial groups? These are all separate questions and it is important to understand the circumstances under which such comparisons are warranted, their inherent limitations and what types of conclusions may be drawn from them.

In social science research, the possibility of making test score comparisons between individuals and groups is a function of the extent to which those individuals, subgroups, or groups are either substantially "alike" or the extent to which their differences can be minimized or controlled (i.e., held constant)—except for the factor(s) being studied. In other words, "apples" must be compared to "apples" not to "oranges" or "pears"—and if there is an observed/measurable difference between these "apples," we should be able to isolate or approximate its cause and/or its meaning. In this context, how can we control for race, i.e., for the differential effects of racial classification and group membership in a society long divided by race?

> *"The issue is not the existence of score differences between racial groups . . . but what, if anything, such differences mean."*

One commonly used approach entails controlling for socio-economic status (SES). To illustrate, since family SES, educational attainment, and IQ are correlated highly with one another, comparing middle- or low-income African Americans to middle- or low-income whites often reduces the degree of racial difference. However, employing such a control assumes that sharing an income range can be equated to sharing a variety of other educational, cultural and life experiences—irrespective of race. In contrast, studies of income and occupational distribution, family structure, attitudes, and values by race indicate that such comparisons have formidable limitations—and that generalizations from such comparisons should be made only with great caution and a clear understanding of larger historical factors.

> *"Students of color will consistently out-perform the predictions of [college admission] tests if afforded an opportunity to do so."*

Another implicit control derives from the assumption of equal educational opportunities by race since the end of legal segregation and that, if educational outcomes (and IQ scores) are unequal, substandard segregated schools can no longer be blamed. However, desegregation in the United States seldom progressed beyond compliance with numerical ("body count") requirements and moved forward without any serious commitment to the equalization of educational outcomes by race, or to addressing key issues such as *racism among teachers*, in the *curriculum*, and in school culture.

Furthermore, many whites have opted out of public education altogether—a step that African Americans, as a relatively poor population, could seldom afford, while significant internal segregation has been maintained in nominally non-segregated public schools through the use of "homogeneous ability grouping," or "tracking." Ironically, even when academic "track" is held constant, students of color *still* earn lower grades and achieve lower test scores than their white classmates. Thus, African Americans and whites still attend largely segregated schools—although often in the same school buildings.

The Effect of Racism

Beyond the problem of how to control for race, there is another, more fundamental problem: Can we isolate race itself as the *only* possible cause of observed differences? Although many differences between individuals and within racial groups (e.g., class) can be controlled, the major differences *between* racial groups in American society—i.e., racism and racial inequality—can neither be controlled nor held constant nor can their effects be *reversed*. For example, given the definition of race in American society, we cannot *randomly* assign people to racial groups. Therefore, we cannot shift an experimental group of whites to the African American category and then compare their IQ test scores to those of whites who have always lived as white Americans—nor can we shift African Americans to the white category, and so on. In other words, we can identify and acknowledge, but we cannot control for, the effects of racial definition, racism and the realities of racial inequality.

This limitation is not an insurmountable obstacle to the measurement of these particular effects—but it confounds any attempts to measure something that is essential to race itself. However, when this limitation is ignored, as it is in *The Bell Curve*, and we assume that we can control what cannot be controlled, then we produce Model 1:

$$\text{Race} \longrightarrow \text{IQ}$$

Model 1 assumes, of course, that differences in IQ are "caused" by genetic racial inferiority. However, what if another and historically valid term is inserted that represents variables that cannot be controlled? Then Model 2 emerges:

$$\text{Race} \longrightarrow \text{Opportunities, Treatment} \longrightarrow \text{Learning}$$

In contrast to Model 1, Model 2 assumes that, although racial groups are inherently equal, the manner in which different racial groups are treated, in a given society at a given time, will produce measurable advantages for the favored group.

Thus, this interpretation (Model 2) which may seem, initially, most counter-intuitive becomes, once again, the best and most logical explanation of all the available facts: *Racial differences in average IQ scores are simply one measure of the impact of racism and racial inequality.*

The Ideology of Racism and the Genetic Argument

Since the ideology of racism evolved before the development of the modern science of genetics (and biology), most of its core beliefs are pre- or pseudo-scientific. Consequently, the contention that there are or can be genetic differences in IQ between racial groups rests on several faulty assumptions regarding both race and human genetics.

As might be expected, the first assumption deals with race itself, i.e., whether "races" exist and whether their boundaries can be defined and clearly delineated. Because "races" are the result of mutation, natural selection and isolation over time, there are no fixed racial categories. Moreover, even the practice of using race as an organizing and classifying principle has a comparatively short history and originated only with the expansion of Europe, beginning in the 1440s.

The second related assumption holds that different "racial" groups have radically different gene pools.

> *"Achievement tests measure what has been learned prior to the date of testing, not intelligence or aptitude per se."*

However, human beings are predominantly and profoundly "alike." Specifically, there is only a .2 percent difference in the genetic material of any two people, chosen at random, from any two locations on earth. Only 6 percent of that .2 percent—*.012 percent*—is attributable to race. Those who argue that test score differences can be explained by genetic differences in intelligence expect a great deal from that .012 percent.

No "Pure" Races

Another similar assumption relates to the pre-scientific notion that racial groups are different biological species or sub-species. However, the simple test of whether two individuals belong to the same species is whether they can breed and produce fertile offspring. By this definition, African Americans, Native Americans, whites, et al., certainly belong to the same species. We are all cousins and all, originally, children of Africa.

Related to this premise is yet another that, while obviously erroneous, is seldom addressed. European Americans, African Americans and other persons of color are not *"pure"* racial groups. Clearly, Americans of European descent are not a "pure" racial group; many (15 percent or more) are part African and/or part Native American genetically, but not visibly so. Furthermore, given the rule of "hypo-descent," or the "one-drop" rule, most (probably 80 percent or more) African

> *"Achievement tests are far more likely to reflect differences in the quality of schooling and life experiences."*

Americans represent some blend of African, European and Native American genetic material. Consequently, in the United States, race is defined by appearance, not genetics—and appearances can be deceiving.

As a corollary, there is also the supposition that persons of mixed race (or racial hybrids or "mongrels") inherit the worst traits or weaknesses associated with both parent racial groups. However, there is strong evidence that the "mulatto hypothesis"—so often employed against African Americans, Brazilians and other Latin Americans—is also false. Since those of mixed race draw from a more diversified gene pool, they are certainly equal to and may, in some cases, be stronger than either parent racial group, e.g., in immunity to a broader range of diseases (not in IQ).

In any case, the degree of "genetic purity" of particular racial groups is important only if a genetic argument or interpretation is being advanced. Since the meaning of race is *constructed* politically and socially—political, social, economic, cultural and historical interpretations of comparisons between racial groups are legitimate. But how meaningful can biological interpretations be? How "African" must one be before, presumably, the mind dims? How "African" must one be before, presumably, jumping/running/dancing ability is enhanced? And how could people whose ancestors demonstrated such genius in other times and places experience sudden brain-death in the Americas? Furthermore what gene is the "switch" that turns these abilities on and off?

Hence, from the perspective of both social science and genetics, comparisons between racial groups which cite *the essence of race itself* as the cause or explanation of IQ differences are as valid as comparing the sum of two apples and three flying fish to the sum of five pebbles and two crickets. Obviously, we get an answer—but does the answer make sense? . . .

The Problem of the Color Line

In 1903, the great African American scholar and political activist W.E.B. Du Bois stated prophetically that "the problem of the twentieth century" would be "the problem of the color line." As this century draws to a close, the United States and the global community have failed rather miserably to resolve this problem. Throughout this society and across this planet, race still divides the powerful from the powerless, and the haves from the have-nots.

That there has been change is undeniable—as colonialism, legal segregation and, most recently, its African counterpart of apartheid have ended. However, new structures of domination have evolved to supplant the old and racial inequality has persisted and deepened—despite the assurances of scholars, politicians and social commentators that "race was declining in significance."

The United States now finds itself at a fateful crossroads. The national and global political economy are changing inexorably and, against this backdrop, the nation is becoming increasingly non-white—with projections that whites will be a minority population in a generation or two. Whether we recognize it or not, these fundamental economic and demographic shifts are defining how and where the color line of the twenty-first century will be drawn—and contested.

One of two possible futures is likely to emerge from this confluence of historical and social forces. In one, human diversity and human equality will be the organizing principles of society—and all groups will share equally (or far more equally) in the bounty of a uniquely multi-racial, pluralistic nation. In the other, racial hierarchy and human inequality will be the organizing principles—and one group, a former majority that has become a minority, will monopolize wealth, power and prestige at the expense of its fellow citizens.

> *"Racial differences in average IQ scores are simply one measure of the impact of racism and racial inequality."*

In this context, while the conclusions of *The Bell Curve* can be dismissed on logical, social science and genetic grounds, they restate a racial myth as old as Thomas Jefferson's *Notes on the State of Virginia* and as contemporary as the guiding assumptions of the neo-conservative movement—a myth which remains a potent ideological weapon in the service of reaction and fear. Thus, this peculiar exercise in combining and comparing unlike "things" is far more than a sterile academic or scientific debate, but a question of the relationship between human value, human diversity, human equality, and power.

For these reasons, the genetic argument must not only be *rejected* as a proposition of pseudo-science, but the racial project it serves must be actively and firmly *opposed*.

147

"Race" Is Not a Valid Scientific Concept

by Donna Alvarado

About the author: *Donna Alvarado is a reporter for the Knight-Ridder News Service.*

Other than skin color, what separates black people from white?

Not much, a growing number of scientists say. In fact—genetically speaking—there is no such thing as race.

Such a startling conclusion is emerging from studies undertaken by a Stanford University researcher and others on genetic diversity in human populations.

"I find the term 'race' pretty useless," said Luca Cavalli-Sforza, a Stanford population geneticist.

Race Is Only Skin-Deep

Evidence from his own studies and those of others is mounting that what we think of as "race" is only skin-deep—and below the surface lies a range of genetic variability that shows no link to skin color or other superficial physical traits.

For example, the sickle cell anemia trait, long viewed as something found in black people, has also been found among some southern Europeans but is not found in some south African tribes. The Rh negative blood type is found most often in the Basque people of France and Spain, and also surfaces among north Africans but not south Africans.

Cavalli-Sforza's studies raise a fundamental challenge to claims in a best-seller, *The Bell Curve*, that genetics explains why black people score lower on IQ tests than whites.

The best-seller, published in 1994 by two conservative scholars, has become a lightning rod for arguments about whether some federal government programs that serve a high proportion of low-income blacks, such as Head Start, are doomed to failure and should be abandoned.

Donna Alvarado, " 'Race' an Empty Idea in Genetics, Scientists Report," *San Diego Union-Tribune*, February 21, 1995. Reprinted by permission: Tribune Media Services.

Cavalli-Sforza and other researchers gathered for the 1995 annual meeting of the American Association for the Advancement of Science wasted no time in denouncing such genetic claims as scientifically weak.

"We have no basis to claim there is any genetic basis for differences in intelligence in any racial group," said Joseph Graves, a geneticist from the University of Arizona.

Cavalli-Sforza, in a book on human genetic diversity that synthesizes 50 years of research in population genetics, found such a wide range of genetic variation in both African and non-African groups that it makes the conventional notion of race meaningless.

In short, looks can be deceiving.

"There are some superficial traits like skin color and body build," Cavalli-Sforza said. "They are striking, and we notice them.

"That is what misleads us. It makes us think races are very different. They are not, when we look under the skin."

Cavalli-Sforza found that the genetic diversity of populations was better explained by geographic origin than by skin color. His book includes more than 500 maps color-coded to show areas of genetic similarity.

He found the biggest genetic differences between African and Australian populations. Yet many Australian aborigines have skin as black as Africans.

Commenting on the notion that genetics has made one race more intelligent than another, Cavalli-Sforza has said previously, "The truth is that there is no documented biological superiority of any race, however defined. Nowhere is there purity of races, except in plants and in some domestic animals that have undergone a special inbreeding process for laboratory purposes."

> *"Genetically speaking—there is no such thing as race."*

Skin color or facial characteristics of Asian people, for example, have developed over time as a response to climate. Black skin protects against strong sunlight. A flat nose and eyelid skin folds seen in Asians are adaptations to freezing weather of Siberian populations.

But none of these superficial adaptations show a link to other underlying genetic traits, Cavalli-Sforza said.

Not a Valid Scientific Concept

Cavalli-Sforza is not the first to reveal the scientific weakness of categorizing people by skin color. Accumulating evidence had already prompted the American Association of Physical Anthropologists to issue a statement that said "pure races" do not exist now—and probably never did.

"Biologically . . . the use of race is no longer a valid scientific concept," said Solomon Katz, a physical anthropologist at the University of Pennsylvania. "We're putting it to rest after so many years."

Yet all these scientists agreed that the term "race" may have valid social meaning even if it isn't biologically based. Most people would find life confusing if they couldn't identify somehow with a group.

"Race is such an important part of how we think about and navigate our lives," said Michael Omi, a sociologist at the University of California Berkeley. "It's acquired such a potent meaning in our society."

Even without a biological basis, it is likely that racial distinctions will continue because social scientists want categories for the study of social and political trends, Omi said.

And Rhett Jones, a professor of African-American studies at Brown University, said most American blacks would not want to abandon their black identity.

Some researchers suggested identifying people by the geographic origin of their ancestors, rather than by skin color.

But even calling someone African-American does not tell the whole story. C. Loring Brace, a biological

> *"'Pure races' do not exist now—and probably never did."*

anthropologist at the University of Michigan, pointed out that 30 percent of the genes in the average person with black skin in the United States originated in Europe. About 8 percent of the genetic traits originated in Asia.

That led Graves, the Arizona geneticist, who is black, to quip that it might be more accurate to call such a person "West African-European-Asian-American."

IQ Differences Between Races Are Genetic

by J. Philippe Rushton

About the author: *J. Philippe Rushton is a developmental psychologist at the University of Western Ontario in London, Canada. He has written numerous books and articles about race and IQ, including* Race, Evolution, and Behavior.

The historical record shows that an African cultural disadvantage has existed, relative to Europeans and Asians, ever since Europeans first made contact 2,000 years ago. However, until recently, it was not possible to be certain about the cause of the Black-White difference. Today the evidence has increased so much that it is almost certain that only evolutionary (and thereby genetic) theories can explain it. Surveys show that a plurality of experts in psychological testing and behavioral genetics think that a portion of the Black-White difference in IQ scores is genetic in origin.

The IQ debate became international in scope when research showed that Asians scored higher on tests of mental ability than did Whites, whereas Africans and Caribbeans scored lower. The debate was also widened by data showing the same worldwide racial ordering in activity level, personality, speed of maturation, crime, family structure, and health. I explored these and other variables and found that East Asians consistently averaged at one end of a continuum, Africans consistently at the other, and Caucasians consistently in between. There is, of course, enormous overlap in the distributions and thus, it is highly problematic to generalize from a group average to an individual.

The central theoretical questions are: Why should Caucasoids average so consistently between Negroids and Mongoloids on so many dimensions? And, why is there an inverse relation between brain size and gamete production across the races? It is not simply differences in cognitive ability that require explanation. A network of evidence allows more chance of finding powerful theories than do single dimensions drawn from the set.

I reviewed 100 years of scientific literature and found that across a triangula-

Excerpted from J. Philippe Rushton, "The Equalitarian Dogma Revisited," *Intelligence*, November/December 1994. Reprinted by permission of the Ablex Publishing Company.

tion of procedures, brains of Mongoloids average about 17 cm³ (1 in.³) larger than those of Caucasoids, whose brains average about 80 cm³ (5 in.³) larger than those of Negroids. For example, using brain mass at autopsy, K.C. Ho, U. Roessmann, J.V. Straumfjord, and G. Monroe summarized data for 1,261 Americans aged 25 to 80 after excluding obviously damaged brains. They reported a significant sex-combined difference between 811 Whites with a mean of 1,323 grams (Standard Deviation = 146) and 450 Blacks with a mean of 1,223 g (*SD* = 144). Using endocranial volume, K.I. Beals, C.L. Smith, and S.M. Dodd analyzed 20,000 crania and found sex-combined brain cases differed by continental area. Excluding Caucasoid areas of Asia (e.g., India) and Africa (e.g., Egypt), 19 Asian populations averaged 1,415 cm³ (*SD* = 51), 10 European groups averaged 1,362 cm³ (*SD* = 35) and 9 African groups averaged 1,268 cm³ (*SD* = 85). Using external head measurements, I found, in a stratified random sample of 6,325 U.S. Army personnel measured in 1988 to determine head size for fitting helmets, Asian Americans, White Americans, and Black Americans averaged 1,416 cm³, 1,380 cm³, and 1,359 cm³, respectively. With data on tens of thousands of men and women collated by the International Labour Office in Geneva, Asians, Europeans, and Africans averaged, respectively, 1,308 cm³, 1,297 cm³, and 1,241 cm³.

The racial differences in cranial size are consistent across procedures. The world database from autopsies, endocranial volume, head measurements, and head measurements corrected for body size, were, respectively, in cm³: Mongoloids = 1,351; 1,415; 1,335; 1,356 (Mean = 1,364); Caucasoids = 1,356; 1,362; 1,341; 1,329 (*M* = 1,347); and Negroids = 1,223; 1,268; 1,284; 1,294 (*M* = 1,267). The world average cranial size was 1,326 cm³. Within-race differences due to method of estimation averaged only 31 cm³.

Intelligence

The global literature on cognitive ability was reviewed by Richard Lynn. Caucasoids in North America, Europe, and Australasia had mean IQs of around 100. Mongoloids, measured in North America and in Pacific Rim countries, had higher means, in the range of 101 to 111. Africans living south of the Sahara, African Americans, and African Caribbeans (including those living in Britain), had mean IQs of from 70 to 90. However, the question remains whether test scores are valid measures of group differences in mental ability. Basically, the answer hinges on whether the tests are culture bound. Doubts about validity linger in many quarters, although considerable technical work has disposed of this problem among those with psychometric expertise. This is because the tests show similar patterns of internal item consistency and predictive validity for all

> *"A plurality of experts ... think that a portion of the Black/White difference in IQ scores is genetic in origin."*

groups, and the same differences are found on relatively culture-free tests.

Novel data about speed of decision making show that racial differences in mental ability are pervasive. Cross-cultural investigations of reaction time have been done on 9- to 12-year-olds from six countries. In these elementary tasks, children must decide which of several lights is on, or stands out from others, and move a hand to press a button. All children can perform the tasks in less than 1 second, but more intelligent children, as measured by traditional IQ tests, perform the tasks faster than do less intelligent children. Lynn found that Asian children in Hong Kong and Japan process information faster than do White children in Britain and Ireland, who process it faster than do Black children in Africa. Using similar tasks, as well as those involving retrieval of well-learned facts from long-term memory, the three-way racial pattern is also found in California.

> *"Research showed that Asians scored higher on tests of mental ability than did Whites, whereas Africans and Caribbeans scored lower."*

The Brain Size–IQ Link

A positive correlation between mental ability and brain size has been established in studies using magnetic resonance imaging, which *in vivo* construct three-dimensional pictures of the brain. These confirm correlations, reported since the turn of the century, from measurements of head perimeter. The brain size–cognitive ability correlations range from .10 to .40.

Two studies imply that brain size differences underlie the Black-White difference in mental ability. In an adolescent sample, Arthur R. Jensen found that the greater the difference between White and Black children on 17 tests, the higher was the tests' correlation with head size. In a study of 14,000 4- and 7-year-olds, when the White and Black children were matched on IQ, they no longer differed in head size.

The Asian-White-Black racial matrix occurs on a surprisingly wide range of dimensions. For example, the racial pattern in violent crime found within the U.S. holds internationally. I averaged several years of international police statistics to find rates of murder, rape, and serious assault to be three times higher in African and Caribbean countries than in Pacific Rim countries, again with European countries intermediate. These results make it clear that whatever the causes of violent crime turn out to be, they must lie beyond U.S. particulars.

One neurohormonal contributor to crime is testosterone. As I review in my book, *Race, Evolution and Behavior*, studies show 3% to 19% more testosterone in Black college students and military veterans than in their White counterparts, with the Japanese showing lower amounts than Whites. Sex hormones go everywhere in the body and have been shown to activate many brain-behavior systems involving crime, personality, and reproduction. As another example, around the world, the rate of dizygotic twinning per 1,000 births, caused by a double ovulation, is less than 4 among Mongoloids, 8 among Caucasoids, and 16 or greater among Negroids.

Worldwide surveys show more sexual activity in Negroids compared to Caucasoids and especially to Mongoloids. Differences in sexual activity translate into consequences. International fertility rates show the racial pattern; so does the pattern of AIDS. As of January 1, 1994, World Health Organization and Centers for Disease Control and Prevention statistics showed infection rates, per hundred thousand population, for (a) Asian Americans and Asians in the Pacific Rim of less than 1, (b) European Americans and Europeans in Europe, Canada, and Australasia of 86, and (c) African Americans and Africans south of the Sahara and in the Caribbean of 355.

Behavioral Genetics

A first study of the genetic contribution to cranial size, and by inference to brain size, has been made in a study of 236 pairs of adolescent twins (472 individuals) aged 13 to 17 years, White and Black, male and female. Heritability for the total sample ranged from 38% to 51%, depending on particular adjustments made for body size. Environmental effects common to both twins, like parental socioeconomic status, ranged from 6% to 20% and environmental effects unique to each twin, like illness, ranged from 42% to 52%. The heritability estimates did not vary systematically by sex or race, although there was a trend for them to be lower in Blacks than in Whites.

Heritabilities for mental ability range from 50% to 80% and have been established in numerous adoption, twin, and family studies. Noteworthy are the 80% heritabilities found in adult twins reared apart. Genetic influence is also found in studies of non-Whites, including African Americans and Japanese. Quantitative genetic research has also built a strong case for the importance of genetic factors in the domains of personality and psychopathology.

Findings such as these led Sandra Scarr to title her 1986 presidential address to the Behavior Genetics Association, "Three Cheers for Behavioral Genetics." She observed that "the war [between nature and nurture] is largely over." Scarr accepted that genetics underlay existing White social class differences in mental ability in the U.S. and Europe, although this may not have been the case for earlier generations when social mobility was more restricted. Because racial barriers are less permeable than class barriers, Scarr interpreted her own research of 7-year-old Black and mixed-race children adopted into White middle-class families as showing an environmental cause of racial differences.

> *"Transracial adoption studies . . . indicate a genetic contribution to cognitive ability."*

Other transracial adoption studies, including a follow-up to Scarr's 7-year-old

Black children to when they were 17, indicate a genetic contribution to cognitive ability. Studies of Korean and Vietnamese children adopted into White American and White Belgian homes showed that, although as babies many had been hospitalized for malnutrition, they grew to excel in academic ability with IQs 10 points or more higher than their adoptive national norms. By contrast, Richard A. Weinberg, Scarr, and Irwin D. Waldman found that at age 17, Black and mixed-race children adopted into White middle-class families performed at a lower level than did White siblings with whom they had been raised. Adopted White children had an average IQ of 106, an average aptitude based on national norms at the 59th percentile, and a class rank at the 54th percentile; mixed-race children had an average IQ of 99, an aptitude at the 53rd percentile, and a class rank at the 40th percentile; and Black children had an average IQ of 89, an aptitude at the 42nd percentile, and a class rank at the 36th percentile.

Multifarious other sources of evidence suggest that racial differences in intelligence are substantially genetic. For example, Black-White differences are most pronounced on more *g*-loaded subtests; that is, on the general factor common to diverse cognitive tests. The *g*-loadings are correlated with a number of biological variables including brain evoked potentials, heritability coefficients determined from twin studies, and the degree to which children's test scores are depressed by inbreeding and raised by outbreeding. Also, genetic weights established from inbreeding depression studies in the Japanese population directly predict the magnitude of the Black-White differences on the various subtests of the Wechsler Intelligence Scale for Children. There is no other explanation for inbreeding depression than a genetic one.

> *"Multifarious other sources of evidence suggest that racial differences in intelligence are substantially genetic."*

Genetics Is a Primary Factor in IQ Differences Between Races

by Richard J. Herrnstein and Charles Murray

About the authors: The late Richard J. Herrnstein held the Edgar Pierce chair in psychology at Harvard University and is the author of IQ in the Meritocracy. *Charles Murray is a Bradley Fellow at the American Enterprise Institute, a conservative research organization, and the author of* Losing Ground: American Social Policy 1950–1980. *Herrnstein and Murray are coauthors of* The Bell Curve: Intelligence and Class Structure in American Life, *from which this viewpoint is adapted.*

Do Asians have higher I.Q.s than whites? The answer is probably yes, if Asian refers to the Japanese and Chinese (and perhaps also Koreans), whom we will refer to here as East Asians. How much higher is still unclear. The best tests of this have involved identical I.Q. tests given to populations that are comparable except for race. In one test, samples of American, British and Japanese students aged 13 to 15 were given a test of abstract reasoning and spatial relations. The U.S. and U.K. samples had scores within a point of the standardized mean of 100 on both the abstract and spatial relations parts of the test; the Japanese scored 104.5 on the test for abstract reasoning and 114 on the test for spatial relations—a large difference, amounting to a gap similar to the one found by another leading researcher for Asians in America. In a second set of studies, 9-year-olds in Japan, Hong Kong and Britain, drawn from comparable socioeconomic populations, were administered the Ravens Standard Progressive Matrices. The children from Hong Kong averaged 113; from Japan, 110; and from Britain, 100.

Different Test Results

Not everyone accepts that the East Asian–white difference exists. Another set of studies gave a battery of mental tests to elementary school children in Japan,

Abridged from Richard J. Herrnstein and Charles Murray, "Race, Genes, and I.Q.—an Apologia," *New Republic*, October 31, 1994. Reprinted by permission of Charles Murray, for the authors.

Taiwan and Minneapolis, Minnesota. The key difference between this study and the other two was that the children were matched carefully on many socioeconomic and demographic variables. No significant difference in overall I.Q. was found, and the authors concluded that "this study offers no support for the argument that there are differences in the general cognitive functioning of Chinese, Japanese and American children."

Where does this leave us? The parties in the debate are often confident, and present in their articles are many flat statements that an overall East Asian–white I.Q. difference does, or does not, exist. In our judgment, the balance of the evidence supports the notion that the overall East Asian mean is higher than the white mean. Three I.Q. points most resembles a consensus, tentative though it still is. East Asians have a greater advantage in a particular kind of nonverbal intelligence.

> *"The evidence supports the notion that the overall East Asian [IQ] mean is higher than the white mean."*

The issues become far more fraught, however, in determining the answer to the question: Do African Americans score differently from whites on standardized tests of cognitive ability? If the samples are chosen to be representative of the American population, the answer has been yes for every known test of cognitive ability that meets basic psychometric standards. The answer is also yes for almost all studies in which the black and white samples are matched on some special characteristics—juvenile delinquents, for example, or graduate students—but there are exceptions.

How large is the black-white difference? The usual answer is what statisticians call one standard deviation. In discussing I.Q. tests, for example, the black mean is commonly given as 85, the white mean as 100 and the standard deviation as fifteen points. But the differences observed in any given study seldom conform exactly to one standard deviation. In 156 American studies conducted during this century that have reported the I.Q. means of a black sample and a white sample, and that meet basic requirements of interpretability, the mean black-white difference is 1.1 standard deviations, or about sixteen I.Q. points. . . .

Genetics, I.Q., and Race

This brings us to the flashpoint of intelligence as a public topic: the question of genetic differences between the races. Expert opinion, when it is expressed at all, diverges widely. In the 1980s Mark Snyderman, a psychologist, and Stanley Rothman, a political scientist, sent a questionnaire to a broad sample of 1,020 scholars, mostly academicians, whose specialties give them reason to be knowledgeable about I.Q. Among other questions, they asked, "Which of the following best characterizes your opinion of the heritability of the black-white difference in I.Q.?" The answers were divided as follows: The difference is entirely due to environmental variation: 15 percent. The difference is entirely due to genetic variation: 1 percent. The difference is a product of both genetic and environmental variation: 45 percent. The data are insufficient to support any reasonable opinion: 24 percent. No response: 14 percent.

This pretty well sums up the professional judgment on the matter. But it doesn't explain anything about the environment/genetic debate as it has played out in the profession and in the general public. And the question, of course, is fascinating. So what could help us understand the connection between heritability and group differences? A good place to start is by correcting a common confusion about the role of genes in individuals and in groups.

Most scholars accept that I.Q. in the human species as a whole is substantially heritable, somewhere between 40 percent and 80 percent, meaning that much of the observed variation in I.Q. is genetic. And yet this information tells us nothing for sure about the origin of the differences between groups of humans in measured intelligence. This point is so basic, and so misunderstood, that it deserves emphasis: that a trait is genetically transmitted in a population does not mean that group differences in that trait are also genetic in origin. Anyone who doubts this assertion may take two handfuls of genetically identical seed corn and plant one handful in Iowa, the other in the Mojave Desert, and let nature (i.e., the environment) take its course. The seeds will grow in Iowa, not in the Mojave, and the result will have nothing to do with genetic differences.

The environment for American blacks has been closer to the Mojave and the environment for American whites has been closer to Iowa. We may apply this general observation to the available data and see where the results lead. Suppose that all the observed ethnic differences in tested intelligence originate in some mysterious environmental differences—mysterious, because socioeconomic factors cannot be much of the explanation. We further stipulate that one standard deviation (fifteen I.Q. points) separates American blacks and whites and that one-fifth of a standard deviation (three I.Q. points) separates East Asians and whites. Finally, we assume that I.Q. is 60 percent heritable (a middle-ground estimate). Given these parameters, how different would the environments for the three groups have to be in order to explain the observed difference in these scores?

Explaining Ethnic Differences in I.Q.

The observed ethnic differences in I.Q. could be explained solely by the environment if the mean environment of whites is 1.58 standard deviations better than the mean environment of blacks and .32 standard deviation worse than the mean environment for East Asians, when environments are measured along the continuum of their capacity to nurture intelligence. Let's state these conclusions in percentile terms: the average environment of blacks would have to be at the sixth percentile of the distribution of environments among

"Most scholars accept that I.Q. in the human species as a whole is substantially heritable."

158

whites and the average environment of East Asians would have to be at the sixty-third percentile of environments among whites for the racial differences to be entirely environmental.

Environmental differences of this magnitude and pattern are wildly out of line with all objective measures of the differences in black, Asian and white environments. The black-white difference is smallest at the lowest socioeconomic levels. Why, if the black-white difference is entirely environmental, should the advantage of the "white" environment compared to the "black" be greater among the better-off and better-educated blacks and whites? We have not been able to think of a plausible reason. Can you? An appeal to the effects of racism to explain ethnic differences also requires explaining why environments poisoned by discrimination and racism for some other groups—against the Chinese or the Jews in some regions of America for example—have left them with higher scores than the national average.

> *"Much of the observed variation in I.Q. is genetic."*

Genetics May Be Involved

However discomfiting it may be to consider it, there are reasons to suspect genetic considerations are involved. The evidence is circumstantial, but provocative. For example, ethnicities differ not just in average scores but in the profile of intellectual capacities. A full-scale I.Q. score is the aggregate of many subtests. There are thirteen of them in the Wechsler Intelligence Scale for Children, for example. The most basic division of the subtests is into a verbal I.Q. and a performance I.Q. In white samples the verbal and performance I.Q. subscores tend to have about the same mean, because I.Q. tests have been standardized on predominantly white populations. But individuals can have imbalances between these two I.Q.s. People with high verbal abilities are likely to do well with words and logic. In school they excel in history and literature; in choosing a career to draw on those talents, they tend to choose law or journalism or advertising or politics. In contrast, people with high performance I.Q.s—or, using a more descriptive phrase, "visuospatial abilities"—are likely to do well in the physical and biological sciences, mathematics, engineering or other subjects that demand mental manipulation in the three physical dimensions or the more numerous dimensions of mathematics.

East Asians living overseas score about the same or slightly lower than whites on verbal I.Q. and substantially higher on visuospatial I.Q. Even in the rare studies that have found overall Japanese or Chinese I.Q.s no higher than white I.Q.s, the discrepancy between verbal and visuospatial I.Q. persists. For Japanese living in Asia, a 1987 review of the literature demonstrated without much question that the verbal-visuospatial difference persists even in examinations that have been thoroughly adapted to the Japanese language and, indeed, in tests developed by the Japanese themselves. A study of a small sample of

Korean infants adopted into white families in Belgium found the familiar elevated visuospatial scores.

This finding has an echo in the United States, where Asian American students abound in science subjects, in engineering and in medical schools, but are scarce in law schools and graduate programs in the humanities and social sciences. Is this just a matter of parental pressures or of Asian immigrants uncomfortable with English? The same pattern of subtest scores is found in Inuits and American Indians (both of Asian origin) and in fully assimilated second- and third-generation Asian Americans. Any simple socioeconomic, cultural or linguistic explanation is out of the question, given the diversity of living conditions, native languages, educational systems and cultural practices experienced by these groups and by East Asians living in Asia. Their common genetic history cannot plausibly be dismissed as irrelevant.

Spearman's Hypothesis

Turning now to blacks and whites (using these terms to refer exclusively to Americans), ability profiles also have been important in understanding the nature, and possible genetic component, of group differences. The argument has been developing around what is known as Spearman's hypothesis. This hypothesis says that if the black-white difference on test scores reflects a real underlying difference in general mental ability (g), then the size of the black-white difference will be related to the degree to which the test is saturated with g. In other words, the better a test measures g, the larger the black-white difference will be.

Spearman's hypothesis has been borne out in fourteen major studies, and no appropriate data set has yet been found that contradicts Spearman's hypothesis. It should be noted that not all group differences behave similarly. For example, deaf children often get lower test scores than hearing children, but the size of the difference is not correlated positively with the test's loading on g. The phenomenon seems peculiarly concentrated in comparisons of ethnic groups. How does this bear on the genetic explanation of ethnic differences? In plain though somewhat imprecise language: the broadest conception of intelligence is embodied in g. At the same time, g typically has the highest heritability (higher than the other factors measured by I.Q. tests). As mental measurement focuses most specifically and reliably on g, the observed black-white mean difference in cognitive ability gets larger. This does not in itself demand a genetic explanation of the ethnic difference but, by asserting that "the better the test, the greater the ethnic difference," Spearman's hypothesis undercuts many of the environmental explanations of the difference that rely on the proposition (again, simplifying) that the apparent black-white difference is the result of bad tests, not good ones.

"Ethnicities differ not just in average [IQ] scores but in the profile of intellectual capacities."

Arguments Against Genetics

There are, of course, many arguments against such a genetic explanation. Many studies have shown that the disadvantaged environment of some blacks has depressed their test scores. In one study, in black families in rural Georgia, the elder sibling typically had a lower I.Q. than the younger. The larger the age difference is between the siblings, the larger is the difference in I.Q. The implication is that something in the rural Georgia environment was depressing the scores of black children as they grew older. In neither the white families of Georgia, nor white or black families in Berkeley, California, were there comparable signs of a depressive effect of the environment.

> *"The better a test measures g [general intelligence], the larger the black-white difference will be."*

Another approach is to say that tests are artifacts of a culture, and a culture may not diffuse equally into every household and community. In a heterogeneous society, subcultures vary in ways that inevitably affect scores on I.Q. tests. Fewer books in the home mean less exposure to the material that a vocabulary subtest measures; the varying ways of socializing children may influence whether a child acquires the skills, or a desire for the skills, that tests test; the "common knowledge" that tests supposedly draw on may not be common in certain households and neighborhoods.

So far, this sounds like a standard argument about cultural bias, and yet it accepts the generalizations about internal evidence of bias. The supporters of this argument are not claiming that less exposure to books means that blacks score lower on vocabulary questions but do as well as whites on culture-free items. Rather, the effects of culture are more diffuse.

Furthermore, strong correlations between home or community life and I.Q. scores are readily found. In a study of 180 Latino and 180 non-Latino white elementary school children in Riverside, California, the researcher examined eight sociocultural variables: (1) mother's participation in formal organizations, (2) living in a segregated neighborhood, (3) home language level, (4) socioeconomic status based on occupation and education of head of household, (5) urbanization, (6) mother's achievement values, (7) home ownership, and (8) intact biological family. She then showed that once these sociocultural variables were taken into account, the remaining group and I.Q. differences among the children fell to near zero.

The problem with this procedure lies in determining what, in fact, these eight variables control for: cultural diffusion, or genetic sources of variation in intelligence as ordinarily understood? By so drastically extending the usual match for socioeconomic status, the possibility is that such studies demonstrate only that parents matched on I.Q. will produce children with similar I.Q.s—not a startling finding. Also, the data used for such studies continue to show the distinctive

161

racial patterns in the subtests. Why should cultural diffusion manifest itself by differences in backward and forward digit span or in completely nonverbal items? If the role of European white cultural diffusion is so important in affecting black I.Q. scores, why is it so unimportant in affecting Asian I.Q. scores?

Other Cultural Bias Arguments

There are other arguments related to cultural bias. In the American context, Wade Boykin is one of the most prominent academic advocates of a distinctive black culture, arguing that nine interrelated dimensions put blacks at odds with the prevailing Eurocentric model. Among them are spirituality (blacks approach life as "essentially vitalistic rather than mechanistic, with the conviction that nonmaterial forces influence people's everyday lives"); a belief in the harmony between humankind and nature; an emphasis on the importance of movement, rhythm, music and dance, "which are taken as central to psychological health"; personal styles that he characterizes as "verve" (high levels of stimulation and energy) and "affect" (emphasis on emotions and expressiveness); and "social time perspective," which he defines as "an orientation in which time is treated as passing through a social space rather than a material one." Such analyses purport to explain how large black-white differences in test scores could coexist with equal predictive validity of the test for such things as academic and job performance and yet still not be based on differences in "intelligence," broadly defined, let alone genetic differences.

John Ogbu, a Berkeley anthropologist, has proposed a more specific version of this argument. He suggests that we look at the history of various minority groups to understand the sources of differing levels of intellectual attainment in America. He distinguishes three types of minorities: "autonomous minorities" such as the Amish, Jews and Mormons, who, while they may be victims of discrimination, are still within the cultural mainstream; "immigrant minorities," such as the Chinese, Filipinos, Japanese and Koreans within the United States, who moved voluntarily to their new societies and, while they may begin in menial jobs, compare themselves favorably with their peers back in the home country; and, finally, "castelike minorities," such as black Americans, who were involuntary immigrants or otherwise are consigned from birth to a distinctively lower place on the social ladder. Ogbu argues that the differences in test scores are an outcome of this historical distinction, pointing to a number of castes around the world—the untouchables in India, the Buraku in Japan and Oriental Jews in Israel—that have exhibited comparable problems in educational achievement despite being of the same racial group as the majority.

> *"The better the test, the greater the ethnic difference."*

The Flynn Effect

Indirect support for the proposition that the observed black-white difference could be the result of environmental factors is provided by the worldwide phenomenon of rising test scores. We call it "the Flynn effect" because of psychologist James Flynn's pivotal role in focusing attention on it, but the phenomenon itself was identified in the 1930s when testers began to notice that I.Q. scores often rose with every successive year after a test was first standardized. For example, when the Stanford-Binet I.Q. was restandardized in the mid-1930s, it was observed that individuals earned lower I.Q.s on the new tests than they got on the Stanford-Binet that had been standardized in the

> *"Parents matched on I.Q. will produce children with similar I.Q.s."*

mid-1910s; in other words, getting a score of 100 (the population average) was harder to do on the later test. This meant that the average person could answer more items on the old test than on the new test. Most of the change has been concentrated in the nonverbal portions of the tests.

The tendency for I.Q. scores to drift upward as a function of years since standardization has now been substantiated in many countries and on many I.Q. tests besides the Stanford-Binet. In some countries, the upward drift since World War II has been as much as a point per year for some spans of years. The national averages have in fact changed by amounts that are comparable to the fifteen or so I.Q. points separating whites and blacks in America. To put it another way, on the average, whites today may differ in I.Q. from whites, say, two generations ago as much as whites today differ from blacks today. Given their size and speed, the shifts in time necessarily have been due more to changes in the environment than to changes in the genes. The question then arises: Couldn't the mean of blacks move fifteen points as well through environmental changes? There seems no reason why not—but also no reason to believe that white and Asian means can be made to stand still while the Flynn effect works its magic.

The Role of Genetics

As of 1994, then, we can say nothing for certain about the relative roles that genetics and environment play in the formation of the black-white difference in I.Q. All the evidence remains indirect. The heritability of individual differences in I.Q. does not necessarily mean that ethnic differences are also heritable. But those who think that ethnic differences are readily explained by environmental differences haven't been tough-minded enough about their own argument. At this complex intersection of complex factors, the easy answers are unsatisfactory ones.

Given the weight of the many circumstantial patterns, it seems improbable to us—though possible—that genes have no role whatsoever. What might the mix of genetic and environmental influences be? We are resolutely agnostic on that.

163

IQ Differences Between Races Are Not Due to Environment

by Richard Lynn

About the author: *Richard Lynn is a professor of psychology at the University of Ulster in Coleraine, Northern Ireland.*

The 1992 article by Richard A. Weinberg, Sandra Scarr and Irwin D. Waldman presented valuable new data on the intelligence and educational attainments of black, interracial (black-white), and white infants adopted by white middle-class families and tested at an average age of 17 years. The new data make important contributions to the debate on the relative contributions of genetic and environmental factors to intelligence and to the information on differences in intelligence between blacks and whites in the United States. However, a number of the authors' interpretations of their results do not appear to be warranted. This viewpoint questions the authors' conclusions on five issues where it is considered that the inferences to be drawn from the data are contrary to those advanced by the authors.

Before considering these issues, it may be useful to summarize briefly the salient points of the data. These concern four groups of children raised in white middle-class families: black adopted, interracial adopted (i.e., with one black and one white parent), white adopted, and white biological. The children were tested for intelligence in 1976 (Time 1), at the average age of 7, with the Progressive Matrices, the Stanford-Binet of the Wechsler Intelligence Scale for Children (WISC), and again in 1986 (Time 2) at an average of 17 years, with the WISC-R or the Wechsler Adult Intelligence Scale-Revised (WAIS-R). There was also a small group of 12 Asian children whose results do not add materially to the issues and who are therefore omitted from this discussion. Only the results of those children for whom intelligence test data are available at both ages 7 and 17 are considered here. The results are summarized in Table 1. There are five inferences drawn by Weinberg, Scarr, and Waldman (WSW) from their data. I believe they are all incorrect and I set out my reasons below their conclusions.

Richard Lynn, "Some Reinterpretations of the Minnesota Transracial Adoption Study," *Intelligence*, July/August 1994 (the original's endnotes have been omitted). Reprinted by permission of the Ablex Publishing Company.

TABLE 1
Mean IQs of Black, Interracial, and White Adopted
Children, with IQ Changes from Ages 7 to 17

Children	IQ Age 7	IQ Age 17	IQ Change
Black	95	89	−6
Interracial	109	98	−11
White	118	106	−12
Biological	116	109	−7

Source: Richard Lynn, *Intelligence*, July–August 1994.

Adoption into White Middle-Class Families

WSW: "These results are congruent with those of other recent adoption studies . . . in demonstrating the strong effects of the rearing environment on IQ."

Critic: None of the mean IQs at age 17 of the three adopted groups of black, black-white, and white children gives any support to this claim. In their earlier report on these children at an average age of 7 years, Scarr and Weinberg compared the mean IQs of the three groups with the IQs of children in the respective general populations and argued that the IQs of the adopted children were appreciably higher. In their later report, Weinberg et al. no longer make this comparison, but it is certainly the appropriate one to use.

The three groups need to be considered separately. First, the black children at age 17 have a mean IQ of 89. A casual reader might suppose that the mean black IQ is 85 and, therefore, that the adopted black children had made a gain of 4 IQ points. This would be wrong and two corrections need to be made. The first is because the majority of the black children came from the north central and northeast regions of the United States, where the mean IQs of black children obtained in the WISC-R standardization sample are not 85 but 88.1 and 93.0, as Scarr has herself noted. Most of the black children apparently came from the north central region, so the appropriate comparison group has a minimum IQ of 88.1. There is, therefore, virtually no difference between the mean IQ of the adopted black children (89) and that of black children reared in their own communities in the north central United States. But a second correction is also required. Allowance must be made for the secular increase in population IQs from the dates of the standardization of the WISC-R and WAIS-R (1972 and 1978) to 1986, when the adopted children were tested. American IQs have been increasing at approximately 3 IQ points per decade since the 1930s, and this rate of increase has been maintained in recent years. Both tests were used for the assessment of the IQs of the adopted children, so we can take the average of the 2 years as 1975 and add 3.3 IQ points to the mean of the general population, to allow for the intelligence increase

> *"The adoptive experience had no beneficial effect at all on the intelligence level of any of the three groups."*

165

over the 11 years 1975–1986. This brings the mean IQ of the general black northern population up to 91.4. Compared with this figure, the mean IQ of 89 of the Weinberg et al. sample of black infants adopted by white middle-class families shows a small deficit and certainly indicates that they made no intelligence gains as a result of their adoptive experience.

> *"The social environment in which the black children were reared had no effect on narrowing the gap between black and white IQs."*

Consider now the adopted white children. Their mean IQ at the age of 17 is 106. Have they, therefore, made a 6-point IQ gain, as compared with a white mean IQ of 100? Surely not. The mean IQ of white children in the WISC-R standardization sample was 102.2. (On any test standardized on the total population of the United States the mean white IQ is necessarily a little higher than 100). Add 3.3 IQ points for the secular increase of intelligence 1975–1986, which brings the mean IQ of the general population of white children up to 105.7, the same as that of the white adopted children.

Finally, the interracial children at age 17 had a mean IQ of 98. There is no good comparison group in the normal population, but the IQ of the interracial group falls midway between the IQs of the white and the black children. The simplest assumption is that the IQ of the normal population of interracial children also falls midway between the IQs of the black and white populations and, hence, that the IQ of the adopted interracial children is also the same as that of the general population. The upshot is that the adoptive experience had no beneficial effect at all on the intelligence level of any of the three groups at the age of 17. Yet, Weinberg et al. claim that their results show strong effects of the rearing environment on IQ.

Race Differences in IQ

WSW: "The results of the longitudinal follow-up continue to support the view that the social environment maintains a dominant role in determining the average IQ level of black and interracial children."

Critic: The study shows mean IQs of 89 and 106, respectively, of black and white children reared in matched social environments. This 17-point IQ difference is the same as, or perhaps fractionally greater than, that of black and white children reared in their own natural environments, which numerous studies place at approximately one standard deviation, or 15 IQ points. This shows that the social environment in which the black children were reared had no effect on narrowing the gap between black and white IQs. The difference between the two groups supports the genetic theory of the origin of these differences, because it apparently makes no difference to their IQs whether they are raised in their own environments or in white middle-class environments.

The results of the interracial group add further support to the genetic explanation for the origin of the race differences in intelligence. The mean IQ of the interracial group at age 17 was 98, halfway between that of the black and the white children. This result is inexplicable in terms of environmental theory but is precisely what would be expected from genetic theory, because the interracial group's IQ should fall halfway between the IQs of the black and the white parent populations. The predominant effect of race, rather than social environment, on the children's IQs is confirmed by Weinberg et al.'s regression analysis, which shows "biological mother's race the best single predictor of adopted child's IQ when other variables are controlled."

Age at Adoption

WSW: "The early adopted group continued to show high IQ test performance at Time 2" (i.e., at age 17). "If genetic background but not social environment contributed to the average follow-up IQ of black/interracial adoptees . . . we would not expect their Time 2 IQ to be correlated with adoptive experiences such as age at placement and time in adoptive home."

Critic: The relevant correlations are –.30 between age at placement and IQ at age 17, and + .20 between time in adoptive homes and IQ at age 17. These correlations may appear to suggest that the younger the child is adopted, the higher the IQ at age 17 and, hence, the beneficial effect of early placement.

There are two problems with this claim: (a) The correlations are given only for the black and interracial adoptees and not for the white adoptees. If early placement has a beneficial effect on the later intelligence of black and interracial adoptees, surely it must have the same beneficial effect on white adoptees? Why, therefore, have the white adoptees been excluded? (b) The correlations presented are confounded with race differences because the black children had lower mean IQs, later ages at placement, and shorter times in the adoptive home, as compared with the interracial children. Thus, what appears to be an age-of-adoption effect may be only a race-differences effect. This is suggested by the multiple regression analysis, because, when race is entered first in the multiple regression, it appears as a significant predictor of adopted children's IQs, and adoptive experience variables, entered second, make no significant contribution to children's IQs. What Weinberg et al. need to do to establish their point is to give the correlations between age of adoption and IQ within each of the three racial groups.

> *"It apparently makes no difference to [black children's] IQs whether they are raised in their own environments or in white middle-class environments."*

Regression Effects of IQ Decline

WSW: "If genetic background but not social environment contributed to the average follow-up IQ of black/interracial adoptees . . . we would expect them to show greater IQ decline than biological offspring, because their Time 2 IQ would regress back to their biological, but not their adoptive, parents' IQ levels."

167

Critic: No confidence can be placed in the IQ decline figures because different tests were used at Time 1 and Time 2 and the IQs are not corrected for secular increases in intelligence in the general population. IQs at Time 1 and Time 2 cannot be meaningfully compared. There may have been no decline at all. The authors could adjust the IQs for the secular increase of intelligence and this would throw useful light on the question.

Parental Education and IQ Correlation

WSW: "If genetic background but not social environment contributed to the average follow-up IQ of black/interracial adoptees . . . we should expect . . . their Time 2 IQ to be correlated with their biological parents' education but not their adoptive parents' education or IQs."

Critic: Weinberg et al. assert that their results do not support the genetic hypothesis, but this is wrong. The correlations are as would be ex-

> *"The quality of the adoptive home has no effect on the IQs of adopted children at the age of 17 years."*

pected from genetic theory; that is, the correlations between biological parents' education and adopted children's IQs are greater than those between adoptive parents' education and children's IQs (.23 and .28 for biological mothers and fathers, as compared with .11 and .14 for adoptive mothers and fathers). A comparison of correlations of the IQs of the biological and adoptive parents with the children's IQs cannot be made because there are no data for the IQs of the biological parents.

The correlations between the IQs of the adoptive parents and the black-interracial children are given (.18 and .20 for mothers and fathers). These are lower than the correlations between the education of the biological parents and the IQs of the children, once again supporting the genetic hypothesis. Nevertheless, these positive correlations do suggest that quality of the adoptive home (indexed by the IQs of the adopting parents) does have a beneficial effect on the intelligence of the adopted children. However, the reader is inevitably curious as to why the correlation is not given for the white adopted children, and this omission places a question mark over the claim. The correlations should be given separately for the three groups of adopted children.

There is an interesting feature of the correlations between the IQs of the adoptive parents and their adopted children that Weinberg et al. do not mention. Mothers typically play a greater part in child rearing than fathers, that is to say, in cognitive stimulation and selection of diet. If the quality of the adoptive home has an advantageous effect on children's IQs, we should expect that the mothers' IQ and education would show higher correlations with the children's IQs than would the fathers' IQs and education. Yet this is not the case. The correlations for IQ and education for mothers are .23 and .18 and for fathers, .28 and .20. This is a prediction failure of the theory that the quality of the adoptive home affects the child's IQ. It provides further evidence that the quality of the adoptive home has no effect on the IQs of adopted children at the age of 17 years.

Results Support Genetic Hypothesis

In their first report on these children, Scarr and Weinberg argued that a transracial adoption study in which black children were reared in white middle-class homes would provide direct evidence on the issue of the relative contribution of environmental and genetic factors to the low mean IQ of black children. If this adoptive experience raised the IQs of black children, the result would indicate the importance of environmental factors. If it failed to raise the IQs of black children, the result would indicate the importance of genetic factors. Others have accepted that this is the crucial investigation required to differentiate between the environmental and the genetic hypotheses.

We now have the results of the study and they support the genetic hypothesis. Five items of evidence lead to this conclusion: (a) black children raised by white graduates with a mean IQ of 119.5 have the same mean IQ at age 17 as black children reared in their own communities, thereby showing that the black environment from the age of adoption at the age of approximately 1 year cannot be a cause of the low black IQ, and being adopted by white graduates, although the ultimate in headstarts yet has no effect in raising the black IQ; (b) the IQ gap between the black and white 17-year-olds reared in these matched environments of white graduate parents is 17 IQ points, the same as that in the general population, again showing that environmental factors operating after adoption have no effect on the race difference in intelligence; (c) the IQ of the adopted interracial children falls halfway between that of the black and white children, as would be predicted by a genetic theory of the origin of these differences but not by an environmental theory; (d) regression analysis shows that the race of the biological mother is the best predictor of the adopted children's IQs at the age of 17; (e) there are no differences between the correlations of IQs and the education of the adoptive mothers and fathers and the adopted children's IQs, contrary to the prediction from environmental theory that the mothers' correlations would be higher and consistent with genetic theory that the quality of the adoptive experience has no effect. Set against these five items of evidence there is one anomalous result, namely, the positive correlations between the IQs of the adoptive parents and those of the black and interracial adopted children. This anomaly should be examined more fully and the correlation for the white adopted children given. However, this result has no bearing on the problem of the causes of the black-white IQ difference.

All students of the problem of the low mean black IQ are indebted to Weinberg et al. for carrying out and publishing this study. It has provided important new evidence differentiating the environmental and genetic hypotheses, and the results provide strong support for the genetic position. It will no longer be possible to state, in the words of a 1992 textbook, that "there is no convincing direct or indirect evidence in favor of a genetic hypothesis of racial differences in IQ."

Chapter 4

How Should IQ Research Affect Social Policies?

CURRENT CONTROVERSIES

Chapter Preface

In their controversial book *The Bell Curve: Intelligence and Class Structure in American Life*, authors Richard J. Herrnstein and Charles Murray maintain that intelligence is an inherited and fixed property that cannot be permanently changed no matter how long children attend school or how hard they study. Therefore, the authors contend, educational programs whose sole or primary purpose is to raise students' IQ scores are a waste of money and should be eliminated. One of the programs Herrnstein and Murray suggest abolishing is the preschool program Head Start.

Head Start was launched in the 1960s as a way to break the cycle of poverty by providing poor children with earlier education opportunities, improving their communication skills, nutrition, and health care, and encouraging parental involvement during their children's formative years. Herrnstein and Murray cite studies that suggest, however, that Head Start and other similar preschool programs have little or no effect on a child's intelligence. According to these studies, children involved in preschool programs may increase their IQ scores by as much as 10 points in the early years, but these gains entirely disappear by the sixth grade. Since Head Start and similar programs do not offer any lasting gains for children with low IQs, Herrnstein and Murray recommend cutting these plans. The money saved by eliminating failed educational programs such as Head Start, they assert, should be applied toward programs for gifted students.

Many of Herrnstein and Murray's critics disagree with their proposals concerning Head Start and education. Alan Ryan, who teaches in the politics department at Princeton University, maintains that Herrnstein and Murray have reached the wrong conclusions regarding the studies about Head Start's effectiveness. The studies cited by Herrnstein and Murray prove only that there is no easy, one-step solution to raising and maintaining a child's IQ level, Ryan argues. "Environmental fixes are possible, but they take much longer to work, or where they work quickly, they need to be repeated so that they keep working," he concludes. Stephen Jay Gould, a Harvard zoology professor and author of *The Mismeasure of Man*, writes that he "would love to see more attention paid to talented students, but not at this cruel price" of eliminating preschool education for children with low IQs. Tim Beardsley, an editor for *Scientific American*, concedes that raising IQ scores may be difficult and expensive but asserts that Head Start may offer children other benefits that justify the continuance of such programs. He contends that policymakers should be concerned not about IQ scores but about providing children with an education that can later help them succeed in life.

The controversy over the value and role of preschool programs such as Head Start is just one aspect of the debate about the part IQ research should play in the formation of social policies. The viewpoints in the following chapter explore other proposed policy changes that concern the issue of IQ.

Social Policies Should Accommodate IQ Differences

by Richard J. Herrnstein and Charles Murray

About the authors: *The late Richard J. Herrnstein held the Edgar Pierce chair in psychology at Harvard University and is the author of* IQ in the Meritocracy. *Charles Murray, the author of* Losing Ground: American Social Policy 1950–1980, *is a Bradley Fellow at the American Enterprise Institute, a conservative research and education organization. Herrnstein and Murray are co-authors of* The Bell Curve: Intelligence and Class Structure in American Life, *from which the following viewpoint is taken.*

How should policy deal with the twin realities that people differ in intelligence for reasons that are not their fault, and that intelligence has a powerful bearing on how well people do in life? . . .

Simplifying Rules

The thesis of this viewpoint may be summarized quickly: As of the end of the twentieth century, the United States is run by rules that are congenial to people with high IQs and that make life more difficult for everyone else. This is true in the areas of criminal justice, marriage and divorce, welfare and tax policy, and business law, among others. It is true of rules that have been intended to help ordinary people—rules that govern schooling, medical practice, the labeling of goods, to pick some examples. It has happened not because the cognitive elite [highly educated intellectuals and policymakers] consciously usurped the writing of the rules but because of cognitive stratification [the separation of American classes by intellectual ability]. The trend has affected not just those at the low end of the cognitive distribution but just about everybody who is not part of the cognitive and economic elites.

The systems have been created, bit by bit, over decades, by people who think that complicated, sophisticated operationalizations of fairness, justice, and right and wrong are ethically superior to simple, black-and-white versions. The cognitive elite may not be satisfied with these systems as they stand at any given point, but however they may reform them, the systems are sure to become more complex. Additionally, complex systems are precisely the ones that give the cognitive elite the greatest competitive advantage. Deciphering complexity is one of the things that cognitive ability is most directly good for.

We have in mind two ways in which the rules generated by the cognitive elite are making life more difficult for everyone else. Each requires somewhat more detailed explanation.

Making It Easier to Make a Living

First come all the rules that make life more difficult for people who are trying to navigate everyday life. In looking for examples, the 1040 income tax form is such an easy target that it need only be mentioned to make the point. But the same complications and confusions apply to a single woman with children seeking government assistance or a person who is trying to open a dry-cleaning shop. As the cognitive elite busily goes about making the world a better place, it is not so important to them that they are complicating ordinary lives. It's not so complicated to *them*.

The same burden of complications that are only a nuisance to people who are smart are much more of a barrier to people who are not. In many cases, such barriers effectively block off avenues for people who are not cognitively equipped to struggle through the bureaucracy. In other cases, they reduce the margin of success so much that they make the difference between success and failure. "Sweat equity," though the phrase itself has been recently coined, is as distinctively an American concept as "equality before the law" and "liberty." You could get ahead by plain hard work. No one would stand in your way. Today that is no longer true. American society has erected barriers to individual sweat equity, by saying, in effect, "Only people who are good at navigating complex rules need apply." Anyone who has tried to open or run a small business in recent years can supply evidence of how formidable those barriers have become.

Credentialism is a closely related problem. It goes all the way up the cognitive range—the Ph.D. is often referred to as "the union card" by graduate students who want to become college professors—but it is especially irksome and obstructive for occupations further down the ladder.

"Life is more complicated than it used to be."

Increasingly, occupations must be licensed, whether the service involves barbering or taking care of neighborhood children. The theory is persuasive—do you want someone taking care of your child who is not qualified?—but the practice typically means jumping through bureaucratic hoops that have little to do with one's ability to do the job. The rise of licensing is both a symptom and a cause of diminishing personal ties, along with the mutual trust that goes with those ties. The licensing may have some small capacity to filter out the least competent, but the benefits are often outweighed by the costs of the increased bureaucratization.

> *"Return to the assumption that in America the government has no business getting in people's way except for the most compelling reasons."*

Enough examples. American society is rife with them. In many ways, life is more complicated than it used to be, and there's nothing to be done about it. But as the cognitive elite has come to power, it has trailed in its wake a detritus of complexities as well, individually minor, that together have reshaped society so that the average person has a much tougher time running his own life. Our policy recommendation is to stop it and strip away the nonsense. Consider the costs of complexity itself. Return to the assumption that in America the government has no business getting in people's way except for the most compelling reasons, with "compelling" required to meet a stiff definition.

Making It Easier to Live a Virtuous Life

We start with the supposition that almost everyone is capable of being a morally autonomous human being most of the time and given suitable circumstances. Political scientist James Q. Wilson has put this case eloquently in *The Moral Sense*, calling on a wide range of social science findings to support an old but lately unfashionable truth: Human beings in general are capable of deciding between right and wrong. This does not mean, however, that everyone is capable of deciding between right and wrong with the same sophistication and nuances. The difference between people of low cognitive ability and the rest of society may be put in terms of a metaphor: Everyone has a moral compass, but some of those compasses are more susceptible to magnetic storms than others. First, consider crime, then marriage.

Imagine living in a society where the rules about crime are simple and the consequences are equally simple. "Crime" consists of a few obviously wrong acts: assault, rape, murder, robbery, theft, trespass, destruction of another's property, fraud. Someone who commits a crime is probably caught—and almost certainly punished. The punishment almost certainly hurts (it is meaningful). Punishment follows arrest quickly, within a matter of days or weeks. The members of the society subscribe to the underlying codes of conduct with enthusiasm and near unanimity. They teach and enforce them whenever appropriate. Living in such a world, the moral compass shows simple, easily understood directions. North is north, south is south, right is right, wrong is wrong.

Now imagine that all the rules are made more complicated. The number of acts defined as crimes has multiplied, so that many things that are crimes are not nearly as obviously "wrong" as something like robbery or assault. The link between moral transgression and committing crime is made harder to understand. Fewer crimes lead to an arrest. Fewer arrests lead to prosecution. Many times, the prosecutions are not for something the accused person did but for an offense that the defense lawyer and the prosecutor agreed upon. Many times, people who are prosecuted are let off, though everyone (including the accused) acknowledges that the person was guilty. When people are convicted, the consequences have no apparent connection to how much harm they have done. These events are typically spread out over months and sometimes years. To top it all off, even the "wrongness" of the basic crimes is called into question. In the society at large (and translated onto the television and movie screens), it is commonly argued that robbery, for example, is not always wrong if it is in a good cause (stealing medicine to save a dying wife) or if it is in response to some external condition (exploitation, racism, etc.). At every level, it becomes fashionable to point out the complexities of moral decisions, and all the ways in which things that might seem "wrong" at first glance are really "right" when properly analyzed.

Simplify the Criminal Justice System

The two worlds we have described are not far removed from the contrast between the criminal justice system in the United States as recently as the 1950s and that system as of the 1990s. We are arguing that a person with comparatively low intelligence, whose time horizon is short and ability to balance many competing and complex incentives is low, has much more difficulty following a moral compass in the 1990s than he would have in the 1950s. Put aside your feelings about whether these changes in the criminal justice system represent progress. Simply consider them as a magnetic storm—as a set of changes that make the needle pointing to right and wrong waver erratically if you happen to be looking at the criminal justice system from the perspective of a person who is not especially bright. People of limited intelligence can lead moral lives in a society that is run on the basis of "Thou shalt not steal." They find it much harder to lead moral lives in a society that is run on the basis of "Thou shalt not steal unless there is a really good reason to."

> *"The policy prescription is that the criminal justice system should be made* **simpler.***"*

The policy prescription is that the criminal justice system should be made *simpler*. The meaning of criminal offenses used to be clear and objective, and so were the consequences. It is worth trying to make them so again.

Commitment to Marriage

It has become much more difficult for a person of low cognitive ability to figure out why marriage is a good thing, and, once in a marriage, more difficult to figure out why one should stick with it through bad times. The magnetic storm has swept through from many directions.

The sexual revolution is the most obvious culprit. The old bargain from the man's point of view—get married, because that's the only way you're going to be able to sleep with the lady—was the kind of incentive that did not require a lot of intellect to process and had an all-powerful effect on behavior. Restoring it is not feasible by any (reasonable) policy we can think of.

But the state has interfered as well to make it more difficult for people with little intelligence to do that thing—find a compatible partner and get married—that constitutes the most accessible and richest of all valued places. Marriage fills a vital role in people's lives to the extent that it is hallowed as an institution and as a relationship unlike any other. Marriage is satisfying to the extent that society validates these propositions: "Yes, you may have a baby outside marriage if you choose; but it isn't the same." "Yes, you may live with someone without marrying, but it isn't the same." "Yes, you may say that you are committed to someone without marrying, but it isn't the same."

> *"It has become much more difficult for a person of low cognitive ability to figure out why marriage is a good thing."*

Once sex was no longer playing as important a role in the decision to marry, it was essential that these other unique attributes of marriage be highlighted and reinforced. But the opposite has happened. Repeatedly, the prerogatives and responsibilities that used to be limited to marriage have spilled over into nonmarital relationships, whether it is the rights and responsibilities of an unmarried father, medical coverage for same-sex partners, or palimony cases. Once the law says, "Well, in a legal sense, living together is the same," what is the point of getting married?

For most people, there are still answers to that question. Even given the diminished legal stature of marriage, marriage continues to have unique value. But to see those values takes forethought about the long-term differences between living together and being married, sensitivity to many intangibles, and an appreciation of second-hand and third-hand consequences. As evidence about marriage rates implies, people low on the intelligence distribution are less likely to think through those issues than others.

Our policy prescription in this instance is to return marriage to its formerly unique legal status. If you are married, you take on obligations. If you are not married, you don't. In particular, we urge that marriage once again become the sole legal institution through which rights and responsibilities regarding children are exercised. If you are an unmarried mother, you have no legal basis for demanding that the father of the child provide support. If you are an unmarried father, you have no legal standing regarding the child—not even a right to see the child, let alone any basis honored by society for claiming he or she is "yours" or that you are a "father."

We do not expect such changes miraculously to resuscitate marriage in the lowest cognitive classes, but they are a step in the return to a simpler valuation of it. A family is unique and highly desirable. To start one, you have to get married. The role of the state in restoring the rewards of marriage is to validate once again the rewards that marriage naturally carries with it.

More General Implications for Policy

Crime and marriage are only examples of a general principle: Modern American society can be simplified. No law of nature says that the increasing complexity of technology must be matched by a new complexity in the way the nation is governed. The increasing complexity of technology follows from the functions it serves. The increasing complexity of government does not. Often the complexities introduced by technology require highly sophisticated *analysis* before good law and regulation can be developed. But as a rule of thumb, the more sophisticated the analysis, the simpler the policies can be. Policy is usually complicated because it has been built incrementally through a political process, not because it has needed to become more complicated. The time has come to make simplification a top priority in reforming policy—not for a handful of regulations but across the board.

More broadly, we urge that it is possible once again to make a core of common law, combined with the original concepts of negligence and liability in tort law, the mechanism for running society—easily understood by all and a basis for the straightforward lessons that parents at all levels of cognitive ability above the lowest can teach their children about how to behave as they grow up. We readily acknowledge that modernity requires some amplifications of this simple mechanism, but the nation needs to think through those amplifications from the legal equivalent of zero-based budgeting. As matters stand, the legal edifice has become a labyrinth that only the rich and the smart can navigate. . . .

Dealing with Income

Ever since most people quit believing that a person's income on earth reflects God's judgment of his worth, it has been argued that income distributions are inherently unfair; most wealthy people do not "deserve" their wealth nor the poor their poverty. That being the case, it is appropriate for societies to take from the rich and give to the poor. The statistical relationship between low cognitive ability and income is more evidence that the world is not fair.

"Marriage [should] once again become the sole legal institution through which rights and responsibilities regarding children are exercised."

But it is not news that the world is unfair. You knew before reading this viewpoint that income differences arise from many arbitrary causes, sociological and psychological, besides differences in intelligence. All of them are reflected in correlations of varying sizes, which mean all of them are riddled with exceptions. This complicates solutions. Whenever individual cases are examined, differences in circumstances will be found that *do* reflect the individual's fault or merit. The data support old arguments for supplementing the income of the poor without giving any new guidance for how to do it.

> **"Modern American society can be simplified."**

The evidence about cognitive ability causes us to be sympathetic to the straightforward proposition that "trying hard" ought to be rewarded. Our prescription, borrowing from the case made by political scientist David Ellwood, is that people who work full time should not be too poor to have a decent standard of living, even if the kinds of work they can do are not highly valued in the marketplace. We do not put this as a principle of government for all countries—getting everybody out of poverty is not an option in most of the world—but it is appropriate for rich countries to try to do.

How? There is no economically perfect alternative. Any government supplement of wages produces negative effects of many kinds. Such defects are not the results of bad policy design but inherent. The least damaging strategies are the simplest ones, which do not try to oversee or manipulate the labor market behavior of low-income people, but rather augment their earned income up to a floor. The earned income tax credit, already in place, seems to be a generally good strategy, albeit with the unavoidable drawbacks of any income supplement.

We will not try to elaborate on these arguments here. We leave the income issue with this: As America enters the twenty-first century, it is inconceivable that it will return to a laissez-faire system regarding income. Some sort of redistribution is here to stay. The question is how to redistribute in ways that increase the chances for people at the bottom of society to take control of their lives, to be engaged meaningfully in their communities, and to find valued places for themselves. Cash supplements need not compete with that goal, whereas the social welfare system that the nation has developed in the twentieth century most definitely does. We should be looking for ways to replace the latter with the former.

Dealing with Demography

Of all the uncomfortable topics we have explored, a pair of the most uncomfortable ones are that a society with a higher mean IQ is also likely to be a society with fewer social ills and brighter economic prospects, and that the most efficient way to raise the IQ of a society is for smarter women to have higher birth rates than duller women. Instead, America is going in the opposite direction, and the implication is a future America with more social ills and gloomier economic prospects. . . . Yet we have so far been silent on what to do about it.

We are silent partly because we are as apprehensive as most other people about what might happen when a government decides to social-engineer who has babies and who doesn't. We can imagine no recommendation for using the government to manipulate fertility that does not have dangers. But this highlights the problem: The United States already has policies that inadvertently social-engineer who has babies, and it is encouraging the wrong women. *If the United States did as much to encourage high-IQ women to have babies as it now does to encourage low-IQ women, it would rightly be described as engaging in aggressive manipulation of fertility.* The technically precise description of America's fertility policy is that it subsidizes births among poor women, who are also disproportionately at the low end of the intelligence distribution. We urge generally that these policies, represented by the extensive network of cash and services for low-income women who have babies, be ended.

The government should stop subsidizing births to anyone, rich or poor. The other generic recommendation, as close to harmless as any government program we can imagine, is to make it easy for women to make good on their prior decision not to get pregnant by making available birth control mechanisms that are increasingly flexible, foolproof, inexpensive, and safe.

The other demographic factor is immigration and the evidence that recent waves of immigrants are, on the average, less successful and probably less able, than earlier waves. There is no reason to assume that the hazards associated with low cognitive ability in America are somehow circumvented by having been born abroad or having parents or grandparents who were. An immigrant population with low cognitive ability will—again, on the average—have trouble not only in finding good work but in school, at home, and with the law.

> **"The time has come to make simplification a top priority in reforming policy."**

This is not the place, nor are we the people, to try to rewrite immigration law. But we believe that the main purpose of immigration law should be to serve America's interests. It should be among the goals of public policy to shift the flow of immigrants away from those admitted under the nepotistic rules (which broadly encourage the reunification of relatives) and toward those admitted under competency rules, already established in immigration law—not to the total exclusion of nepotistic and humanitarian criteria but a shift. Perhaps our central thought about immigration is that present policy assumes an indifference to the individual characteristics of immigrants that no society can indefinitely maintain without danger.

Social Policy Should Not Accommodate Perceived IQ Differences

by Glenn C. Loury

About the author: *Glenn C. Loury is a professor of economics at Boston University.*

Reading Richard J. Herrnstein and Charles Murray's treatise [*The Bell Curve*] causes me once again to reflect on the limited utility in the management of human affairs of that academic endeavor generously termed social science. The authors of *The Bell Curve* undertake to pronounce upon what is possible for human beings to do while failing to consider that which most makes us human. They begin by seeking the causes of behavior and end by reducing the human subject to a mechanism whose horizon is fixed by some combination of genetic endowment and social law. Yet we, even the "dullest" of us, are so much more than that.

Different Levels of Mental Ability

Now, as an economist I am a card-carrying member of the social scientists' cabal; so these doubts now creeping over me have far-reaching personal implications. But entertain them I must, for the stakes in the discussion this book has engendered are too high. The question on the table, central to our nation's future and, I might add, to the future success of a conservative politics in America, is this: Can we sensibly aspire to a more complete social integration than has yet been achieved of those who now languish at the bottom of American society? A political movement that answers "no" to this question must fail, and richly deserves to.

Herrnstein and Murray are not entirely direct on this point. They stress, plausibly enough, that we must be realistic in formulating policy, taking due account of the unequal distribution of intellectual aptitudes in the population,

Glenn C. Loury, "Dispirited," *National Review*, December 5, 1994; © 1994 by National Review, Inc., 150 E. 35th St., New York, NY 10016. Reprinted by permission.

recognizing that limitations of mental ability constrain what sorts of policies are likely to make a difference and how much of a difference they can make. But implicit in their argument is the judgment that we shall have to get used to there being a substantial minority of our fellows who, because of their low intelligence, may fail to perform adequately in their roles as workers, parents, and citizens. I think this is quite wrong. Social science ultimately leads the authors astray on the political and moral fundamentals.

For example, in chapters on parenting, crime, and citizenship they document that performance in these areas is correlated in their samples with cognitive ability. Though they stress that IQ is not destiny, they also stress that it is often a more important "cause" of one's level of personal achievement than factors that liberal social scientists typically invoke, such as family background and economic opportunity. Liberal analysts, they say, offer false hope by suggesting that with improved economic opportunity one can induce underclass youths to live within the law. Some citizens simply lack the wits to manage their affairs so as to avoid criminal violence, be responsive to their children, and exercise the franchise, Herrnstein and Murray argue. If we want our "duller" citizens to obey our laws, we must change the laws (by, e.g., restoring simple rules and certain, severe punishments). Thus: "People of limited intelligence can lead moral lives in a society that is run on the basis of 'Thou shalt not steal.' They find it much harder to lead moral lives in a society that is run on the basis of 'Thou shalt not steal unless there is a really good reason to.'"

No Reason to Base Policy on Mental Ability

There is a case to be made—a conservative case—for simplifying the laws, for making criminals anticipate certain and swift punishment as the consequence of their crimes, and for adhering to traditional notions about right and wrong as exemplified in the commandment "Thou shalt not steal." Indeed, a case can be made for much of the policy advice given in this book—for limiting affirmative action, for seeking a less centralized and more citizen-friendly administration of government, for halting the encouragement now given to out-of-wedlock childbearing, and so on. But there is no reason that I can see to rest such a case on the presumed mental limitations of a sizable number of citizens. In every instance there are political arguments for these policy prescriptions that are both more compelling and more likely to succeed in the public arena than the generalizations about human capacities that Herrnstein and Murray claim to have established with their data.

> *"There is no reason [to base public policy] on the presumed mental limitations of a sizable number of citizens."*

Observing a correlation between a noisy measure of parenting skills, say, and some score on an ability test is a far cry from discovering an immutable law of nature. Social scientists are a long way from producing a definitive account of the causes of human performance in educational attainment and economic success, the areas that have been most intensively studied by economists and sociologists over the last half-century. The claim implicitly advanced in this book to have achieved a scientific understanding of the *moral* performance of

> *"Try telling the . . . Christian Right that access to morality is contingent on mental ability."*

the citizenry adequate to provide a foundation for social policy is breathtakingly audacious.

I urge Republican politicians and conservative intellectuals to think long and hard before chanting this IQ mantra in public discourses. Herrnstein and Murray frame their policy discussion so as to guarantee that its appeal will be limited to an electoral minority. Try telling the newly energized Christian Right that access to morality is contingent on mental ability. Their response is likely to be, "God is not finished with us when he deals us our genetic hand."

This is surely right. We human beings are spiritual creatures; we have souls; we have free will. We are, of course, constrained in various ways by biological and environmental realities. But we can, with effort, make ourselves morally fit members of our political communities. If we fully exploit our material and spiritual inheritance, we can become decent citizens and loving parents, despite the constraints. We deserve from our political leaders a vision of our humanity that recognizes and celebrates this potential.

The Matters of the Spirit

Such a spiritual argument is one that a social scientist may find hard to understand. Yet the spiritual resources of human beings are key to the maintenance of social stability and progress. They are the ultimate foundation of any hope we can have of overcoming the social malaise of the underclass. This is why the mechanistic determinism of science is, in the end, inadequate to the task of social prescription. Political science has no account of why people vote; psychology has yet to identify the material basis of religious exhilaration; economics can say only that people give to charities because it makes them feel good to do so. No analyst predicted that the people of Eastern Europe would, in Vaclav Havel's memorable phrase, rise to achieve "a sense of transcendence over the world of existences." With the understanding of causality in social science so limited, and the importance of matters of the spirit so palpable, one might expect a bit of humble circumspection from analysts who presume to pronounce upon what is possible for human beings to accomplish.

Whatever the merits of their social science, Herrnstein and Murray are in a moral and political cul de sac. I see no reason for serious conservatives to join them there. This difficulty is most clearly illustrated with the fierce debate about racial differences in intelligence that *The Bell Curve* has spawned. The authors will surely get more grief than they deserve for having stated the facts of this matter—that on the average blacks lag significantly behind whites in cognitive functioning. That is not my objection. What I find problematic is their suggestion that we accommodate ourselves to the inevitability of the difference in mental performance among the races in America. This posture of resignation is an unacceptable response to today's tragic reality. We can be prudent and hard-headed about what government can and cannot accomplish through its various instruments of policy without abandoning hope of achieving racial reconciliation within our national community.

In reality, the record of black American economic and educational achievement in the post-civil-rights era has been ambiguous—great success mixed with shocking failure. Myriad explanations for the failure have been advanced, but the account that attributes it to the limited mental abilities of blacks is singular in its suggestion that we must learn to live with current racial disparities. It is true that for too long the loudest voices of African-American authenticity offered discrimination by whites as the excuse for every black disability; they treated evidence of limited black achievement as an automatic indictment of the American social order. These racialists are hoist on their own petard by the arguments and data in *The Bell Curve*. Having taught us to examine each individual life first through a racial lens, they must now confront the specter of a racial-intelligence accountancy that suggests a rather different explanation for the ambiguous achievements of blacks in the last generation.

A Poisonous Question

So the question now on the floor, in the minds of blacks as well as whites, is whether blacks are capable of gaining equal status, given equality of opportunity. It is a peculiar mind that fails to fathom how poisonous a question this is for our democracy. Let me state my unequivocal belief that blacks are, indeed, so capable. Still, any assertion of equal black capacity is a hypothesis or an axiom, not a fact. The fact is that blacks have something to prove, to ourselves and to what W.E.B. Du Bois once characterized as "a world that looks on in amused contempt and pity." This is not fair; it is not right; but it is the way things are.

> *"God is not finished with us when he deals us our genetic hand."*

Some conservatives are not above signaling, in more or less overt ways, their belief that blacks can never pass this test. Some radical black nationalists agree, arguing increasingly more openly now that blacks can never make it in "white America" and so should stop trying, go our own way, and maybe burn a few things down in the process. At bottom these parties share the belief that the magnitude of the challenge facing blacks is beyond what we can manage. I insist, to the contrary, that we can and must meet this challenge. I find it spectacularly unhelpful to be told, "Success is unlikely given your average mental equipment, but never mind, because cognitive ability is not the only currency for measuring human worth." This is, in fact, precisely what Herrnstein and Murray say. I shudder at the prospect that this could be the animating vision of a governing conservative coalition in this country. But I take comfort in the certainty that, should conservatives be unwise enough to embrace it, the American people will be decent enough to reject it.

Social Policies Should Be Based on Valid Science

by Kenneth Aizawa

About the author: *Kenneth Aizawa is the Charles T. Beaird Professor of Philosophy at Centenary College in Shreveport, Louisiana.*

Commentators have often observed gaps between the scientific conclusions in *The Bell Curve* and the social policy recommendations that Richard Herrnstein and Charles Murray wish to make in light of them. In other words, even if the scientific conclusions of *The Bell Curve* were true, there would remain a number of viable policy options. The most familiar, and perhaps clearest, illustration of this kind of gap centers on Head Start. Herrnstein and Murray observe that the Head Start program is able to increase the IQ scores of children, but that these advances are lost over time. Here is a scientific conclusion that is largely uncontested. But what consequence does this have for social policy? By itself, very little. One might, for example, adopt a conservative policy, such as Herrnstein and Murray favor, that simply abandons Head Start altogether. A more liberal policy would hold that even a few years of increased IQ is worth preserving, if only because children may learn more in those few years of higher IQ. Another liberal policy would be to try to fight "IQ fade out" with greater investments in education. Yet another liberal policy might involve earlier interventions in a child's life. The obvious point is that the conservative position that Herrnstein and Murray favor is far from being dictated by scientific findings. Indeed, Herrnstein and Murray do not even consider the possibility of maintaining or extending a Head Start program. Rather, they examine other more elaborate projects, the Abecedarian and Milwaukee Projects; challenge the experimental evidence that supports the cognitive improvements these programs claim to provide; then assert that there are not enough teachers or money to provide such programs for all children who might benefit from them. In other words, other programs come in for their fair share of abuse, but nothing is said about Head Start per se. . . .

Excerpted from Kenneth Aizawa, "The Gap Between Science and Policy in *The Bell Curve*," *American Behavioral Scientist*, September/October 1995, pp. 84-97. Copyright © 1995 by Sage Publications, Inc. Reprinted by permission of Sage Publications, Inc.

Chapter 4

The Irrelevant *Bell Curve* Policies

It is hard to treat *The Bell Curve* as a serious discussion of social policy rather than simply a statement of a conservative political agenda. It is more what one might expect of a candidate for political office than a serious scholar. There is, of course, the poor treatment accorded Head Start, alluded to above. Herrnstein and Murray also tell us that "As crime grows, society must substitute coercion for co-operation." Here again, Herrnstein and Murray ignore the possibility of preventing crimes through noncoercive means. For example, there is never any discussion of, say, the decriminalization or legalization of drugs. Aside from these occasional comments that betray conservative blinders, there is the fact that the principal policy recommendations that Herrnstein and Murray make are not even plausibly construed as solutions to [many social] problems.

> *"The conservative position that Herrnstein and Murray favor is far from being dictated by scientific findings."*

In Chapter 17 of *The Bell Curve*, Herrnstein and Murray suggest that, although there might be some hope in raising children's IQs through better nutrition, they discourage further investments in schooling, including preschool programs such as Head Start, the Milwaukee Project, and the Abecedarian Project. In Chapter 18, Herrnstein and Murray argue that the American education system ought to spend less money on those with low IQ, which is essentially a waste of time, and more money on those with high IQ, who might actually benefit from it. In Chapters 19 and 20, they favor reducing the help of affirmative action, so that only those minorities who are cognitively slightly below the standards set by White males will be helped.

Social Mores and Laws

Chapter 21 offers two general policy recommendations. First, we should transfer functions of the federal government back to local neighborhoods; do away with a remote federal bureaucracy in favor of the "good old days" when local school boards, churches, and the like saw to the effective implementation of the social contract. Second, Herrnstein and Murray propose that we simplify the legal and moral rules of life. A number of more specific policy recommendations fall under this heading. There are simplifications in the laws concerning business. Although is it difficult for a person of ordinary intelligence to handle the IRS 1040 form, seek government assistance, and open and run a business, it is all the more difficult for persons of low IQ. There are also simplifications of the judicial system to be considered:

> People of limited intelligence can lead moral lives in a society that is run on the basis of "Thou shalt not steal." They find it much harder to lead moral lives in a society that is run on the basis of "Thou shalt not steal unless there is a really good reason to."

Laws concerning marriage ought to be made simpler as well, because those with low IQ are supposed to have greater difficulty in appreciating why they should get married or remain married. After all, the "very dull" are supposed to reason, why be married, if you can have sex without marriage? And what about the rights and responsibilities of unmarried fathers? Palimony cases? Medical coverage for same-sex partners? This too must be confusing for the very dull. Herrnstein and Murray propose the following "solution":

> Our policy prescription in this instance is to return marriage to its formerly unique legal status. If you are married, you take on obligations. If you are not married, you don't. In particular, we urge that marriage once again become the sole legal institution through which rights and responsibilities regarding children are exercised. If you are an unmarried mother, you have no legal basis for demanding that the father of the child provide support. If you are an unmarried father, you have no legal standing regarding the child—not even a right to see the child, let alone any basis honored by society for claiming he or she is "yours" or that you are a "father."

Here, then, are three principal simplifications of society: laws regulating business and finance, moral principles, and marriage law.

Questioning Herrnstein and Murray's Recommendations

There is much to question in these policy recommendations. For example, regarding improved education for the brightest, if, as Herrnstein and Murray suggest, part of the problem of IQ is that it induces disparities in income and quality of life, why should we invest in efforts that will exacerbate the problem? If, as Herrnstein and Murray suggest, the aim of better education for the brightest is to produce "educated men" who will feel greater compassion for others, especially their intellectual inferiors, why not promote compassion for others, at all levels of intelligence? Or consider the transfer of functions from the federal government to local organizations. Herrnstein and Murray suggest that without the federal government, there are some tasks that local organizations will have to do or they will not get done. But, isn't there good reason to think that in crime-ridden neighborhoods, where citizens are afraid to go out at night, the tasks simply will not get done? And, why does there have to be a transfer of function anyway? Why not develop policies that will encourage neighborhoods to complement the existing efforts of federal government? The transfer idea is more a scheme to help affluent people keep their money in their affluent local communities, while leaving the unfortunate poor to their own devices in their poor local communities. As important as these questions are, I should keep to my central concern with *The*

> *"The principal policy recommendations . . . are not even plausibly construed as solutions to [many social] problems."*

187

Bell Curve's gap between science and policy.

When one juxtaposes the putative causal connections between IQ and job-related accidents, illegitimacy, good parenting, low-birth-weight babies, infant mortality, and civility from Part 2 of *The Bell Curve* and the various policy prescriptions found in Part 4, one sees the science/policy gap quite clearly. For many of the cognitive problems and challenges discussed in Part 2, the policy recommendations in Part 4 simply fail to address the cognitive as-

> *"If . . . part of the problem of IQ is that it induces disparities in income and quality of life, why should we invest in efforts that will exacerbate the problem?"*

pects of the problem, the very aspect of social problems Herrnstein and Murray set themselves out to address. Recall their saying that "to try to come to grips with the nation's problems without understanding the role of intelligence is to see through a glass darkly indeed, to grope with symptoms instead of causes, to stumble into supposed remedies that have no chance of working" (pp. xxii-xxiii). The policies they offer are not always completely irrelevant to the problems discussed in Part 2, but generally they are. Consider job-related accidents. Cutting back on preschool educational programs will not help make those of low IQ safer at work. More spending on those with high IQs will not make the workplace safer for those of low IQ. Reducing affirmative action will not make those with low IQ safer at work. Transfer of functions from the federal level to the local level will also not make the workplace safer. Legal simplifications will not much help safety in the workplace, especially if the simplification involves eliminating federal regulations enforcing safety standards.

A reduction in remedial education spending, an increase in spending on high-IQ schooling, a weakening of affirmative action, transfers to neighborhoods, and many of the simplification measures do not directly address the cognitive problem of illegitimacy. Only the proposal concerning a "simplification" of the rewards for marriage has any prima facie relevance. But, even if relevant, the proposal leaves many questions unanswered. What deterrent value is there in depriving a poor woman of a poor man's financial support? What impact would a redefinition of fatherhood and visitation rights mean to those affected? Would they care? And what about the consequences for women and children left completely abandoned by biological fathers, as well as the government? Of these policy recommendations, only the increase in neighborhood strength might increase good parenting, decrease the incidence of low-birth-weight babies, lower infant mortality, and increase civility. Friends and family in a neighborhood might help and guide a mother or prospective mother. But, again, these benefits might be had through the help of a federal program that makes for better informed neighborhoods, rather than by federal pullout. Across the board, even a cursory glance at the policies and problems reveals what should be for Herrnstein and Murray an embarrassing incongruity.

Some Steps Toward Better Policy Making

In the preface to *The Bell Curve*, Herrnstein and Murray tell us that the nation's social scientists, journalists, and politicians have ignored the role of intelligence in shaping the American economy, demographics, and culture. They tell us that good social policy requires that we understand the bearing of intelligence on social structure and public policy. In response, I say that even were we to know the putative effects of IQ on social problems, we would be far from having to adopt the policy recommendations that Herrnstein and Murray propose. Indeed, even were we to know the putative effects of IQ on social problems, there would still remain many important classes of facts that would appear to be essential before we could address social policy armed with the sort of scientific evidence we would ideally, or even reasonably, like to have. Here I will try to make this point by indicating some of the policy options that remain open to us in the face of *Bell Curve* science, as well as some of the kinds of scientific developments that would be necessary for a scientifically sound social policy.

It is clear that finding a causal role for IQ in some social problems goes a very little way toward determining social policy when we recall that IQ plays its causal role in a specific environment. In one environment, a low IQ may produce an undesirable result, and in another environment, it may not. In evaluating policy options, therefore, one needs to consider to what extent social interventions can prevent or mitigate undesirable effects. The point here is not that environment can be manipulated to raise IQ levels. Perhaps it can; perhaps it cannot. The point is rather that, even with fixed IQ, some environments may be better than others. Whether or not this is true involves examining cases in detail. So, let us examine one of the hypothetical mechanisms that Herrnstein and Murray suggest underlie the putative causal connections.

Suppose it is true that low IQ promotes job-related injuries, that people with low IQs are more accident prone. Clearly nothing in Herrnstein and Murray's policy recommendations will touch on this, but here is an idea. We might better engineer the workplace for safety. Are low-IQ workers more likely to put their fingers into places in machinery they should not put them? If so, then design the machinery so fingers cannot get there. Are low-IQ workers more likely to lift loads that are too heavy for them? If so, then design the loads so they are not too heavy and establish firm policies concerning the proper handling of freight. Are low-IQ workers more likely to experience repetitive stress disorders? If so, then design their computers to warn them to take a break and suggest exercises they might perform. Design keyboards to reduce stress in the first place. Workers should demand safe working conditions and employers might even find some economic

> *"Cutting back on preschool educational programs will not help make those of low IQ safer at work."*

189

incentives in this area. A natural complement to better workplace engineering is better workplace safety education. Something as simple as a once-a-week safety discussion session might do a great deal to reduce accidents, even for those with low IQs. . . .

Cognitive Stratification

Some of the problems that Herrnstein and Murray see arising from IQ stem from simply having low IQs. People with low IQs tend not to know all they need to know. But, IQ is supposed to figure into social problems in other ways as well via cognitive stratification. At present, people with high IQs tend to intermarry, while people with low IQs tend to intermarry. As a result, we might find *The Bell Curve* distribution of intelligence distorted toward a bimodal distribution with many very dull people and many very bright people. If, however, the very dull are more prolific than the very bright, the intelligence distribution will become

> *"Finding a causal role for IQ in some social problems goes a very little way toward determining social policy."*

weighted toward the very dull end of the distribution. At the same time as there is cognitive stratification, there is supposed to be financial stratification as well. Fewer and fewer smart people will come to have more and more of the wealth in society. As a result, society will be forced to create high-tech reservations on which the masses of people with low IQ will live in poor, crime-infested, unhealthy conditions. This relates to the various proposals to improve education, in that according to Herrnstein and Murray, improvements or alterations in education may lead to greater disparities in achievement, hence exacerbate the problems that intellectual disparity causes.

Suppose, for a moment, that cognitive stratification is taking place. What is to be done? As far as social problems such as crime, unemployment, and out-of-wedlock births, it is not clear. Perhaps nothing. Other highly technological industrialized nations, such as Japan, appear to have much the same mechanisms in place for cognitive stratification as does the United States, but they are not beset by the levels of crime, unemployment, and so forth as is the United States. Although Japan is in many respects not a good model for American society, it does serve to show that a nation can endure cognitive stratification without the sorts of social problems we face in the United States. So, perhaps cognitive stratification per se is not a problem. If society can be organized in such a way as to preserve a low crime rate, a low unemployment rate, and so on in the face of cognitive stratification, then to that extent cognitive stratification is perhaps not a bad thing. The connection between financial and cognitive stratification is another matter. Salaries and the accumulation of wealth are most obviously influenced by social arrangements that, in the face of the human suffering that Herrnstein and Murray predict, we might decide ought be changed. It is common enough to ask why we should pay someone $15 an hour to operate heavy equipment, when we can get away with paying much less. The additional salary costs eat into corporation profits and have to be passed on to customers.

But, the same might be said about, say, investment bankers. Why should we pay such a person a percentage of a multimillion-dollar transaction, when we can pay a smaller fixed fee? The additional salary costs eat into corporation profits and have to be passed on to customers. Herrnstein and Murray suggest that we must pay the corporate executive more than the ditch digger for the well-being of the economy, but why? Given the same salary, aren't there plenty of people who would prefer working in an office to working in a ditch? Might they not be roughly the same people who now work in offices rather than ditches? Salary structures can be changed and so can tax policy. Income tax rates, the home mortgage interest deduction, corporate tax rates, depreciation on corporate assets, inheritance taxes, and so forth are all social policy concerns that are subject to change. Any link between IQ and financial success is literally what we make it.

The Reckoning of Social Policy

IQ and social policy are a volatile mix. One can be sure that even after *The Bell Curve* stands largely repudiated, much the same cluster of ideas will one day reappear much to the detriment of those who are worst off in society. When that day comes, there will be a scientific reckoning, wherein scientists will review the quality of data presented, wherein they will challenge inferences from correlations to causation, wherein reasoning about nature versus nurture will be closely scrutinized, wherein the concept of heritability will again be hashed out. But, alongside the scientific reckoning, there will be a policy reckoning. When that reckoning comes, we will have to consider what, if anything, the science of that day will really dictate to us. As far as I can see, it will be a good long time, some hundreds of years perhaps, before we could possibly amass the sorts of scientific evidence that would require us to acquiesce in *Bell Curve* policies.

> *"IQ and social policy are a volatile mix."*

Aside from the very important and complicated current debates over the causes of IQ, the effects of IQ on social problems, interracial differences in IQ, there will have to be a determination of the mechanisms by which IQ brings about its putative effects and how these mechanisms might be most effectively dealt with. It is not enough to know that low IQ has certain effects. We need to know how it has those effects. Until we begin to understand this, which will take quite some time, we will continue to have a wide gap between social science and social policy.

Social Policies Should Not Be Based on IQ or Race

by Samuel Francis

About the author: *Samuel Francis is a nationally syndicated columnist for the* Washington Times.

The second week in October 1994 must have been National Intelligence Week, since at least three major journals all happened to publish important articles about the role of intelligence in society, who's got the smarts and who hasn't. To judge from the results, you don't need an IQ test to learn that some writers for these major journals seem to burn their mental headlights on low beam.

Intelligence Is Genetic

First, there was a *New York Times Magazine* piece about Charles Murray, co-author with the late Richard Herrnstein of Harvard of *The Bell Curve*, a hefty tome that argues, among other things, that intelligence is largely determined genetically and that the presence or absence of the right genes explains success or failure in the funhouse of life.

Then there was Mr. Murray and Professor Herrnstein explaining themselves on virtually the whole *Wall Street Journal* editorial page. And finally there was an insipid little screed published in *Rolling Stone* in its annual "Back to College" issue about other experts who do research on intelligence. Just to let you know what the *Stone* wants its sophomoric readers to think, the screed is subtly titled "Professors of Hate."

If perchance you perused these articles to learn about the nature and role of intelligence, you probably were disappointed. The best of the three, by Mr. Murray and Mr. Herrnstein, unloads much data, but when it comes to the really sexy stuff—namely, IQ and race—it seems to dance artfully around the subject. Nonetheless, the implication of what they say is clear enough.

What they say is that (a) "IQ is substantially heritable," between 40 and 80

Samuel Francis, "Race, IQ, and Big Government," *Washington Times*, October 18, 1994, p. A17. Reprinted by permission of the *Washington Times*.

percent, they estimate; (b) "racial differences in means and distributions on IQ tests are a reality" and "as far as anyone can tell, they are not artifacts of test bias"; and (c) therefore—which they do not quite say, at least in the *Journal*—races differ in their intelligence because of inherent, genetic reasons.

Not long ago, that would have been the last of Mr. Murray and Mr. Herrnstein. The giant sucking sound you heard would have been their careers gurgling down the academic drainpipes. But in the last few years they're not the only ones to have reached these conclusions. The "Professors of Hate" at whom *Rolling Stone* spits are in fact among the pioneers in building the case that intelligence is inherited and the races differ in it.

In the event you're wondering who really hates whom, it's interesting that the first paragraph of the *Rolling Stone* piece tells how one prof at the City College of New York can't have his name on his office door because it keeps getting "swastikas and ethnic slurs" smeared on it. Presumably, while the prof is a "professor of hate," those who chalk up the swastikas are disciples of brotherly love.

There are some (though nowadays fewer) who raise serious arguments against the conclusion that the races differ in intelligence. Not being a scientist, I can hardly pass authoritative judgment on the question, though a lot of others who aren't scientists either are awfully quick to reject that conclusion. What really frightens people is that racial differences in intelligence might be used to justify racial repression.

Rights Are Not Based on Intelligence

But whatever the implications of the IQ research, racial repression doesn't follow. The basic rights that American and Western society recognizes do not differ according to intelligence. In a letter of 1809, Thomas Jefferson wrote of blacks, "whatever be their degree of talent it is no measure of their rights. Because Sir Isaac Newton was superior to others in understanding, he was not therefore lord of the person or property of others." Jefferson had less than egalitarian beliefs about blacks, but he saw clearly that, just as being smart confers no special rights, so not being smart doesn't mean you have fewer rights.

Mr. Murray and Mr. Herrnstein say racial IQ differences "call for a re-thinking of policy, especially affirmative action." Well, maybe. Some of us (including me) have opposed affirmative action regardless of the truth about race and IQ. But the larger point is this: What you think the state ought to do about race has little to do with what you think about race. It has everything to do with what you think about the state.

> *"The basic rights that American and Western society recognizes do not differ according to intelligence."*

Under the properly limited federal government with which this country started out and to which it should return, the state would be unable to do very much at all about race. In the modern leviathan created by liberals, where smoking, sexual beliefs and guns are approved targets of federal meat-grinding, there's no limit to what the state might do about race or those of whose IQs it doesn't approve.

I very much doubt that any of the savants whose research on race and intelligence is making headlines these days hate anyone, but it doesn't really matter if they do. Their findings seem to offer a valuable explanation of differences in racial behavior and achievement, but as a guide to what the government should do about those differences, it's no more useful than the failed egalitarian dogmas from which the modern leviathan lurched into life.

More Research Is Needed to Study IQ, Race, and Social Policy

by Christopher Winship

About the author: *Christopher Winship is a professor of sociology at Harvard University in Cambridge, Massachusetts.*

At a meeting of social scientists at the Harvard Business School in October 1994, Richard Herrnstein and Charles Murray's controversial book *The Bell Curve* came up. One group reported that in an earlier conversation they had thoroughly "trashed" it. Heads around the room nodded in approval. I asked the room at large—about 20 people—how many had actually read the book. Two raised their hands.

The condemnation of *The Bell Curve* in the media has been equally definitive, if presumably better informed.

Most of the analysis has focused on the question raised in the book of whether I.Q. is hereditary and whether racial differences in I.Q. are predominantly due to environmental or genetic factors. The consensus appears to be that the book's argument is inherently racist and that Mr. Herrnstein (who died in September 1994) and Mr. Murray are academic charlatans.

Yet, while their treatment of these issues has been justly criticized, much of *The Bell Curve* is not about race at all, and parts of it have been misrepresented.

Intelligence Is Essentially Inherited

For example, a frequent assertion about *The Bell Curve* is that it argues that intelligence is essentially inherited. In fact, the authors make the weaker claim that, according to existing research, between 40 and 80 percent of intelligence is in the genes. They adopt the middle of this range, 60 percent, as reasonable. (If you think this amounts to arguing that intelligence is "essentially" inherited, ask yourself whether you would be "essentially" receiving the same pay if you received a 40 percent cut in salary.)

Mr. Herrnstein and Mr. Murray have been rightfully attacked for their shoddy and sometimes contradictory analysis of the relationship between race and intelligence. They acknowledge, for example, that there is no scientific way to determine even within broad ranges what proportion of the difference is due to environment and what proportion due to genes. After offering this critical warning, however, the authors conclude that the racial gap is more likely genetic than environmental—a divisive and irresponsible line of argument.

Three Valuable Insights

Yet, in spite of its serious flaws, *The Bell Curve* offers three potentially valuable insights that should not easily be dismissed. The first is that as a society we are becoming increasingly socially and economically stratified by level of cognitive ability. This is an observation that has been made by others from widely different political perspectives, including Secretary of Labor Robert Reich. The dramatic increase since the 1970s in the difference in incomes between high school and college graduates is strong evidence of this trend.

The second important assertion is that limited cognitive skills are strongly associated with myriad social problems. The authors find that among the poor, the unemployed, high school dropouts, those in prison, women on welfare and unwed mothers, 40 to 65 percent fall in the bottom 20 percent of measured I.Q.

Most of these groups, by the way, contain more whites than blacks. Indeed, seeking to sidestep the race question altogether, the authors restricted a large part of their analysis to whites. They find, as other social scientists have using the same data, that cognitive ability is a strong predictor of various social problems even when other factors such as family background are taken into account. Given the strong suggestion of a link between intelligence and behavior, isn't further study of a possible causal relationship needed?

The third important claim in *The Bell Curve* is that cognitive ability is largely immutable. Although the authors may well be overly pessimistic about the possibility of improving intellectual ability, surely we would be naïve to think that simply increasing federal funding for early childhood education, say, or for job-training programs would be sufficient to compensate for the increasing gap between the highly educated and the barely literate in American society.

> *"We are missing two decades of research that could have informed current policy."*

What are the consequences of ignoring such controversial but potentially important observations about our society? In 1965, Daniel Patrick Moynihan, then an aide in the Labor Department, wrote a report that argued for an aggressive social policy to address the rising number of out-of-wedlock births in the African-American community, then about 30 percent of the total. Today, nearly 70 percent of African-American children are born out of wedlock (as are 30 percent of white children, compared to about 12 percent in 1965).

However valid the warning, after the report was published Mr. Moynihan and his defenders were denounced as racists and the African-American family became a taboo subject for scholars for the next 20 years. As we now try to grapple with the desperate situation of many black families in this country, we are missing two decades of research that could have informed current policy.

The furor about *The Bell Curve* risks the same perils. Many scholars are likely to back away from research on cognitive skills and social outcomes; others will be inclined to present only findings consistent with the thesis that I.Q. and race differences of any kind are largely environmentally determined. This is hardly an atmosphere conducive to objective, rigorous scientific study.

> *"It is critical that we understand what the relationship is . . . between intelligence and entrenched social problems."*

Few of the most controversial assertions in *The Bell Curve* can be shown with any certainty to be either true or false. Only better, more unbiased and more sophisticated research can help us do this. We need to insure that neither the irresponsible statements in *The Bell Curve*—nor the media's vitriolic response to the book as a whole—prevents this research from being done.

In an era of increasing stratification by level of ability and income, it is critical that we understand what the relationship is, if any, between intelligence and entrenched social problems if we are to develop sensible public policy.

Bibliography

Books

N.J. Block and Gerald Dworkin	*The IQ Controversy: Critical Readings.* New York: Pantheon, 1976.
Carl C. Brigham	*A Study of American Intelligence.* Princeton, NJ: Princeton University Press, 1923.
Farai Chideya	*Don't Believe the Hype: Fighting Cultural Misinformation About African-Americans.* New York: Penguin, 1995.
Dinesh D'Souza	*The End of Racism: Principles for a Multiracial Society.* New York: Free Press, 1995.
Douglas Lee Eckberg	*Intelligence and Race: The Origins and Dimensions of the IQ Controversy.* New York: Praeger, 1979.
H.J. Eysenck and Leon J. Kamin	*The Intelligence Controversy.* New York: Wiley, 1981.
James R. Flynn	*Asian Americans: Achievement Beyond IQ.* Hillsdale, NJ: Lawrence Erlbaum Associates, 1991.
Steven Fraser, ed.	*The Bell Curve Wars: Race, Intelligence, and the Future of America.* New York: BasicBooks, 1995.
Francis Galton	*Hereditary Genius: An Inquiry into Its Laws and Consequences.* Cleveland: World, 1962.
Daniel Goleman	*Emotional Intelligence: Why It Can Matter More Than IQ.* New York: Bantam, 1995.
William A. Henry III	*In Defense of Elitism.* New York: Doubleday, 1994.
Richard J. Herrnstein and Charles Murray	*The Bell Curve: Intelligence and Class Structure in American Life.* New York: Free Press, 1994.
Seymour W. Itzkoff	*The Decline of Intelligence in America: A Strategy for National Renewal.* Westport, CT: Praeger, 1994.
Russell Jacoby and Naomi Glauberman, eds.	*The Bell Curve Debate: History, Documents, Opinions.* New York: Times Books, 1995.
Arthur R. Jensen	*Bias in Mental Testing.* New York: Free Press, 1980.
Leon J. Kamin	*The Science and Politics of IQ.* Potomac, MD: Lawrence Erlbaum Associates, 1974.
R.C. Lewontin, Steven Rose, and Leon J. Kamin	*Not in Our Genes: Biology, Ideology, and Human Nature.* New York: Pantheon, 1984.

David Perkins   *Outsmarting IQ: The Emerging Science of Learnable Intelligence*. New York: Free Press, 1995.

J. Philippe Rushton   *Race, Evolution, and Behavior*. New Brunswick, NJ: Transaction, 1995.

Sandra Scarr   *Race, Social Class, and Individual Differences in I.Q.* Hillsdale, NJ: Lawrence Erlbaum Associates, 1981.

Carl Senna, ed.   *The Fallacy of I.Q.* New York: Third Press, 1973.

Pat Shipman   *The Evolution of Racism: Human Differences and the Use and Abuse of Science*. New York: Simon & Schuster, 1994.

Thomas Sowell   *Race and Culture: A World View*. New York: BasicBooks, 1994.

William H. Tucker   *The Science and Politics of Racial Research*. Urbana: University of Illinois Press, 1994.

Philip E. Vernon   *Intelligence: Heredity and Environment*. San Francisco: W.H. Freeman, 1979.

Periodicals

Richard D. Arvey et al.   "Mainstream Science on Intelligence," *Wall Street Journal*, December 13, 1994.

Black Scholar   Entire issue on race and intelligence, Winter 1995.

Fred Bruning   "Writing Off the Black Race," *Maclean's*, November 21, 1994.

Jason DeParle   "Daring Research or 'Social Science Pornography'?" *New York Times Magazine*, October 9, 1994.

Linda S. Gottfredson   "What Do We Know About Intelligence?" *American Scholar*, Winter 1996.

Stephen Jay Gould   "Curveball," *New Yorker*, November 28, 1994.

Leon J. Kamin   "Behind the Curve," *Scientific American*, February 1995.

Richard Lacayo   "For Whom the Bell Curves," *Time*, October 24, 1994.

Adam Miller   "Professors of Hate," *Rolling Stone*, October 20, 1994.

Charles Murray   "*The Bell Curve* and Its Critics," *Commentary*, May 1995.

Charles Murray   "The Real *Bell Curve*," *Wall Street Journal*, December 2, 1994.

National Review   "A Symposium," special section on race and intelligence, December 5, 1994.

New Republic   "Race and I.Q.," October 31, 1994.

Psychology Today   "Race, Intelligence, and Genetics," December 1973.

Thomas Sowell   "Ethnicity and IQ," *American Spectator*, February 1995.

Organizations to Contact

The editors have compiled the following list of organizations concerned with the issues debated in this book. The descriptions are derived from materials provided by the organizations. All have publications or information available for interested readers. The list was compiled on the date of publication of the present volume; names, addresses, fax numbers, and phone numbers may change. Be aware that many organizations take several weeks or longer to respond to inquiries, so allow as much time as possible.

American Psychological Association (APA)
750 First St. NE
Washington, DC 20002-4242
(202) 336-5500

The APA is a professional society that works to advance psychology as a science, as a profession, and as a means to promote human welfare. One branch of the APA includes psychometrics, which studies intelligence and IQ. The association produces numerous publications, including the monthly journal *American Psychologist* and the monthly newspaper *APA Monitor*.

American Society of Human Genetics (ASHG)
9650 Rockville Pike
Bethesda, MD 20814-3998
(301) 571-1825
fax: (301) 530-7079

ASHG is a professional society of physicians, researchers, genetic counselors, and others interested in human genetics. Committees within the organization deal with issues concerning the human genome project, human genetics education, public policy, and social issues. ASHG publishes the monthly *American Journal of Human Genetics*.

Institute for the Study of Man (ISM)
1133 13th St. NW, Suite C-2
Washington, DC 20005
(202) 371-2700
fax: (202) 371-1523

Founded in 1975, ISM is a nonprofit educational organization that publishes books, journals, and monographs related to anthropology and the human sciences. It has numerous publications concerning heredity and intelligence, including the journal *Mankind Quarterly* and the books *Evolution, Creative Intelligence, and Inter-Group Competition* and *The Nature of Intelligence and Essays on the Analysis of Racial Differences in IQ*.

International Genetics Federation (IGF)
Dept. of Botany
University of British Columbia
6270 University Blvd.
Vancouver, BC V6T 1Z4
CANADA
(604) 822-5629
fax: (604) 822-9179

Through its international network of genetics societies, IGF works to further the science of genetics. The federation provides information about genetics and offers referrals to local genetics societies.

National Center for Fair and Open Testing (FairTest)
342 Broadway
Cambridge, MA 02139
(617) 864-4810
fax: (617) 497-2224

FairTest works to ensure that standardized tests are fair, open, and educationally sound. It seeks to eliminate racially, culturally, and sexually biased tests, including aptitude and intelligence tests and professional certification exams. FairTest organizes testing reform campaigns, educates the public, and serves as a national clearinghouse for assessment information. Its publications include the *Annotated Bibliography on Assessment of Young Children*, the quarterly *FairTest Examiner*, and the books *Fallout from the Testing Explosion* and *Standardized Tests and Children: A Guide to Testing Reform*.

Society for the Study of Social Biology (SSSB)
c/o Jacci L. Rodgers
Oklahoma City University
Meinders School of Business
Oklahoma City, OK 73106
(405) 521-5824
fax: (405) 225-4511

SSSB is an association of biological, behavioral, and social science scholars interested in the study of heredity and population. It promotes discussion, advancement, and sharing of knowledge about the biological and sociocultural forces affecting human populations and their evolution. The society publishes the quarterly journal *Social Biology*.

Index